America, from Client State to World Power

America, from Client State to World Power

Six Major Transitions in United States Foreign Relations

By Paul A. Varg

University of Oklahoma Press : Norman and London

By Paul A. Varg

Open Door Diplomat: The Life of W. W. Rockhill (Urbana, Ill., 1952)

Missionaries, Chinese, and Diplomats (Princeton, N.J., 1958)

The Foreign Policies of the Founding Fathers (East Lansing, Mich., 1964)

The Making of a Myth: The United States and China, 1897– 1912 (East Lansing, Mich., 1968)

The Closing of the Door: Sino-American Relations, 1936–1946 (East Lansing, Mich., 1973)

United States Foreign Relations, 1820–1860 (East Lansing, Mich., 1979)

New England and Foreign Relations, 1789–1850 (Hanover, Me., 1983)

America, from Client State to World Power: Six Major Transitions in United States Foreign Relations (Norman, 1990)

Library of Congress Cataloging-in-Publication Data

Varg, Paul A.
    America, from client state to world power : six major transitions in United States foreign relations / by Paul A. Varg. — 1st ed.
        p.   cm.
    Includes bibliographical references.
    ISBN 0-8061-2251-X (alk. paper)
    1. United States—Foreign relations.   I. Title.
E183.7.V26   1990
327.73—dc20   89-29012
                                                                          CIP

The paper in this book meets the guidelines for permanence and durability of the Committee on Production Guidelines for Book Longevity of the Council on Library Resources, Inc. ∞

To Cozette

Contents

Acknowledgments

A study extending from 1763 to 1947 necessarily requires use of an array of secondary sources. I am deeply indebted to the historians who have enriched our knowledge and understanding of specialized topics and important personalities who were participants. Their writings are cited in the notes. I am particularly indebted to those many historians who have edited the private papers of presidents and others who contributed to the shaping of history. There is also extensive use of primary sources used by me in my earlier writings. Needless to say, this book could not have been written had it not been for the many excellent books on American diplomatic history.

The staff in the Michigan State University Library has been most helpful in assisting me. I owe them a sincere thanks. All of us in the field of the history of American foreign relations owe much to the fine editions of diplomatic correspondence and related materials in the United States Foreign Relations Series. This series not only has greatly expanded its coverage of the twentieth century; it has adhered to high stands of scholarship. Limited funds have often delayed the publications, but excellence has been maintained.

I am especially indebted to two of my colleagues, Paul Sweet and David Jones, of the Department of Political Science, Michigan State University. Paul Sweet, now retired, has patiently answered scores of inquiries and has raised challenging questions in his area of specialization and experience in the foreign service. David Jones spent hours with me in thoughtful discussions and encouraged me when that was important.

The editorial staff of the University of Oklahoma Press has been particularly helpful by their careful editing of the manuscript.

Finally, I am indebted to Julie Ecker, who typed the manuscript and patiently endured my calls for retyping what had to be rewritten.

PAUL A. VARG

East Lansing, Michigan

America, from Client State to World Power

Prologue

THE major objective of this book is to advance understanding of how the nation's policy emerged out of the inexorable process of foreign relations in response to changing interests and pressure. Terms such as the Monroe Doctrine, Open Door policy, and isolationism lack specificity, and their meanings change greatly over time. Emphasis on the process of national policy-making leads to the real factors in the major transitions that are the focus of this book.

Foreign relations are integral to the nature of American society and to the always-changing neighborhood of nations. The drives in our society are multiple: honor, pride, economic interests, security, party rivalry, a willingness to make pronouncements that satisfy the public appetite for spicy rhetoric, myths based partly on facts but embroidered by pride and fancy, special interests, moralism, and genuine challenges—all of these have entered into shaping a consensus of opinion on the national interest.

During the first transition, extending from the colonial period to the years immediately following the War of 1812, the major drive was for security. The second stage embraced the years between 1820 and the 1850's, a period devoted to extending settlement and expanding the nation's boundaries. After victory in the Mexican War, the American republic was no longer an experiment in representative government; it had become a nation recognized by European states as dominant in the western hemisphere. After 1850 expansionism focused upon Cuba, Central America, and Mexico. The Pierce and Buchanan

administrations supported ambitious and reckless projects that were premature and adventurous. Had not the
Civil War intervened, the nation might have moved from
continental expansionism to imperialism.

In the 1890's came the third stage of foreign-policy development, with the annexation of the Philippines, the
establishment of protectorates in the Caribbean, and a
turnabout from anglophobia toward a tacit alliance with
Great Britain. Presidents Theodore Roosevelt and Woodrow Wilson shared basic political views, and at the same
time they were men of different temperaments. Both were
pro-British and both were expansionists in the Caribbean.
Wilson was not ready to accept the balance-of-power system, but he was deeply concerned about the prospect of
changes in the existing balance in Europe. Caught between his ideals of pacifism and his horror of war and the
probable defeat of Great Britain, he called for war, protesting that, God willing, he could do no other.

The world depression brought about the rise of totalitarian governments, closely followed by threats to the
existing structure of international relations. The prospective rise of Germany to a position of dominance in Europe
and the simultaneous aim of Japan to achieve hegemony
in East Asia, brought the United States to a realization of
what the change could bring about. Americans had long
denounced the balance-of-power system, but they were
now compelled to recognize it as the determinant of political authority. The new challenge brought an end to
the faith in isolationism and recognition that the United
States had much at stake in supporting the Allied cause.
The transition ushered in a revolution in diplomacy.

The final stage followed World War II. Germany and
Japan were defeated, western Europe was a scene of destruction, Japan was in ashes, and China was embroiled
in civil war. Only two strong powers emerged. The United
States had a greatly expanded industry and the financial
resources to promote reconstruction and extend its influence. The Soviet Union, in spite of destruction, had made
great strides in industrialization behind the battle lines

and possessed a powerful army. The irreconcilable aims and interests of these two powers ushered in the cold war and a new struggle for a favorable balance of power.

Each of the transitions had unique factors, but it was the coming of ever-new interests and pressures that shaped policy.

Foreign Policy Rooted in Society
1763–1783

THE colonial experience before the winning of independence dictated a set of aims and points of view that would
determine the character of American foreign policy well
before independence was achieved. The vast unoccupied
lands west of the Appalachian mountains gave birth to a
vigorous expansionism long before 1776. The colonists, a
society of doers with an adventurous spirit and pride in
their achievements, often ignored the legitimate interests of other nations. In Europe the proximity of powerful
neighbors had caused each nation to take careful account
of the limits of its power. America, by contrast, lacked
powerful neighbors; thus the colonists made light of the
need for defense and showed no great concern about limit-
ing their national aspirations.

Besides geography, the political order was also a major
determinant of colonial policy. American society dedicated itself without reservation to the ideology of the
British Glorious Revolution. Abuse of power would be
checked by the division of that power among three
branches of government. Civic rights, the rule of reason,
and natural law were exalted. Religious teachings, prominent in the prevailing Protestantism, buttressed political
doctrines. These provided the colonists with faith that a
new and more just society would replace the system of
absolute monarchies. A prominent corollary of these
ideals was that nations, as well as individuals, were subject to the moral laws grounded in natural law. Nations,
too, should be moral. The new republic was pervaded by

a strong strain of moralism that, Americans assumed, had universal validity.

A third major determinant of foreign policy was economic interest. From the middle of the eighteenth century the colonial economy was inextricably intertwined with the new business world. Merchants and counting houses had their interests. There was more than one kind of future that Americans looked forward to. There was the society envisioned by Thomas Jefferson in which democracy had sway, but there was also the anticipation of economic growth, of wealth, and of monetary advancement. In this land of plenty, financial opportunities placed their stamp on politics.

The society that emerged along the east coast of North America was a product of individual enterprise. The metropolis of London imposed only limited regulations with the consequence that ingenuity, self-confidence, and unbridled energies created thriving settlements leavened by opportunity and individual ambition. Settlers from England, Scotland, and the German states responded to their own felt needs rather than to imperial ambitions in the mother country.

The rivalry of European imperialism began in the eighteenth century, and the greatest stake in a long series of wars was control of North America. British settlers along the coast from Maine to Georgia were as much participants in the struggle as were Englishmen at home. Their involvement was of great importance in shaping attitudes that would endure after they had achieved independence. The neighboring colonies were French and Spanish, but British settlers had no hesitation in trading with their prospective enemies. Economic motives likewise led them to trade with the colonies of other European powers in the West Indies. Self-interest easily overrode British mercantile regulations.

British imperial relations gradually loosened, leaving the colonies largely self-governing. As a consequence, occupied as they were with pushing back the forests and learning to cultivate the soil in a new climate, the colonists gradually became as much American as British. The new environment bent old habits of doing and thinking, and the political phrases the colonists had brought with them came to have different meanings. At the same time, because the rivalry between Great Britain and France, and diplomacy accompanying the rivalry, rested on imperial interests as understood in England, Americans began promoting their own views with vigor through their London agents. Thus, long before independence, Americans had developed their own idea of foreign relations.

However, the colonists' fears for security at the same time strengthened their British heritage. The French threat, combined as it was with the French alliances with the Indians, was a major concern. The seaboard colonists were totally dependent on British protection. The heavy burdens of carving out their farms, and their limited financial resources, allowed little time or money for assuming the challenges of defense. New Englanders lived in dread of Indian raids, and saw in the French control of Acadia great danger that the French would drive them from the fishing grounds in the Bay of Fundy and off the coasts of Nova Scotia. Colonists in the province of New York had equally good reason to be uneasy. French forces held Crown Point at the southern end of Lake Champlain, not far from Albany, and the French were also in control of settlements on the shores of Lake Ontario. This would allow the French in some future war to seize the lands of the Iroquois in the western part of the province. Southward in Virginia there was a vital interest in the lands across the mountains and the Ohio valley. And still further southward, in the Carolinas and Georgia, dreams focused on settlement of the lower Mississippi valley.

Interest in these areas rested on deeply rooted feelings. Thoughts of a French conquest raised the specter of domination by the French absolute monarchy and its ally, Catholicism. Fear raised alarms not only from the clergy but officials, doctors, and lawyers. William Livingston, representative in the Continental Congress from New Jersey, attributed all the iniquities of the French to the Catholic church. He described Catholicism as impious and absurd, disgraceful to human understanding, a religion "chiefly calculated to support the tyrannical Power, and the insatiable Avarice of the Clergy."[1] A contributor to the *American Magazine* declared himself "an irreconcilable foe of *French* power, *French* customs, *French* policy, and every species of slavery." Comments of this type abounded in the public literature of the day.

The important fisheries of New England, the visions of rich lands to the west, and profits to be made in the Indian trade undergirded an imperialism that was as much colonial as it was British. There was no conflict over expansion between London officials and the colonists. On that issue they stood together.

No such harmony existed on questions of foreign trade. To the enterprising merchants of the port towns, the freedom to trade beyond the channels laid down by the imperial authorities was often the difference between success and failure. Merchants in Albany suffered no pangs as they violated British regulations and carried on a lively trade with the French in Montreal. This enabled French merchants to undersell the Iroquois in trade with the Indians further west.[2] The governors of New York sought to suppress the trade because it alienated the Iroquois, who were being squeezed out. They pleaded with the Crown to suppress the trade, but this only served to stir up ardent criticism from the merchants who argued in favor of free trade.

Trade on a much larger scale was carried on with the French, Spanish, and Dutch colonies in the West Indies. This too was in direct violation of British mercantilism, but even during the Seven Years War, when the French were the enemy, the trade continued. This trade was of sufficient importance that it could be contended that the future prosperity of the American colonies depended upon it. Such an argument was advanced with boldness in communications with the British Crown by colonial agents in London and by colonial leaders at home. The Pennsylvania Assembly warned that not to revise the laws and permit the trade "would be a vast Diminution to the Navigation of Great Britain, an increase of the Shipping of Our Foreign Neighbors, a large reduction to the Exportation of the British Manufactures, and by the Decay of their Trade would impoverish these your Majesty's colonies, and by that means not only render us useless to Our Mother Country but expose us to great Dangers from our powerful Neighbors, the French, by whom we are now surrounded."[3] Thomas Hutchinson of Massachusetts presented the same argument. If the question be which is most for the interest of the dominions, he wrote, the answer was freedom to trade with the foreign colonies. This, he added, would stimulate the growth of British manufactures.[4] The lieutenant governor of New York, Cadwallader Colden, noted that it was difficult to enforce the regulations "because the people are of the opinion that a preference has been given to the sugar islands."[5] An interest in free trade and neutral rights was present well before the Revolution.

Anglo-Americans lived in dread of French conquests, but this did not create a recognition of the need for colonial unity. Of all the many characteristics of colonial culture none gained a firmer hold than intercolonial rivalry. No one colony showed an interest in the security of its neighbors. Their attention focused on the dangers near at hand, and the instances of cooperation were rare. Pennsylvania aided Massachusetts with a grant of £3000 in 1745 to help meet the expenses of an expedition against Acadia.[6] During the Seven Years War, when Massachusetts asked for assistance to support an expedition to attack Crown Point, Pennsylvania again voted a grant of £10,000 sterling.[7] Both instances were the work of Benjamin Franklin, who stood forth as a defender of the empire and recognized the need for cooperation.

Absence of a unified defense policy played into the hands of the French and their Indian allies. The conse-

quences were evident by 1750 as thousands of immigrants, finding the coastal areas occupied, moved across
the mountains, where they became prey to attacks. As
the dangers mounted, the Board of Trade in London called
for a conference to consider a plan of union. In 1754,
when the Congress met, New York faced the threat that
the Six Nations (due to bold intrusions by land speculators) would align with the French. The prospect was
sufficiently alarming that the delegates reached new and
more generous agreements with the Iroquois. Otherwise,
the Congress was a failure. The Plan of Union agreed
upon promised more to assure each colony's freedom of
action than to meet the pressing needs for cooperation
and defense. Even this cautious step was rejected by the
Board of Trade.

However, Thomas Hutchinson led the way in drafting
a document entitled *Representation of the Present State
of the Colonies,* and Congress reaffirmed the earlier British claim that the coast from Georgia to the St. Lawrence
River belonged to the Crown. The only exceptions to this
sweeping claim were the Cape Breton Island and the islands of the Gulf of St. Lawrence. In addition, the Congress declared that the territory between the Atlantic
Ocean and the Pacific between 34° and 48° belonged to
Great Britain, plus Lake Champlain, Lake Erie, and Lake
Ontario. The spirit of manifest destiny was already
present.[8]

The tightening of British mercantile regulations after the
Seven Years War affected all parts of the population in the
rapidly growing American towns. The wealthy merchant
suffered as regulations long in abeyance were imposed,
sales of British goods were made directly to the shop-
keepers, and the issuing of paper money was disallowed.
The middle class, suffering from postwar depression and
changes wrought by the war, experienced unemployment.
This is not to say that the causes of the revolutionary
movement were wholly economic. As Gary Nash, well-
known historian, writes, "in fact, there was no compart-

mentalization in their minds between England's onerous new economic regulation and its encroachment upon the political rights of American subjects."[9]

Before the Stamp Act of 1765 there was political unrest due to the significant social changes that were taking place. The wealthy had been fearful of an uprising by the lower middle classes. Mob violence more than once frightened conservatives, who were, in large part, in both political and economic control. In 1763 and 1764 the middle classes demonstrated a new assertiveness and challenged the traditional leadership. The movement against the stringent British regulations coincided with a search for a new social order in a society that had undergone great changes.

Not until late 1765 did public protest turn against the British. Already the basic postulates of disagreement had been formed. Expansion, non-involvement in the European balance-of-power system, and a firm conviction in support of free trade were basic interests on which there could be no compromise. The general acceptance of free enterprise, particularly the vested interests of the business class, guaranteed that Americans would assiduously seek the advancement of their interests. The prevailing sense that the colonies of British America represented a political order true to the principles of the Glorious Revolution and the British Constitution accompanied devotion to economic interests. The two were not separated. Embedded in this philosophy was the moralism and idealism of the day. Any thoughts of independence were not yet entertained. Faith that the empire would return to the true teachings of the British Constitution remained strong. It was at the Stamp Act Congress in 1765 that the colonies found a common ground in opposition to taxation without representation. This marked the beginning of the end of each colony's going it alone.

Necessity rather than preference dictated the Declaration of Independence and the alliance with France. Later generations long overlooked how very reluctant the colonists were to break with the mother country. To resist imperious interference was one thing; to sail forth on the uncharted sea of independence was quite another. That there were reefs in that sea the colonists well knew, and one danger was the probability that they might to some degree become supplicants of France. This and other uncertainties created a period of excruciating indecision.

Necessity dictated a search for foreign supplies as early as 1775. This would endanger the possibility of reconciliation that the great majority expected. Slowly it was recognized that not to seek foreign aid would in all probability result in submission. Concern over the possible domestic consequences of independence added to the reluctance. Many feared an internecine war over western lands. Some, like John Rutledge of South Carolina, at first opposed independence because a purely American government might be subverted by scheming New Englanders who favored democracy. "I dread their low Cunning," wrote Rutledge, "and those leveling principles which men without Character and without Fortune in general possess, which are so captivating to the lower class of Mankind, and which will occasion such a fluctuation of Property as to introduce the greatest disorder."[10]

The primary deterrents to seeking foreign aid lay in the popular attitude toward France and Great Britain. John Adams ranked sentimental ties to Great Britain as the greatest obstacle. The frightening prospects of having to turn to France probably played as significant a role. For a hundred years that nation had been a determined enemy of Great Britain and her colonies. In public addresses, sermons and in writings, France had appeared as a nation of despotism and intrigue, the citadel of Roman Catholicism, and the scheming encroacher on British territories in the new world. To cast oneself on the mercy of such a nation required a sense of desperation.

Committees in the Congress, however, were ready to seek French aid long before the people agreed. In the autumn of 1775, the Committee on Trade arranged for the purchase of $200,000 worth of provisions to be sold to

France for the purpose of establishing credit which could be used for the purchase of supplies. On November 29, Congress established the Committee of Correspondence, and in December the committee directed Arthur Lee, who was already in London, to inquire as to the disposition of foreign powers.

The following March, the committee named Silas Deane to go to Paris as its agent. To avoid giving offense, Deane was to pose as a merchant buying goods for the Indian trade. If Count Vergennes, the French minister for Foreign Affairs, gave him any encouragement, he was to explain that the trade with the colonies that had made England wealthy was now open to France. "France," read the instructions, "had been pitched on for the first application, from an opinion that if we should, as there is a great appearance that we shall, come to a total separation from Great Britain, France would be looked on as the power whose friendship it would be fittest for us to obtain and cultivate."[11] Vergennes was to be sounded out on the question of diplomatic recognition and an "alliance," a term that meant no more than a commercial treaty.

Pressures of the moment also led Congress to take steps that added up to independence even while its members denied it. In April, Congress declared American ports open to ships of all nations, authorized American warships to sail against the enemy, and sanctioned privateering. These were acts of a sovereign power.

The necessity of securing foreign assistance finally forced the hand of the reluctant rebels. Richard Henry Lee observed: *"It is not choice then but necessity that calls for Independence, as the only means by which foreign Alliance can be obtained,* and a proper Confederation by which internal peace and union may be secured."[12] Progress on the question of independence and an alliance went hand in hand. On the same day that Congress established a committee to draft a declaration of independence it also set up a committee to draw up a "Plan of Treaties."

As the flirtation with France began, Adams had already

asked the question "What connection may we safely form with her?" Adams and Franklin opposed political ties. They were isolationists. This is evident in the three rules Adams laid down. He wrote: "1st. No Political Connection. Submit to none of her authority—receive no Governors, or officers from her. 2nd. No Military Connection. Receive no Troops from her. 3rd. Only a Commercial Connection, i.e. make a Treaty, to receive her Ships into our Ports—furnish Us with Arms, Cannon, Salt Petre, Powder, Duck, Steel."[13]

When the committee met, they debated the question of how far it would be necessary to go if the colonies were to secure French support. Adams argued that they should "avoid all Alliance, which might embarrass Us in after times and involve Us in future European Wars. . . ." A treaty of commerce, he maintained, would be ample compensation, for by it France would increase her commerce, encourage her manufactures and agriculture, stimulate the growth of her merchant marine, and "raise her from her present deep humiliation, distress and decay, and place her on a more equal footing with England, for the protection of her foreign Possessions."[14] Adams drafted the committee report, but it was not debated until late August. A faction led by Samuel Adams thought that a simple treaty of commerce would not be sufficient to secure French support, and they proposed additional provisions that were political and would have included future obligations. Both Franklin and Adams were opposed. Franklin held firmly to the position that a commercial treaty alone opening trade with France would enfeeble England and prevent her from extending her empire and making it the most powerful that Europe had ever seen.

The Plan of Treaties foreshadowed the future policy of no entangling alliances. It bound the new nation to nothing in the way of support of France in a future war and offered her no favored treatment in regard to commerce. The plan as proposed would bind France not to seek territory on the continent of North America and not to extend the fishing rights she already enjoyed in the area of New Foundland.

The gravity of the situation soon led to a compromise. Some months later the commissioners were instructed to offer France assistance in the conquest of the British West Indies and diplomatic support of the islands if she acquired them. Spain was to be promised assistance in a campaign against the British in the Floridas, and the United States was to accede to her possession of them in return for support of the American cause and for Spain's acknowledging the Americans' right to free navigation on the Mississippi River and free entry into the harbor of Pensacola.

Congress entertained the hope of establishing commercial relations with as many nations as possible, somewhat overlooking the fact that any nation trading with the colonies would be in serious difficulty with the British. Benjamin Franklin opposed the move but was overruled; he foresaw that it could only result in embarrassing rejections. Ignoring Franklin, Arthur Lee set out from Paris to inform the governments of Spain and Prussia that trade with the United States would make them rich and powerful. Silas Deane joined in the effort and sent word to the Dutch that the United States "only ask for what nature surely entitles all men to, a free and uninterrupted commerce and exchange of the superfluities of one country for those of another."[15] He hoped that the Dutch would recognize that "the first power in Europe which takes advantage of the present favorable occasion must exceed every other in commerce." The optimistic commissioners were unceremoniously shunted aside in each effort. The final chapter in this militia diplomacy ended in the dreary capital city of St. Petersburg, where Francis Dana and young John Quincy Adams arrived after receiving encouragement from John Adams, who assured them that, should the Russian court reject the overture, it would leave a mark of moral odium on Russia. The two Americans lingered there for two years, and they learned among other things that England was the most important market for Russian wheat. That market counted heavily with the landed aristocrats who were Catherine's chief support. The energetic effort, although a failure, signaled that major emphasis in the years ahead would be on the negotiation of commercial treaties.

Short of French assistance in the early years of the struggle, and with a large contingent of French troops in the battle of Yorktown, an American victory would have been long delayed and perhaps postponed it indefinitely. But the alliance with France would expose the rebellious colonies to great dangers when the days of peacemaking arrived.

Russia, Austria, Hungary, Prussia, and the Italian states had no direct interest at stake in how the New World was to be divided. Neither did the absolute monarchies ruling those states have any sympathy with rebels who were challenging the old order. They were indifferent in their regard of the Americans, but the war between Great Britain and her enemies France and Spain did concern them. The balance of power in Europe was of vital concern. Catherine the Great of Russia had no wish to strengthen France at the expense of Great Britain. France repeatedly stood as a barrier to the expanding Russian influence and control in Turkey, Poland, and Sweden. Should Great Britain decline, France would be supreme on the continent. Austria too had grievances against France. The two countries had long been in alliance, but France had recently been a party to dislodging the Austrian troops from Bavaria, where Emperor Joseph had hoped to extend his realm. Consequently, Queen Maria Theresa was on the alert to recover national honor and reestablish herself as a first-rate power. Frederick of Prussia had earlier made a clear stand regarding the colonies when Arthur Lee journeyed to Berlin to seek recognition of the new republic. The king of Prussia was no great friend of the British, but he did not find it to his interest to antagonize Great Britain by offering a friendly hand to a set of mere upstart rebels who were threatening her empire. He looked on the full-scale war that arose in 1779 with indifference.[16]

Territorial expansion, the other major colonial aim, had an urgency about it that would brook neither compromise nor postponement. A victory short of acquisition of some considerable portion of the west would have been a hollow one. It was this ambition that greatly complicated the relations with France, for Spain fully expected her ally to hold the Americans in check and prevent their drive in the direction of Spain's colonies.

From the beginning of the Revolution, Americans assumed that the new nation would include all of the territory held by Great Britain on the North American continent. Not only to win independence but to gain additional territory far surpassing the original thirteen colonies constituted the goal.

In 1776, Congress wrote this expansionist dream into a draft of the proposed treaty. The king of France was to agree never to

> invade, not under any pretence "attempt to possess himself of Labradore, New Britain, Nova Scotia, Acadia, Canada, Florida, nor any of the Countries, Cities, or Towns, on the Continent of North America, nor of the islands of New-foundland, Cape Breton, St. John's, Anticosti, nor of any other Island lying near to the said Continent, in the Seas, or in any Gulph, Bay, or River, it being the true Intent and meaning of this Treaty, that the said United States, shall have the sole, exclusive, undivided and perpetual Possession of the Countries, Cities, and Towns, on the said Continent, and of all Islands near to it, which now are, or lately were under the Jurisdiction of or Subject to the King or Crown of Great Britain, whenever they shall be United or confederated with the said United States."[17]

When the treaty of alliance was signed, it specified that the United States was to have possession of any territory formerly British that it conquered on the continent of

North America and also Bermuda, should that island be taken. Any other islands that might be subdued during the course of the war would go to France. These treaty provisions represented promises rather than accomplished facts. The hard pressed American army could not hope to conquer and occupy these vast territories. Americans had to place their faith in diplomacy, which gave them little comfort, for they had great fear that the European belligerents would barter away what the Americans claimed but did not possess.

American ambitions clashed further with those of Spain. Spain not only rejected the French thesis that an independent America, by weakening England, would create a situation in Europe favorable to Spain as well as France, but she also was convinced the new republic would threaten her territory. The Marquis de Castejon observed in February 1777 that, in regard to America, Spain "should be the last country in all Europe to recognize any sovereign and independent state in North America." An independent America, he warned, would soon become powerful, was already ambitious, and when free to ignore considerations of balance-of-power politics in Europe, would have a free hand to threaten Spain's empire.[18]

In September 1779, Congress appointed John Jay minister to Spain. Jay's residence there simply served to illuminate the gulf between American and Spanish interests. His instructions did nothing to conceal the ambitions of the United States, which would guarantee Spain's possession of the Floridas if she captured them, "provided always that the United States shall enjoy the free navigation of the river Mississippi into and from the Sea." Jay was "particularly to endeavour to obtain some convenient port or ports below the 31st degree of north latitude on the river Mississippi free for all merchant vessels, goods, wares and merchandise, belonging to the inhabitants of these states."[19] Well aware that Spain feared the United States would expand to the south and west, Jay warned the secretary, William Carmichael, of his mission:

In speaking of American affairs, remember to do justice to Virginia, and the western country near the Mississippi. Recount their achievements against the savages, their growing numbers, extensive settlements, and aversion to Britain for attempting to involve them in the horrors of an Indian war. Let it appear also from your representations, that ages will be necessary to settle those extensive regions.[20]

In his first meeting with Jay, the Spanish minister, Floridablanca, spoke of America's pretensions to the navigation of the Mississippi as a great diplomatic obstacle.[21] Jay was first of the opinion that the United States could afford to sacrifice these interests for the time being in return for Spain's recognition of American independence, financial aid, and military assistance.[22] But when Spain went to war with England and not only disregarded the United States but "declared war for objects that did not include ours, and in a manner not very civil to our independence," Jay decided "that we ought not to cede to her any of our rights, and of course that we should retain and insist upon our right to the navigation of the Mississippi." Before Jay had been in Spain many months, he advised Diego, Gardoqui, the Spanish envoy:

> that the Americans, almost to a man, believed that God Almighty had made that river a highway for the people of the upper country to go to the sea by; that this country was extensive and fertile; that the General, many officers, and others of distinction and influence in America, were deeply interested in it; that it would rapidly settle, and that the inhabitants would not readily be convinced of the justice of being obliged, either to live without foreign commodities, and lose the surplus of their productions, or be obliged to transport both over rugged mountains and through an immense wilderness to and from the sea, when daily they saw a fine river flowing before their doors and offering to save them all that trouble and expense, and that without injury to Spain.[23]

Congress had to weigh the possibility of gaining Spanish loans against Spain's insistence on full control of the Floridas and the Mississippi River. The Floridas presented no great obstacle. In 1778, Congress gave its approval to Spain's taking Florida and in 1779 promised assistance in the conquest, but the Mississippi dispute found Congress unyielding. The French ministers at Philadelphia repeatedly urged Congress to make the necessary concessions.[24] France, in her desire for Spain's naval help, thought she could only get it if Spain got what she wanted in the New World.

Congress, desperate for funds to purchase supplies in Europe, persisted in seeking Spanish aid. Even if the territorial issue had not stood in the way, Spain's own financial difficulties after declaring war on England in June 1779 militated against an extension of loans. The British cut off the shipment of treasure from her colonies, and Spain was forced to borrow from France. Despite stringent finances, the Spanish government encouraged Jay to expect that a loan was forthcoming. Jay reported this to Congress, and Congress took the hazardous step of underwriting orders of supplies to be paid for out of these prospective funds. Spain, in the meantime, made available only a part of the money agreed upon. Consequently, Jay faced a critical situation in which merchants held bills payable by him.[25] In July, 1780, Jay was told by a representative of Floridablanca not to accept any further bills until Spain's agent at Philadelphia, Miralles, returned. The Spanish government was waiting to see if Congress would come to an agreement on the western boundary. When Jay had a conference with Gardoqui in September, the Spanish official made it clear that Americans could scarcely expect financial aid unless they offered something in return, and he raised the question of the Mississippi, and Spain's needs for ship timber and vessels.

The following day Del Campo, secretary to Floridablanca, lectured Jay on the evil of underwriting purchases for which he had no funds. He told Jay "that the king must first take care of his own people before he gave supplies to others; that Spain, instead of deriving advantage from America, heard of nothing but demands."[26] America, Del Campo charged, was in a ruinous condition and some of the states were secretly suing for peace. The Spaniard's brusque talk deeply offended Jay. Only Franklin among the Americans avoided pique. He confided to Jay that Spain owed the Americans nothing and that it would be best to be patient and accept in a gracious spirit the minor advantages Spain might bestow.[27]

On February 15, 1781, Congress agreed to concede Spain's control of the Mississippi if that would serve to make her an effective ally.[28] Jay soon learned of this step from the French ambassador and concluded that Spain knew of his new instructions. After mulling over his situation from every point of view, Jay decided not to adhere to the decision of Congress. He came to the conclusion that Spain would not commit herself to an alliance, and that she merely sought to pry offers from the United States which could be used in some future negotiation. Jay explained to Congress that he would have used the instruction as a trump card to prevent a separate peace between Spain and Britain but as the situation stood he could not justify using it. His reasoning had a ring of realpolitik: Why, he asked, make concessions to secure an alliance when Spain, already at war with Great Britain, when they would not "render her exertions more vigorous or her aids to us much more liberal?" Jay concluded: "The cession of this navigation will, in my opinion, render a future war with Spain unavoidable, and I shall look upon my subscribing to the one as fixing the certainty of the other."[29] He did inform Floridablanca of the concession but made it contingent on Spain's recognition of American independence and agreement to the Mississippi as the western boundary of the United States.

Spanish coolness stemmed not only from fear of a hardy race of American settlers pushing on their own colonies, but from the more immediate danger of American commercial competition in the Gulf of Mexico. In 1781 the Spanish minister candidly explained that Spain must have an exclusive monopoly of the trade there.[30] To admit one nation would be as contrary to Spanish interests as admitting several, for she would not be able to compete. Here lay the great fear that guided Spanish policy.

On the eve of peace negotiations the Reverend John Witherspoon, member of Congress, observed that the territorial ambitions of Americans had already made Europeans uneasy.[31] He was quite content to confine the United States to the territory whose rivers flowed into the Atlantic, but in this respect Witherspoon was unique. Congress agreed almost unanimously that the western boundary should be the Mississippi River, and declared that under the English charters these lands already rightfully belonged to the colonies. Economic considerations strengthened this conviction, as did fear of powerful neighbors. This gave rise to nightmarish protests in which the United States was portrayed as grimly hanging on to a narrow strip of coastal territory, its independence made subject to mockery.

In their first venture into diplomacy Americans knew exactly what they wanted: independence, fishing rights, the territory from west of the Alleghenies to the Mississippi River, and free access down that outlet to the sea. For a new nation, as yet uncertain of internal unity and dependent in large part on foreign sources of arms, these were ambitious aims. The European scene with which they must deal was one of rivalry in which they could become victims of sharp bargaining. They had much to receive and nothing to give except bright promises of the future.

There was both a rigid persistency and vanity in John Adams, but he was also a man of complete integrity and a superfluity of frankness that made him an undiplomatic diplomat. He was possessed by an unilateral point of view. The national interests of other powers received scarcely any attention from the inflexible Massachusetts patriot, and he was certainly strongly disinclined to bend in their favor if those interests in any degree conflicted with the interests of the United States. But he was a man deserving of respect, highly intelligent, skillful in presenting the American side, and able and ever ready to seize on any weakness in the argument of an opponent.

On the other hand, restraint was foreign to John Adams whenever he detected wrong doing. When he attacked Siles Deane, he was, in fact, lecturing Benjamin Franklin, who had been a friend of Deane, and worse still in Adams' eyes, appeared to be guilty of servility to Count Vergennes.

Adams was guided by the maxim "Virtue is not always amiable." "Integrity is sometimes ruined by Prejudices and by Passions," he observed. In a reference to Arthur Lee and Ralph Izard he said that they were men of honor but their "prejudices and violent Tempers would raise Quarrells in the Elysian Fields if not in Heaven." Passions and bad temper were great evils, but it appears that Adams was equally disturbed by what he saw as Franklin's love of ease and dissipation. These qualities in a man made reformation difficult. Perhaps Franklin in his quiet musings might well have asked why Congress should have burdened him with such a colleague.

Except for Benjamin Franklin, this unilateral approach was also true of John Jay and Henry Laurens. Jay, like Adams, was brilliant and also a staunch defender of national interests, but in other respects he had a radically different personality. Priding himself on good manners and graciousness, Jay was legalistic in his approach, but after his experience as minister to Spain, he was likewise distrustful of his opposites.

A sharp contrast to his fellow peacemakers, Benjamin Franklin could overlook human frailty, never expected perfection, chose to live life to the full, and was a master at winning the confidence of Vergennes. His wit, enjoyment of human foibles, flirtations with female acquaintances and a lackadaisical attitude at times, led to misunderstanding. But Franklin was not a man who would sell his country short. He flattered Vergennes and time and again praised the French for their support. More was to be gained by an attitude of trust and cordiality than by lecturing Vergennes at length as John Adams did. The sophisticated, worldly, playful and witty Franklin, the most popular man in France, disgusted the stern and ever serious Adams.

Adams' jealousy of Franklin's popularity and his objections to Franklin's lifestyle might have created a hostility that could have been destructive, but in the negotiations Franklin was as rigid as Adams and Jay in his assertion of American interests. As Richard Morris, historian and author of *The Peacemakers*, observes: "There was about Benjamin Franklin a certain suppleness and depth that set him apart from his two more unbending and less complicated colleagues in the peacemaking, John Jay and John Adams, neither of whom had his capacity for indolence nor his gift for enjoying the fine art of frivolity."[32] Both Jay and Adams were able negotiators, and they were to find that Franklin, whose "saltiness, ribald streak, and long spells of apathy and inattention to official correspondence, reticence and inscrutable ways contrasted sharply with their own lifestyles, was as rigid and adamant as they on such issues as the Tories and perhaps surpassed them as an expansionist." As Gerald Stourzh points out, in his study of Franklin and foreign policy, Franklin thought of expansion in terms of power.[33] An ultimate hope was the annexation of Canada, not because the nation needed more land or because Canada had resources the United States needed, but because it would eliminate the possibility of border rivalry with the British and deprive Great Britain of a launching pad for an invasion or the threat of invasion. Franklin made little use of the term "rights," he thought in terms of interests and power.

The American victory at Yorktown in October 1781 opened the way to the making of peace. The French contributed approximately half of the troops, and when the British sought to escape by sea, the French fleet under Comte François Joseph Paul de Grasse blocked the way. Six thousand British troops had no choice but to surrender. George III now faced strong demands to agree to make peace.

Since peacemaking involved France, Spain, and Great Britain as well as the United States, the military victory at Yorktown did not assure achievement of American peace aims. The United States was bound to France and obligated as an ally not to make a separate peace. France, in turn, was bound to Spain and obligated not to make peace until Spain's aims were achieved. It appeared that not only must Great Britain be won over to accepting American independence and American claims, but also some way must be found to reconcile the sharply conflicting interests of the United States and Spain.

A major block to arranging the peace was the set of ambitious demands of the United States formulated by Congress in Philadelphia, and the even more ambitious aims of Spain. Aside from an unqualified recognition of independence, Congress called for fishing rights and the right to dry fish off the shores of Nova Scotia, a western boundary at the Mississippi River, free access for American navigation of the mouth of the Mississippi through territory controlled by Spain, and the annexation of Canada. These claims had no other basis than that what had once been England's now belonged to the United States. The United States had carried out only one military thrust into the Northwest Territory under George Rogers Clark and had captured Vincennes, but had not established control across the mountains. Only a thin line of American settlements crossed the Appalachian mountains into what was then known as the state of Franklin. Who was to possess these territories was still to be decided.

Spain's significant contribution to American victory, forcing the British to disperse some of their military forces to the Floridas, was of no account. Americans assumed that their long held colonial charters bestowed upon them the right to the first claim. At stake for Spain was commercial dominance of the Gulf of Mexico and security from American expansion westward.

France had entered the alliance with the United States hoping to weaken the British empire. She had not committed herself to supporting the western claims of the

Americans. Vergennes viewed the American claims as extravagant, but he was more shocked by the lavish Spanish demands calling for the recovery of Gibraltar. Both stood in the way of making peace. He was prepared to sacrifice the American claims. By the time of the final peace negotiations in the fall of 1782, he not only favored British retention of Canada, but he was ready to support British claims in the backlands of the Northwest. Such a division would allow for rivalry between the United States and England, which would promote an American disposition to side with France in future difficulties.[34]

In the final negotiations during the fall of 1782, the British, suffering from charges at home that they were capitulating to the Americans, sought to have the boundary between Canada and the United States moved southward unless the United States would agree to compensate the loyalists.

The boundary question received no attention during the first soundings for peace between Franklin and Richard Oswald, who represented the Earl of Shelburne, the British secretary of state for Home and Colonial Affairs. Franklin proposed the accession of all of Canada, suggesting that such a settlement would foster friendly relations in the years ahead, and Oswald viewed the proposal with some favor. Otherwise, Franklin adhered to ambiguity in his discussions, preferring to entice the British into continuing the argument but avoiding any observations that the British might seize upon as commitments once serious negotiations got underway.

Relations between France and the American peace commissioners in Paris during the summer opened a breach that was to have significant consequences. The United States, including Congress and the peace commissioners, counted on France to support their boundary claims. John Jay, distrustful because of the shabby treatment he had received in Spain and, as a lawyer, intent on looking behind eloquent words for hidden meanings, was prepared to believe the worst. John Adams, guided by the maxim that virtue is not always amiable and integrity is often sacrificed to self-interest, stood guard over American interests. Adams had engaged Vergennes in a heated argument in the spring of 1781, when he learned that Vergennes had agreed to mediation by Austria and Russia. At that time Vergennes had no hope that the British would set aside pride and grant the Americans independence. He believed that mediation would be a useful face-saving device enabling the British to make peace. The terms of the mediation included a provision that the United States should be represented and granted independence, but the terms also included a provision that peace should be based on the principles of *uti possidetis*, whereby the British would retain control of territories still in her military possession. The British forces held parts of Maine, New York, and Georgia, and this would leave the United States a truncated union of noncontiguous parts. Adams was shocked on finding that France was ready to accept such a proposal. The Americans escaped from this danger thanks to George III, who rejected mediation on the ground that he could not admit the right of foreign powers to intervene in the empire.

Adams' distrust of the French was more than matched by John Jay's feelings. Adams said of Jay that he did not like Frenchmen: "He says they are not a Moral People. They know not what it is. He don't like any Frenchman—the Marquis de la Fayette is clever but he is a Frenchman."[35]

What Vergennes saw as a necessity dictated by financial stringency and sharp criticism at home that he had committed a grievous error in making the alliance with the United States, Adams and Jay saw as evidence of moral delinquency. French betrayal was confirmed for Jay and Adams when they met with Aranda, Spanish Ambassador in Paris, who had arrived from Spain, and Rayneval, the close associate of Vergennes. Aranda proposed that Spain should have the territory up to Lake Erie west of the Appalachians and westward to the Mississippi. Rayneval supported the Spanish claim, asserting that the American claims were exaggerated.[36]

Previously, in preliminary negotiations on August 10, Franklin and Jay met with Vergennes. It developed into a meeting with unforeseen consequences. Vergennes encouraged them to go forward with negotiations with the British, adding only that while the negotiations should proceed separately they must finally all be tied together.[37] The meeting also had a second important result. Adams seized the occasion to inform Vergennes of the territorial demands that Aranda had presented. Rayneval, who was also present, promptly defended the Spanish claims and stated once again that the Americans had no basis for their claims. Vergennes sat silently by, thereby giving the impression that he agreed with Rayneval.[38] This further confirmed the suspicions of Adams and Jay, who were ready to pursue separate negotiations with the British. Franklin, who had enjoyed cordial relations with Vergennes, questioned their thinking.

When Jay heard that Rayneval was going on a secret mission to England, he suspected that Rayneval's purpose was to encourage the British to stand firm against the Americans. Historians long believed that this was not the case, but documents now show that, while this was not Rayneval's major purpose, he did sound out the British and it appears that Shelburne agreed that American claims were exaggerated.

Vergennes had been careful in his dealings with the Americans not to give any hint of his willingness to sacrifice the interests of his American ally. However, we know now what Adams and Jay could only suspect. Vergennes had reached the conclusion before this time that the Americans were not justified and that their demands must not stand in the way of making peace. Faced with Vergennes' resort to expediency, the peace commissioners chose to slip out of the noose by going ahead independently with the British, who, as good fortune would have it, reached the decision on the evening of August 28 to move forward and tentatively accept Franklin's necessary articles.

The American-British negotiations confronted touchy

questions concerning fishing rights, compensation for the loyalists, and debts owed to British merchants. Halfway through the negotiations, due to protests from special interests in London, new instructions arrived that, should the Americans refuse to compensate the loyalists, then the British were entitled to the backlands, the territories between the Ohio River and the Great Lakes. Shelburne told Oswald that the Americans, in basing their claims on the old colonial charters, were resorting to "nonsense." This posed a danger of breakup of negotiations, but Jay held firm.[39]

In the course of these negotiations, Franklin proposed that they should keep Vergennes informed. Jay adamantly opposed this. To inform the French court was to assure that the British would have the advantage of full information.[40]

The new nation had now been recognized as independent and had been successful in acquiring the rich lands of the upper Ohio valley and the territory around the Great Lakes. The Americans' certainty that these vast lands were theirs by right had been challenged many times since the victory at Yorktown. Whether it belonged to them by "right" could be disputed, but their "rights" were as good or better than those of their competitors. The Americans had won a diplomatic victory thanks in part to the rivalries in Europe. The first step had been taken toward the eventual creation of an empire.

Making peace in the international sphere is much less a question of the rights than it is of the power of the contestants. So it was in 1782. The alliance of the United States and France, with the aid of the Spanish fleet, dictated the eventual British defeat. The victory of American and French forces at Yorktown reduced British war efforts in North America to a lost cause. The financial weakness of France compelled the French to seek peace. Spain's ambitions extended far beyond her power.

Other nations viewed American claims as extravagant, and to them it was not a question of "rights." National interests were saved when the American peace commissioners violated the instructions of Congress to be guided by Vergennes. This resulted in the peace settlements depending on negotiations with England alone. In this contest the Americans had an upper hand. The British accepted that there was no possibility of realizing their last hope, some kind of an Anglo-American union. They had learned too that the American peace commissioners were intractable as far as independence and the Mississippi boundary were concerned. The British recognized that to continue the war was impossible. After the negotiations came to a close, John Jay went to London, where he met Shelburne, who asked him if the Americans would have fought rather than give up the backlands. Jay answered that he supposed that they would have fought and that he would have so advised them.

In accounting for the success of the colonists, it is well to take note of the judgment of Richard Morris, author of the highly acclaimed book *The Peacemakers*, who wrote:

> Men of little vision and less faith could not discern the shape of things to come. It was this prescience with which the American commissioners were endowed which rendered their diplomacy at once so effectual and by the same token so distasteful to their European counterparts, save for visionaries like Oswald and Hartley. Franklin, Jay and Company were instruments of a new revolutionary society. They were principals in a great confrontation of the Old Order and the New. The Old Order, in which even adversaries were tied together by blood and caste, were unaccustomed to treating as equals men of lesser social rank. With its balance-of-power politics, its pseudo-Machiavellian ethics, and its objectives of limited gains, the Old Order could not comprehend revolutionary ends, which, in the rhetoric of the day so faithfully reported from American by Barbé-Marbois, could accept "no middle ground" between "slavery and liberty."[41]

2

The First Transition: The Difficulties of a Client State, 1789–1815

FROM the beginning, the fragile United States republic faced the difficulties of an underdeveloped state. It needed to achieve financial solvency, to win the confidence of a variety of interests, and, above all to reconcile its close Anglo-American financial and commercial relations with its alliance with France. Troubled by feelings of uncertainty, Americans bolstered their spirits by nurturing the myth that representative government in their republic was the light of the world, and if it failed, then the future of republican principles would give way before a continuation of despotism. The myth gave them courage to face the outside world, but immediate realities demanded their closest attention. Economic interests were important, but they were closely tied to considerations of security, pride and conflicts in the realm of domestic politics.

Parties had yet to emerge, but from the time of settlement there was a conflict between rival political persuasions. Merchants looked forward to a central government able to promote foreign trade, protect merchant ships in the far corners of the world, and able to ensure stability so that the counting houses would not be subject to swirls of unpredictability.

Agrarians, largely dependent on weather and their own efforts, had a different view. For them the national government was far away and their immediate concerns were local. But they too looked to the government to help them achieve access to port cities so that they could market their surpluses. And they expected protection from the Indians and from their other warlike neighbors across the borders. Thomas Jefferson cherished them as independent yeomen, the foundation of a free society. This was at the heart of "republican principles," the ideological construct so dear to both Jefferson and Madison.

The two sides differed sharply about who should be at the controls. Merchants were men of law and order who called for expertise in finance, experience in the marketplace, and administrators who understood the procedures in a counting house. Agrarians, having not only different interests but a different mind-set, could not trust the merchants, who did not produce, but who seemed inherently selfish and often placed their own interests above those of the country. Believers in republican principles were intent on having their representatives in Congress control the purse, and the purse was the Treasury. It must be subject to close scrutiny and be subordinate to the legislative branch. Therein lay the seeds of controversy and irreconcilable disputes.

The differences were as much ideological as they were economic. The Jeffersonians owed much of their thinking to the writings of Lord Bolingbroke, Alexander Pope, and John Dryden, the men of literature in England who saw in the ministry of Horace Walpole a government by manipulation.[1] All three were widely read in America. Jefferson, Madison and their followers believed that, in the train of a consolidated government unchecked by strict adherence to the constitution, there would inevitably follow degeneration, corruption and eventually tyranny. To both Jefferson and Madison the word "corruption" did not mean thievery but taking power from the people by commanding support in the legislature by the use of patronage and special privileges.

James Madison, the most prominent architect in the building of the constitutional structure, had lived through the difficult years during the Revolution and had concluded that, either by a restructuring of the articles of the Constitution or by the establishment of a new government, the rule of passions in state legislatures could be restrained and a firmer posture could be achieved in for-

eign affairs. He was at one and the same time a nationalist and firm believer in republican principles. He favored
strengthening the central government but strictly limit-
ing its powers.[2]

Neither Alexander Hamilton nor his supporters were
the "monarchists" that Jefferson accused them of being,
nor did Hamilton seek to enrich himself. He firmly believed that sound and wise leadership could be crippled
by a zealous adherence to the check-and-balance system
and a literal adherence to the Constitution. He aimed at
creating a consolidated government.[3]

Hamilton believed that the future of the republic depended upon putting its finances in order and promoting
economic growth. Jefferson and Madison dreaded the em-
ulation of the British system that Hamilton so much admired. They too were firm believers in a sound fiscal system and were anxious to pay the debts, but they believed
that this system alone would not suffice to build a strong
republic. Hamilton focused his attention on the merchant class; Jefferson, Madison and Gallatin believed that
a powerful republic must have a broad base of support
from planters in the South, pioneers in the West, and the
eastern merchants. Gallatin, who had lived among the
frontier settlements, knew that if the pioneers were accorded fair treatment they would support the Union.
Jefferson and Madison were southern planters and were
confident of support.

Historians provided later generations with conflicting
interpretations of Hamilton and Jefferson. Henry Adams
saw the difference between the two men in broad perspective and gave both their due. Adams was convinced
that sovereignty rested as much on other factors as on financial credit, although credit was important. The difference, he said, was broader than the issue of credit. The
statesmen represented two great divisions of thought and
were not mere declaimers. They never for a moment mis-
understood each other, says Adams, and "no compromise
between them was or ever will be possible. . . . Mr. Jefferson meant that the American system should be a democ-

racy, and he would let the world perish rather than this principle, which to him represented all that man was worth, should fail. Mr. Hamilton considered democracy a fatal course, and meant to stop its progress."[4]

In 1970, Broadus Mitchell, a liberal, surprised the scholarly world with his admiration for Hamilton. He credited him with devising the solvency of the government and contended that solvency was the basis of sovereignty. Jefferson's forte, said Mitchell, was democracy and Hamilton's was effective organization.

Jefferson and Madison placed a high priority on the check-and-balance system written into the Constitution. Only that system could save the republic for control by the people. Hamilton placed the highest priority on the need of the underdeveloped country for solvency and foreign capital to develop its great natural resources.

Except for his call for a protective tariff, Hamilton's program was adopted by Congress, but only after strong opposition. The creation of a national bank, privately owned, whose notes were granted legal tender status, the only bank to enjoy this great advantage, caused it to be decried as the monopoly of the monied interests. Critics charged that the bank constituted a government within a government, free of public control. Defenders of the national bank pointed out that it was useful as a government depository, could extend loans to the government, and that it would serve as a stabilizer of the currency and thereby prevent violent swings in the business cycle.

The measure creating the greatest outcry was Hamilton's provision for the assumption of state debts. The news spread that insiders sent out agents to buy up almost worthless state script. There were other criticisms. The southern states had already paid their state debts and would not benefit. Against these criticisms Hamilton pointed out that once the United States gained a reputation for paying all its debts, then its credit abroad would be firmly established.

None of Hamilton's measures aroused greater opposition than his creation of the sinking fund. He greatly admired the British government and believed that it was the existence of a sinking fund that made England prosperous. Once put into operation in the United States it became the whipping boy of the Jeffersonians. Albert Gallatin, fully Hamilton's match in financial matters, argued that a sinking fund had no place in a government that was in debt; the most important commitment of the republic should be to pay the debts. In years ahead, as the debt increased, the sinking fund came under ever stronger attack. However, Hamilton made shrewd use of the fund. Whenever government bonds declined in value, he used the fund to buy up the bonds and restore them to par. Some private speculators profited by the measure, but at the same time Hamilton's action encouraged foreigners to invest in the United States.

Too often the difficult financial problems faced by the republic have not received full attention. When Hamilton became secretary of the treasury the federal government had a foreign debt of $11.7 million, federal domestic debts of $40.4 million, and state debts assumed by the federal government were estimated at $25 million. The annual interest on this debt was $4,587,444. The operating expenses of the government totaled $1,600,000.

Government revenues were far from adequate to meet expenses. The revenue from import duties, constituting 98 percent of its income, was $6,634,263.84 in 1790. Three years later these revenues declined to $4,615,559.36. In the spring of that year Hamilton faced the prospect of having only $43,000 in the treasury unless he was able to borrow abroad.[5] Only foreign loans kept the government afloat. There was no feasible way to cut expenses and no way to increase funding short of direct taxes, which ran counter to public feelings.

Thanks to Hamilton's measures, the government was able to borrow abroad, and to borrow at lower interest rates than other countries. The Jeffersonians denounced the sinking fund, stating that the money should have been used to pay the debt. They also advised boldly that direct taxes should be levied.

There were dangers in the course that Hamilton pursued. Should war come to Europe, then the loans would be cut off. It was this risk that later caused Gallatin, when he became secretary of the treasury, to reduce the debt and stop borrowing abroad.

Central, however, to Hamilton's program was the attraction of foreign capital. The nation was rich in resources waiting to be developed. To bring this about it was necessary to encourage foreign investment. The United States was already a part of the business world. Aspirations for building a sound and strong economy were as viable as the hopes of the Jeffersonians for a democratic republic. A former president of the American Economics Association, E. A. J. Johnson, has said it was "the conscious and unashamed acceptance of a system of politics-economic pluralism that made possible the vigor and the catholicity of our institution." It is quite wrong, he argued, "to assume that ours was merely an experiment with the simple system of natural liberty; it was quite otherwise, a militant, pragmatic, conflict-fashioned variant of neo-libertarian public policy that comprised rather than harmonized the demand of existing and emergent interests."[6]

The conflict between the two persuasions was not over whether the debts should be paid. Jefferson wrote to a business friend in London that, "though one here affects to charge the other with unfriendly disposition towards the public debt, yet I believe there is not a man scarcely in the United States who is not secretly determined to pay it." The difference between the two parties, Jefferson wrote, "is that the republican one wish it could be paid tomorrow, and the fiscal party wish it to be perpetual because they find it an engine for corrupting the legislature."[7] To Jefferson "corrupting the legislature" meant undue influence by the executive; the legislature, elected by the people, must not be subject to manipulation by the executive. Hamilton's measures, particularly the sinking fund, gave him, in Jefferson's view, control over the nation's finances. The republican principles so dear to

Jefferson and Madison stressed the importance of the power of the purse. That authority should not be surrendered to a member of the executive branch, who was not subject to control by the people through Congress.

The powerful figure of Hamilton, who dominated the administration, presided over the controversy. Dedicated to the imperative of financial solvency, he let nothing stand in his way. He did not hesitate to use the prestige of Washington to carry through his program, and often provided members of Congress who were sympathetic to his views with speeches that were persuasive. He shut his eyes to the lines of responsibility of cabinet departments. Jefferson was secretary of state, but Hamilton intruded repeatedly in foreign affairs. He was less concerned about the principles laid down in the Constitution. He was a hard-driving pragmatist of great skill and with the ability to override his opponents. Democracy was not his goal; a powerful state led by a strong executive suited his preferences.

In contrast, the Jeffersonians had a dream. It was to be a republic of self-government. If it were to achieve that goal, the power of the purse must be in the hands of the people. They saw in Hamilton a man who seized control and governed by manipulation. While Hamilton saw as a necessity the executive branch winning influence in the legislature and pushing it along enlightened paths, Jefferson labelled that practice corruption.

The clash between the two men was in part due to a difference in personalities. Jefferson was a languid man and one who took the long view and moved with caution. He was guided by his commitment to the check-and-balance system and fearful of a concentration of power. Hamilton was the epitome of action and energy and was often not slow to feel frustration. To get things done was more important than rigid adherence to the check-and-balance system.

Hamilton was the dominating figure in the administration. Not only did he intrude in Jefferson's Department of State, he used his power to combat Jefferson at every turn. At times he looked on Congress as a committee made up of captious troublemakers who continually insisted on detailed reports on his handling of funds. Congress was jealous of its authority. Hamilton viewed its actions as petty and interfering with his work. Suspicion led to charges that the secretary of the treasury was profiting, but no evidence appeared, then or since, of wrong doing. Nevertheless, the latitude he exercised in his management of funds was in conflict with the popular spirit that identified self-government with control of the purse.

The controversy mounted into a battle of mutual recriminations. In response to criticism of his program in Congress, Hamilton wrote the *Catullus* papers charging that Jefferson had inspired the attacks made upon Hamilton by Freneau's *Gazette*. To be sure, Freneau's criticism was wild and denunciatory and catered to the worst suspicions of the public. Jefferson and Madison had employed Freneau in the Department of State, but his low level of journalism was wholly inconsistent with their thinking. Hamilton declared that Jefferson was both a patron and promoter of disunion, national insignificance, public disorder, and discredit.[8] To destroy what he had done, Hamilton declared, "would be one of the most flagitious acts, that ever stained the annals of a civilized nation."[9]

Madison's major objective was to reduce dependence upon Great Britain and to bolster the alliance with France with economic ties. To achieve this he introduced a bill providing for higher duties on British ships than on ships from countries that had entered into diplomatic relations with the United States. British dominance, he said, was due to "long possession of our trade, their commercial regulations calculated to retain it, their similarity of language and manners, their conformity of laws and other circumstances—all these concurring have made their commerce with us more extensive than their natural situation would require it to be."[10]

The opposition quickly pointed out that the higher rates on British ships could only mean higher prices on the goods Americans bought. Madison replied that the patriotism of Americans would cause them to make the necessary sacrifice, and that Americans in a short time could be induced to build a merchant marine, as American ships would have an advantage over all foreign ships.

Madison's goal was to command the respect of the British, who had so recently carried on a war against Americans and who were violating the treaty of peace by occupying American territory in the northwest and refusing to negotiate. "We have now the power to avail ourselves of our natural superiority," he said, "and I am for beginning with some manifestation of that ability, that foreign nations may or might be taught to pay us that respect which they have neglected on account of our former imbecility."[11] Madison and Jefferson were to go to great lengths to implement this program that would rescue the new republic from its status as a client state of Great Britain. Before resigning as secretary of state late in 1793, Jefferson put together extensive statistics on trade, showed how economic ties to Great Britain placed the republic in a position of dependence, and urged that the republic be freed from the "commercial manacles" by which it was bound to Great Britain.

Here was a challenge to Hamilton's program, and when Jefferson presented it, a member of the Senate delivered a speech prepared by Hamilton that reduced Madison's proposal to a nullity. France had neither the capital nor the manufacturers that were needed, and to engage in commercial warfare with a powerful nation would be dangerous. Madison cherished an illusion that the United States could cripple the British by shutting off food supplies to the British West Indies. This was the British window of vulnerability that Madison looked to for leverage.

Madison's proposals threatened the merchant class and particularly New England, where the merchants depended on British credit. In a later stage of the controversy, Fisher Ames of Massachusetts dismissed the notion that dependence on England was humiliating. Ames asserted that if "our trade is already on a profitable footing, it is on a respectable one."[12]

The outbreak of war between Great Britain and France in February 1793 widened the rift. Ever since the beginning of revolution in France in July of 1789, Americans had focused their attentions on the upheaval. At first it was heralded as an overthrow of absolute rule and as a sign that the American Revolution was the harbinger of a new day. No one had greater confidence in the French Revolution than Thomas Jefferson. He was minister to France in that crucial summer of 1789 and was consulted by its leaders when they drew up the *Declaration of the Rights of Man*. His faith in the revolution continued, and he saw it as the opening of a new era when liberty would prevail. However, as Dumas Malone states in his biography, there was no danger that Jefferson was about to hitch the republic to France and involve the country in war.[13]

War in Europe elevated the question of relations with France to the foremost problem of the day. Treaty commitments to France were far reaching. Articles 11 and 12 of the Treaty of Alliance spelled out the difficulties. Article 11 committed the United States to aid France in the defense of her colonies in the West Indies. Article 12 bound the United States to uphold the principle that free ships make free goods and therefore goods on a neutral ship, regardless of its final destination, were not subject to seizure. Article 23 posed an equal danger. It provided that ships of war and privateers were to be free to enter each other's ports and free to bring into each other's ports ships or goods that they might capture. Strict observance of these treaty provisions would render the republic a cobelligerent and make war with the British inevitable.

Hamilton had long been distrustful of pro-French feelings and had already convinced himself that the Treaty of Alliance was no longer binding. His most vocal critics were admirers of the French, and across the country there were republican societies whose members called each other by the names of leaders of the French Revolution.

Their ardent partisanship ran counter to the views of a small republic that found its interest to be neutrality and peace. Word that a new minister from France was about to arrive prompted Hamilton to urge President Washington to call a cabinet meeting to discuss the now delicate diplomatic position of the United States. Hamilton took the view that the treaty with France was no longer binding since a new government had been established in France and the king with whom the treaty had been made had been decapitated.[14] He called for an immediate breaking off of relations with France. When the cabinet met, it was decided unanimously that the United States should remain neutral. Jefferson thought no proclamation was necessary, and Hamilton did not have his way. Jefferson and Attorney General Edmund Randolph held that the new minister from France, Edmond Charles Édouard Genêt, should be received without reservations. Jefferson also argued that the treaty with France was made with the people of that country and was still binding. The cabinet went along with Jefferson's argument.

Hamilton exaggerated the danger that Jefferson's followers would rally to France, but two of his own supporters, Rufus King and Edward Carrington, advised him that there was no cause for alarm. Both King and Carrington also told Hamilton that the treaty with France was still valid because the new government exercised complete authority. Carrington pointed out that to do otherwise than hold the treaty valid "would manifest more than a spirit of neutrality," it would be to take sides. Carrington saw no danger of the United States becoming involved in the war.[15]

In the exchange of views a question arose that was to trouble the conduct of American foreign relations many times in the future. Jefferson believed that the United States was under a moral obligation to abide by treaties in the same way, he explained, that individuals had an obligation to remain true to their promises. Hamilton took a radically different view: treaties were to be observed only so long as they coincided with national interests. Changing circumstances often demanded that a nation set a treaty aside; the Treaty of Alliance with France was a case in point. Jefferson could not accept this opinion. It reduced treaties to temporary agreements that could be cast aside whenever some advantage was to be gained by doing so. For Jefferson, moral obligation was written in the laws of nature and was the basis of the social order. The moral obligations of nations were likewise the basis of international order. The often-languid Jefferson could not sit quietly by as this was discussed. At stake was the heart of his whole political theory and the intellectual basis of the American political order. "For the reality of these principles," he wrote, "I appeal to the true fountains of evidence, the head and heart of every rational and honest man. It is there Nature has written her moral laws, and where every man may read them for himself."[16] A nation that violates its moral obligations is guilty of perfidy and contributes to the destruction of peace.

There were, however, situations in which the individual was excused from the performance of obligations. When the individual facing a new situation confronts self-destruction if he adheres to the agreement, the law of self-preservation takes over. And so it is between nations. But the danger "must be great, inevitable and imminent."

Jefferson believed that the dangers anticipated from France did not present such a threat. What then were these dangers? Was it that the alliance "may taint us with despotic principles?" The agreement was entered into when France "was a perfect despotism, civil and military." Was it that the French government "may issue in a republic, and too much strengthen our republican principles?" It could not be that because this was the great hope of the mass of constituents. The "doctrine I am combatting, the change the French are undergoing may end in something we know not what, and bring on danger we know not whence . . . it is not the *possibility of danger*, which absolves a party from this contract: for that possibility always exists, and in every case."[17] The moral question was to trouble Americans time and again. Only the age of superpowers did the moral questions and the check-and-balance system lose their hold.

Hamilton was a pragmatist in a hurry, but he raised a most significant question about the moral approach. The rule of morality, he said, is not the same between individuals as between nations. The duty of a nation to promote its own welfare is much greater than the duty of the individual. The greater magnitude of a nation is greater than the happiness of an individual. The measures of government affect an entire society whereas the decisions of the individual are circumscribed within a narrow compass.[18] He might have added that the morals of the individual are often not the morals of a whole society.

Jefferson was not necessarily more moral than Hamilton. In his later years as president he was already to go to war against Spain and exaggerated the danger posed. At this point, in 1804, Albert Gallatin brought him back to face realities.

Genêt, the exuberant Gerondist, aglow with enthusiasm for the French Revolution, was received without reservations, but soon embarked on ventures that could only be tolerated if the republic had been a cobelligerent with France. On his arrival in Charleston in late April 1793 he commissioned four privateers to prey on British commerce. In Boston privateers were also fitted out and cruised outside the harbor, and two prizes were brought into port. At first the United States marshal took possession of the prizes, but then a French consul and an armed band took possession. Privateering was profitable and there was no shortage of Americans who put personal gain above the orders that Washington had issued. Genêt made a triumphal entry into Philadelphia and New York and was lavishly entertained.

The incident of the *Little Sarah* forced a decision. The brigantine had been fitted out in Philadelphia and was ready to go to sea as a privateer. When reports of her presence reached Hamilton, he informed Jefferson, who asked the governor of Pennsylvania to investigate. The governor, in turn, sent Alexander Dallas to request Genêt to delay the sailing until the president returned to Washington and could make a decision. Genêt flew into a rage and refused. Jefferson then called on Genêt and asked that he order the privateer to delay. Genêt would only say that the ship was not ready to sail.

Jefferson had already reached a decision: "Never, in my opinion, was as calamitous an appointment made, as that of the present minister of F. here."[19] Well before the incident of the *Little Sarah*, he had firmly opposed the actions of Genêt, but chose to avoid making the minister's behavior an excuse for breaking off relations with France. He still had hopes of settling the treaty questions that had arisen in negotiations. To break off relations with France would only leave the British freer to treat the United States as a client state.

The cabinet met, in the absence of the president, to decide what to do. Hamilton and Secretary of War Henry Knox wanted to fortify Mud Island to prevent the *Little Sarah* from sailing. Jefferson opposed this, on the grounds that Genêt would order the ship not to sail, and also because, should any blood be shed, it could bring on war. He also contended that the cabinet did not have the authority to act in the president's absence. Should the *Sarah* get away it could be explained satisfactorily to the British. It would, he said, be inconsistent "for a nation which has been patiently bearing for ten years the grossest insults and injuries from their late enemies, to rise at a feather against their friends and benefactors."[20] As it turned out, the *Little Sarah* only sailed down the river a short distance and did not go to sea.

Not until August 1, 1793, did the cabinet meet with the president. All were agreed that the French government should be asked to recall Genêt. Jefferson again stood on the side of caution. He opposed sending a peremptory letter. All except Knox were opposed to sending Genêt home at once. It was decided to send a letter to Genêt informing him of his recall. Again Jefferson opposed this because it would cause Genêt "to become extremely active in his plans." It was at these meetings that

Hamilton took a high tone, speaking for three quarters of an hour on two successive days.[21] During that same month the cabinet drew up a set of regulations prohibiting the equipping of any foreign vessels, whether warships, privateers, or merchant ships which appeared suspicious. This received unanimous approval.[22]

At no time did Jefferson in any way compromise with the actions of Genêt or the French consuls. He adhered with rigidity to a strict and impartial neutrality. Years later George Canning, British foreign secretary, in a speech in the House of Commons, stated: "If I wished for a guide in a system of neutrality, I should take that laid down by America in the days of the presidency of Washington and the secretaryship of Jefferson, in 1793."[23] John Quincy Adams also praised Jefferson. He wrote: "Mr. Jefferson's papers on that controversy present the most perfect model of diplomatic discussion and expostulation of modern times."[24] Jefferson refused to be stampeded into hasty actions in a moment of excitement and subordinated his private pro-French views to the national interest.

The differences between Jefferson and Hamilton partially reflected domestic politics. As the leaders of the future political parties, which were in the process of formation, each gave consideration to the political effects of Genêt's actions. After Genêt had been recalled, Jefferson observed that he had adhered to him as long as he had hope that he might set Genêt aright, because of the weight "we should derive to our scale by keeping it in the love of the people of the French cause and nation, and how important it was to ward off from that cause any just grounds of alienation"; however, "finding that the man was absolutely incorrigible, I saw the necessity of quitting a wreck which could not but sink all who would cling to it."[25]

Hamilton exploited the French issue to undermine Jefferson and his followers. His *Pacificus* letters to the press and his letters written under the pen name "No Jacobin" aimed at undermining gratitude toward France and in portraying what a mistake it would be to become involved in a war in Europe. The writings were aimed at a danger that was remote and at an opponent, Jefferson, who was as much opposed to involvement as Hamilton. In his final installment of "No Jacobin," Hamilton reduced the issue to one of patriotism. He denounced those who had justified Genêt's actions: "What baseness, what prostitution in a citizen of this country, to become the advocate of a pretention so pernicious, so unheard of, so detestable language is too poor to give a name to be abandoned a renunciation of principle."[26]

Hamilton's determination to weaken his critics led by Jefferson and Madison continued well after Genêt had been discredited. A letter from Stephen Higginson, the Boston Federalist, reported that there were only one hundred of the French party in that town.[27] A letter from Virginia informed Hamilton that sentiment in that state was in support of the government and that there was no need of concern. The correspondent, David Ross, a friend of Hamilton, confessed that he had been apprehensive that the members of the opposition party would rally to the French side but they had not. To this he added, "Mr. Genêt's conduct is considered a very lucky circumstance as it has been the means of proving so great a confidence of the people, in, and a desire to support the Dignity of their own Government exceeding the expectations of its earnest friends."[28]

The departure of Genêt and the decision in favor of neutrality had scarcely taken place when a crisis in relations with Great Britain posed new dangers. British seizures of American ships under an order-in-council of July 1793 was followed by an even bolder stroke on November 6 when the British ministry issued another order calling for the seizure of all ships laden with goods, the produce of any colony belonging to France, or carrying provisions or other supplies for use by the French colonies. Not until February did Congress learn that under these orders more than two hundred American ships had been seized.

At the beginning of the session Congress had received

Jefferson's famous report calling for an end to British dominance of American trade. A long and heated debate took place in which each side repeated the arguments that had been presented when Madison first made the proposal to Congress in 1789. Madison had expanded on the evils of British dominance. A sudden derangement of commerce could be brought about by the caprice of the British sovereigns. Should Great Britain face bankruptcy—in 1794 this was a possibility—it would bring a serious shock to the United States, whose financial system was tied to England. Finally Madison spoke of the influence "that may be conveyed in public councils by a nation directing the course of our trade by her capital, and holding so great a share in our pecuniary institutions, and the effect that may finally ensue in our taste, our manners, and our form of government itself."[29] Madison's concern was not to be dismissed lightly.

There was a limit beyond which the most ardent Federalists could no longer tolerate British imperiousness. That limit was reached when it was learned that the British had seized 250 American vessels in the West Indies alone. This alarm pushed aside Jefferson's call for measures to bring an end to the dominance of the British in American trade.

As the Jeffersonians saw it, Hamilton's obsequiousness in dealing with the British had brought about the latest orders-in-council and injuries to the republic. As Henry Adams wrote of these formative years extending to the War of 1812, the British expected their rivals to fight; if they did not, they looked upon them as cowardly or mean. The proud Jeffersonians meant to demand respect. Given the bold British measures, Madison acknowledged that something more was called for than discriminatory duties on British ships. The first week in April, Congress laid an embargo on all foreign shipping for one month. Here was the first intimation of how the Jeffersonians proposed to deal with an antagonist: not by strengthening the defenses to gain a stronger negotiating position, as the Federalists proposed, but by economic coercion.

Should the embargo fail and the British resort to arms, as they recognized could happen, then the United States would rely on militia and privateers.

Jefferson's and Madison's policy of economic coercion was based on their deep distrust. To place military power in the hands of the Federalists would augment their power in domestic affairs and might even be used against dissenters. Concerning the Federalist proposals for strengthening the military, Madison wrote to Jefferson: "You understand the game behind the curtain too well not to perceive the old trick of turning every contingency into a resource for accumulating force in the government."[30]

The ire of Jeffersonians in Congress over British presumption on the high seas burst forth in a proposal by Jonathan Dayton of New Jersey calling for the sequestration of all debts due from the citizens of the United States to subjects of Great Britain. William Giles of Virginia, like Dayton a man given to flamboyant pronouncements, supported the proposal by contending that only if the people of Great Britain were brought to fear for their own interests would they exert pressure on their government to negotiate.[31]

Dayton's measure failed to pass, but it signalled the danger ahead. Hamilton took the lead in proposing negotiation. The president agreed and suggested that Hamilton serve as the special envoy. The astute gentleman knew very well that any undertaking carried on by himself would wither away under a blight of distrust. He proposed that the president send John Jay, who had served as envoy to Spain and later participated in peace negotiations at the close of the War for Independence. Washington appointed Jay to a mission that would inevitably be difficult.

Behind the scenes, Hamilton wrote Jay's instructions. They called for an equitable settlement, one based on give-and-take. Accepting that the British would be unyielding on the seizure of American ships engaged in trade with the French, Hamilton sought to counter this with concessions by the British. Much was to be gained if the British would open their colonies in the West Indies to American ships. He was also hopeful that the British would withdraw from the forts they held in the northwest.

In his letters to Jay, Hamilton recognized that any surrender of legitimate interests or too great leniency toward the British would result in strong public opposition that might defeat the treaty. What worried him most was that the British would not yield on their seizure of ships nor would they accept the strict definition of contraband adhered to by the United States. His approach to this delicate problem lay in placing unpalatable British demands between two layers of pleasing concessions. He wrote to Jay: "If you can effect solid arrangements with regard to the points unexecuted of the treaty of peace, the question of indemnification may be managed with less rigor, and may be still more laxly dealt with if a truly beneficial treaty of commerce, embracing privileges in the West India Islands can be established."[32]

What Jay brought back was a treaty that promised peace but at a high price, so high that it has been viewed by many historians as a degrading and demanding surrender. James Madison and Albert Gallatin judged it that way at the time. Hamilton was disappointed but labored for its approval.

The treaty provided for British surrender of the forts in the northwest. It stipulated that the unsettled boundary controversies in the northwest and northeast be settled by a commission. Concerning the troublesome question of neutral trade, it provided that when goods were seized, a joint commission sitting in London should determine if the American owners were entitled to compensation. The treaty also urged that provisions going to France be treated as contraband.

Madison cited all of his objections to the treaty in a debate in the House of Representatives. Great Britain should have been made to pay for the losses incurred from her continued possession of the military posts. He protested with vigor against the provision that the British would be free to send goods into the northwest duty-free. This would serve to perpetuate a British military alli-

ance with the Indians in that region. Equally objection-
able was that the treaty outlawed future discrimination
against British goods entering the United States. This
nullified the long campaign of Jefferson and Madison to
achieve a better balance of trade and to reduce the influence of the British.[33] The Senate had already eliminated
Article 12, which provided for so limited an opening of
the West Indies that it was meaningless. It narrowed the
entry of American ships to those of less than seventy
tons and prohibited Americans' participation in the export of tropical fruit from the islands.

Jerald Combs, historian of the Jay Treaty, concluded
that Jay could not have secured any further concessions.[34]
John Jay was convinced that although the treaty was un-
satisfactory, it was at least preferable to war.

There was ample room for a difference of opinion.
President Washington held the treaty for months before
sending it to the Senate, and when a new order-in-council
was issued in April 1795 extending the order for the seizure of ships going to French ports, he temporarily decided against the treaty and he did not pass it on to the
Senate until that order was revoked.[35] In the Senate, Article 12 was revoked, and the treaty was only approved by
the vote of Vice President John Adams.

The Republicans in the House, led by Madison and
Gallatin, contended that as the treaty required appro-
priations if it was to be implemented, the House had a
voice. The session was a scene of extreme emotions.
Fisher Ames of Massachusetts, in an eloquent speech
that brought tears to his listeners, pleaded that to reject
the treaty would bring shame on the republic.

It was Gallatin who now came forth and distinguished
himself as a statesman, proclaiming that fear before and
during the negotiations, and now again, had paralyzed sober mindedness. And "now every imaginary mischief
which can alarm our fear is conjured up, in order to deprive us of that discretion which this House thinks it has
a right to exercise, and in order to force us to carry the
treaty into effect . . . ," he said. Fear and feelings were

strong in American life, and they were to make themselves a factor many times in American foreign relations.

Gallatin cited three evils which would result from the rejection of the treaty. The nation would be discredited by receiving no reparations for the spoilations on American trade, there would remain uncertainty over the final adjustment of differences with England, and there would be a further detention of the rightful possession of posts within American boundaries. He added that the divisions of political opinion in the country would be prolonged, and concluded with the words "however injurious and unequal I conceive the treaty to be, however repugnant it may be to my feelings and, perhaps, to my prejudices, I feel induced to vote for it, and will not give my consent to any proposition which would imply its rejection."[36]

The Jay Treaty set aside the internal controversy and opened the way to reconciliation. Both nations had been convinced of the justice of their cause, and the treaty was a compromise of irreconcilable national interests. To have continued the dispute would have been futile, dangerous, and destructive. The treaty was the more remarkable because it was negotiated and then approved in a period of passionate feelings and mutual distrust. The republic was in need of peace at home and abroad. A remarkable quiet pervaded Anglo-American relations during the next ten years. A major factor in the transformation was the undeclared war with France. In the next four years relations between the United States and Great Britain became so close that there was a brief flirtation with establishing a formal alliance.[37]

In 1805 President Jefferson stated that no two nations on earth enjoyed a sounder relation of friendliness than the United States and Great Britain. Prescience is not a common trait, even among talented individuals. There arose disputes over neutral rights, freedom of the seas, and the reexport trade, and these gradually escalated into an irreconcilable conflict during the Napoleonic Wars in Europe. War came in 1812. American grievances justified President Madison's declaration, but he had ignored the axiom that a nation must seek a balance between its power and its aims. It was a hazardous venture which neither England nor America won. The psychological effect of having stood up to the most powerful nation in the world offered adequate reward. The war did bring an end to the militant party warfare that had divided the nation from 1807 to 1812. In that limited sense Madison had saved the republic.

It was during the first Jefferson administration that European rivalries bestowed on the United States the acquisition of a territory west of the Mississippi River equal to the original national domain. Settlers west of the Alleghenies had long been frustrated by Spanish control of the mouth of the Mississippi, the only outlet by which western produce could reach world markets. Jefferson took up the cause, first voiced during the War for Independence, for a guarantee that the Mississippi be open to free trade. He initiated negotiations with France for the purchase of the territory at the mouth of the river, which had just recently been acquired by the French from Spain. That was the claim of France, but Spain, with some justice, held that the French had not lived up to the terms of the deal and that the territory belonged to her. Jefferson's negotiations came to a happy close when Napoleon offered to sell all of Louisiana. The Emperor of the French had readied a fleet to take possession of the Louisiana Territory during the previous fall only to have it prevented from sailing by an ice-bound harbor. He had also met failure in Santo Domingo. The peace with England was temporary, and he planned to renew the war. When that day came, the British fleet could take Louisiana. In his quest for security Jefferson had found an ally in European rivalry.

Spanish possession of the Floridas, a territory that Jefferson compared to a gun aimed at the United States, caused him to justify war by conjuring up the danger posed by Spain with the Floridas and a dilapidated fort in the distant west, but Gallatin argued that there was no threat. The inexorable march of events, plus the expansionist fever thriving on a legitimate concern for security, opened the way for Madison in 1810 to occupy West Florida. There was no danger, as Jefferson and Madison recognized, as long as a weak Spain held the Floridas, but given the rapidity of territorial transfers during the Napoleonic Wars, there was a real possibility that either Great Britain or France might take possession of the Floridas.

A settlement was delayed until after the War of 1812. Spain did not have the resources to develop Florida or to control the Indians within the territory. Restless soldiers and adventurers sought to capitalize on the situation. Similarly, John Quincy Adams had no hesitation in exploiting the helpless Spanish in his negotiations with Spain for the acquisition of the Floridas. When Andrew Jackson was sent to put down Indian border warfare, he swept through in such a swashbuckling fashion that there was a move in Washington to repudiate him. Adams came to his defense. Jackson's actions and Adams' defense convinced Spain that the Floridas were lost and that she could only hope that, in return for transferring the colony, she could drive a bargain for the territories west of the Mississippi. The transcontinental treaty negotiated by Adams yielded what was to become Texas, and carried American claims to rights on the Pacific shore, although it did not transfer territory west of the mountains. Once again, as during the negotiations after the War for Independence and after the War of 1812, the United States was moved by existing and emergent interests alongside of dreams of a model republic.

3

Manifest Destiny and Crisis in the Midnineteenth Century 1820–1850

In the three years from 1845 to 1848 the United States extended its territory by 1.2 million square miles. For the only time in its history, a president provoked one war and approached the brink of a second. The vast gain in territory approximated naked conquest. The war with Mexico disrupted internal peace. With the possible exception of the Vietnam War, no military involvement met with such bold opposition from the American people. Annexations sharpened sectionalism, catapulted the slavery question into the political arena, and eventually hastened the coming of the Civil War.

The politics of annexation provided a test of strength between popular national feelings of an adolescent nature, on the one side, and on the other side, prudence guided by experience, respect for the legitimate interests of other nations, and patient negotiation. Expansionism was not new, but in the past it had taken place in the aftermath of settlement, as the government purchased and by negotiation extended its boundaries.

The urge to settle remote areas was inherent in a country bordering on a largely unoccupied territory, populated by energetic doers, entrepreneurs, and farmers. From their days as colonists along the shores of the Atlantic Ocean, Americans sought lands ever westward across the Alleghenies. The process was peaceful, if we take the unwarranted liberty of overlooking warfare with the Indians.

The expansionism that took over in the 1840's was of a different order. It too was fostered by land hunger and commercial enterprise, but as the biographer of James

Knox Polk has written, it had become something more, an irresistible continental impulse guided by an adolescent and innocent egotism. Gallatin noted this difference. In the midst of the Oregon crisis, he testified that he understood the feelings of the expansionists when the presence of a European power on the continent of North America became an intrusion by a remote power into a nearby neighborhood. The growth of the last fifty years fed upon itself. Now nothing seemed impossible to the westbound pioneers. They measured wealth in terms of land, and "now amid a faltering economy they find themselves unable to pay interest on their debts." But, Gallatin, the cautious statesman who had played a major role in foreign relations, warned: "Feelings do not confer a right and the indulgence of excited feelings is neither virtue nor wisdom."[1]

The westward movement of settlers was the first stage of expansionism. Pioneers in the southern states began their trek into Texas in 1821, after Mexico invited Moses Austin to promote a settlement and granted him huge tracts of land. At this time newly independent Mexico granted a large degree of self-government to the several states that comprised its territory. By the end of 1823 some three hundred American families lived in Austin's colony. Settlement was promoted by allowing American impresarios the right to bring in immigrants and granting them large tracts if they brought in one hundred or more families. The families, in turn, received sizeable parcels of land. By 1835, according to careful estimates, Texas had 30,000 inhabitants, of whom probably one-tenth were Mexicans.[2]

The Mexican frontier was a scene of decay and neglect. The institutions that had provided security, such as the basic agricultural unit, and sustained traditional church teaching and culture, gradually disintegrated after independence. Distrust of Spain persisted, and in 1827 all Spanish priests were expelled. Many of the clergy and bishops had already returned to their native land, and no new ones came to take their places. This resulted in a weakening of the missions, which had served as political and economic foundations of society. Resources of the church were further drained by the imposition of forced loans by hard-pressed political leaders. This general breakdown also thinned the army that had provided protection against Indians in the border areas.[3]

Whereas Americans were migrating into Texas at the rate of a thousand a month by 1835, very few Mexicans settled in the borderlands, a phenomenon rooted in the differences between the two cultures, differences which made conflict almost certain. The immigrants were overwhelmingly Protestant and were accustomed to meeting their needs through local governments controlled by themselves. They brought with them the Anglo-American traditions of law and courts, they were bred in the tradition of self-reliance, and they were accustomed to an upwardly mobile society. Of these differences none was as important as the American desire to establish local self-government.[4]

Mexico prohibited the settlers from establishing Protestant churches and required them to attend mass once a year. With the first newcomers, who had not been exposed to the religious revivals that later swept the frontier, the church question posed no problem and Texas seemed well worth a mass. Both Stephen Austin and Sam Houston became Catholics. But later immigrants found the lack of religious freedom a grievance.

Although the frontier did not change the settlers, the settlers changed the Texas frontier. Ray Billington, historian of the westward movement, has called the transformation of Texas into a cotton culture area "as natural a process as the creation of a wheat-growing empire in Minnesota and Dakota." Following the agricultural boom, American merchants penetrated first to Santa Fe and then through all the Mexican borderlands, where soon an American-oriented economy replaced ties to Mexico City.[5] In these respects what was taking place in Texas was simply a part of the American tradition of moving westward.

Mexico's policy of benign neglect shortly gave way to a policy of control. In 1830 the authorities in Mexico City, alarmed by the influx of Americans, suddenly imposed a decree prohibiting further immigration. This threatened to put an end to the city's rapid growth and the increase of land values, and the settlers protested. Mexico's failure to give way to other demands likewise promoted dissatisfaction. Then, in 1833, the Americans' request for statehood was rejected. This measure, together with the arrest of Stephen Austin when he went to Mexico City hoping to convince General Santa Anna of the need for changes, ended the settlers' hope for accommodation. Mexicans in the borderland provinces, including Texas, also took measures to resist the new policy of centralization imposed by Santa Anna. The two movements, that of the settlers and that of the Mexicans, became intertwined.[6]

The first stirrings of a separatist movement took place in 1832. American settlers were, at that time, divided on the question. The more prosperous and successful were loyal to Mexico, no one more so than Stephen Austin, who believed that the grievances would be corrected. The rebels were centered in the village of Nacogdoches near Louisiana. Their leaders were the Wharton brothers, who were already planning for annexation to the United States. The prohibition against more immigrants coming to Texas had converted the town of Nacogdoches into a center for the admission of illegal aliens. These arrivals were not of the sturdy stock that had settled on Austin's lands. They were largely refugees from the law, vagrants rather than enterprising farmers seeking to improve their lot. Further, the inhabitants of Nacogdoches had little to lose by joining in a revolution. Amenable to the appeals of leaders of the less respectable sort, such as the Wharton brothers, they saw in either an independent Texas or one annexed to the United States, opportunities closed to them as long as Austin and his large following pursued a peaceful course and abided by their loyalty to Mexico, where landholdings had enabled them to prosper.

Among these leaders was General Sam Houston, whose

erratic career included sojourns with Indian tribes, duels, membership in Congress, a censure by the House of Representatives because of his beating a fellow member with a cane, a sudden resignation as governor of Tennessee, and travels in Texas as an agent of President Jackson. His determination to win glory in this remote territory defy easy characterization. In 1833 at the first signs of revolt, Houston appeared in the front ranks rousing the populace with charges against the tyranny of military power and claims that "war is our only alternative." He was soon in command of an army that did not yet exist, and sent appeals to New Orleans that urged American support of the rebels in Texas as a matter of patriotism. To attract volunteers he promised that they would receive liberal bounties of free land.

By 1836 separatism was moving toward a direct conflict with Santa Anna's plans for concentrating control in his own hands. A revolt in the state of Coahuila and the overthrow of its government led Santa Anna to send General Cos, his brother-in-law, to restore order. A messenger from Cos was intercepted by the people of San Felipe and letters he was carrying exposed plans for sending an army into Texas to put down the agitation for reform. This incident placed before the public, hitherto content to resist peacefully, the stark reality that their appeals were futile and that they must resort to arms.

Sam Houston had already become commander of the untrained and undisciplined bands of volunteers who were ready to waste their ammunition in raids that would only enable the oncoming forces to destroy them one at a time. Houston's major problem was to control impetuous spirits and bring them to order. This he did with great success enabling him to defeat the army of Santa Anna in the battle of San Jacinto.[7] During the brief war for Texas independence the United States did its best to enforce the laws of neutrality, but volunteers and supplies from the United States contributed to the victory, although they do not account for the success of the Texans. In the eyes of Mexico, the victory of the rebels was possible only because of the support they had received. Mexicans looked upon the war as only a temporary setback and they believed that someday they would recover their territory to the north.

The pioneer trek to Oregon was of a far different order than settlement of Texas. Texas was contiguous with the already-settled territory of Arkansas, and the trails from the old southern states and from Missouri traversed the Texas flatlands. Oregon was remote. Between the westernmost settlements along the Mississippi valley and Oregon lay hundreds of miles of prairie lands inhabited by unfriendly Indians, and then came the Rocky Mountains. Months of danger and severe hardships lay between St. Louis and the valleys of the Columbia and Willamette rivers. So remote did Oregon appear to several generations that it was not at first viewed as a prospective part of the Union, but rather as a future independent republic.

Both the United States and Great Britain had legitimate claims to parts of the Oregon Territory. An American, Captain Gray, was the first to venture through the rough waters at the mouth of the Columbia River. The British were the first to explore the region of Puget Sound. Conflicting claims led to the convention of 1815 providing for joint occupancy, a compact that was renewed in 1827. These agreements limited the activities of both nations. Neither was free to exercise sovereignty, and the entire Territory was closed to private ownership of lands. The British, however, carried on a lucrative fur trade, an enterprise that was soon monopolized by the Hudson's Bay Company, around whose posts sprang up several settlements. In lieu of any government, the company provided regulations necessary to maintain order.

The efforts of Nathaniel Wyeth to establish a business enterprise for the catching and selling of salmon failed in 1832 and again in 1834. Wyeth's reports, however, gained wide publicity and provided easterners with the first information on the nature of the Oregon Country and its possibilities. On his second trip over the difficult transmountain route, Wyeth agreed to take along the first of several missionaries, who were unfortunately misled into believing that the native Indians were hungry for the Christian gospel.

Four Indians, who had travelled to St. Louis, were curious about the white civilization, but had no real interest in it, and they became the center of a legend manufactured by one William Walker, an agent from the East, who was in St. Louis arranging for a migration of people to Missouri. Walker, who never met the Indians, wrote a letter adorned with a dramatic account of how the Indians had asked for the "Book of Heaven." This letter found its way to New England and to the Methodist Board of Missions, where this tale of ignorant heathens thirsting for the gospel led to the first of several campaigns to raise funds and send ministers to Oregon.[8]

Missionaries were to play a major role in the settlement of Oregon and in awakening political interest in the remote territory. The first of these was Jason Lee, who combined a sincere piety with a secular interest in promoting settlement by whites from the East who could transform the country surrounding missions into thriving agricultural communities. Lee believed that the natives living in this environment would be amenable to Christian nurture. Quite predictably, the harvest of souls was largely a failure, but Lee and other missionaries publicised a new description of Oregon as a land of promise for pioneers interested in improving their harsh situation in the Middle West, where the depression of 1837 left them struggling between heavy debts and sharply reduced prices.

In that year the federal government, now alert to future possibilities in Oregon, commissioned W. A. Slacum to investigate conditions there. He was impressed with the missionary settlements he visited and gave a full and encouraging report. He also learned that a major shortcoming of the new communities was the absence of cattle in country that appeared ideal for grazing. Out of his efforts came the establishment of the Willamette

Cattle Company. The following year the company brought in some six hundred cattle from California.[9] The enterprise received publicity in the Middle West and promoted migration.

By early 1843 the stream of settlers was fully underway, and so was congressional action to provide protection for the migrants both on their way and once there. The Oregon question—posed by the assertion that the territory rightfully belonged to the United States—demanded the end of the treaty of joint occupation. In geographic terms, the question concerned control of the Oregon triangle, the territory between the Columbia River on the south, the forty-ninth parallel on the north, and the western boundary of the United States on the east.

The Oregon question involved obtaining not only the fertile lands of the Willamette valley but also a port on the Pacific, in Oregon or California. These goals were uppermost in the minds of commercial interests.

This was the golden age of New England's shipping industry. The trade in hides from Brazil and California was of significant value. The imported hides supplied a thriving shoe industry. In return for them, New Englanders exported cotton and lumber.

Also, the prospect of future trade with China was bright. The importance of the China trade measured in terms of total foreign trade or compared with trade with western Europe or all of North America was not great, but imports from China exceeded in value those from any one country with the exception of Great Britain and France, and in public estimates the future value outweighed statistics. It was virtually agreed that trade across the Pacific would eventually surpass all other trade.[10]

Fascination with China owed almost as much to stories of American success and experiences in Canton as it did to the fortunes that were made there. There was the legend of the fabulous Chinese merchant Houqua, who had torn up a promissory note for $72,000 from a Boston merchant. Chinese traders were known for their fairness in business dealings. Russell Sturgis, who carried on at least half the China trade between 1820 and 1840 testified that he never knew better tradesmen than the Hong merchants. Another prominent importer, John P. Cushing, described the Chinese salesmen and advised that the way to success was to treat them uprightly and as gentlemen.[11] Of all the Boston merchants, Cushing achieved the greatest success and reputation. He first went to China at the age of sixteen, took over the management of Thomas Handasyd Perkins' office in Canton, and with the exception of two brief visits home, remained there for thirty years. He returned a fabulously rich man.

It was this trade with China that first directed attention to the future of Oregon. Had Oregon been next door to his home in Quincy, John Quincy Adams could not have been more convinced of its future importance and that it must eventually become a part of the United States. Adams had seen the finger of God pointed toward Oregon. Another determined friend of the western territory was Caleb Cushing of Salem, who maintained a regular correspondence with the merchants of Canton and who predicted that the greatest trade in the future would be across the Pacific. In 1839, Cushing addressed Congress and called for action. He warned that the British had a broad overall plan for hemming in the United States and holding her hostage. The title to Oregon, Cushing contended, was sufficient "to be justly maintained, if necessary, by force." Oregon, said Cushing, "is a country ours by right; ours by necessities of geographical position; ours by every consideration of national safety."[12] It was Cushing who first introduced a bill providing for the protection of American settlers.

The interests of the China trade and in Oregon rode in tandem. A seaport in Oregon or in California, or in both, constituted a vital national priority. Merchants engaged in the China trade were well aware that the entrance to the Columbia River was inaccessible, so that the port must be either somewhere north of there in the Puget Sound area or southward in San Francisco. When Daniel

Webster entered into his negotiations with Lord Ashburton in 1842, without any previous interest in acquiring Oregon, he was troubled when Ashburton, who had been instructed by Lord Aberdeen to seek a settlement of the Oregon question, proposed drawing the line at the Columbia River. Webster, thanks to his interest in a possible seaport to the north of the river, rejected the British proposal but explained that if some plan could be worked out whereby Mexico would sell Upper California, including San Francisco, then perhaps a settlement could be reached.[13]

In the 1840's, the annexation of Texas and a settlement of the Oregon question were issues that became immersed in politics. The Texas question lay dormant in large part after 1837. Texas had applied for admission to the United States and been refused because President Van Buren assumed that it would divide his party between northern and southern sympathies. In 1837, William Ellery Channing, Boston's prominent Unitarian minister, addressed a letter that was widely published, denouncing annexation as a plot contrived by the holders of Texas land script and by the slavocracy bent on gaining control of the Union. The subject, he wrote, belongs to the realm of morals and religion. A small minority of men, almost wholly Americans, complained about the requirement that they become Catholics, and that they were denied trial by jury. This they knew was the order in Mexico when they entered the country. Those who revolted, Channing explained, were a minority who had moved to Texas. The people at large were being misled by a small group of incendiary men, political adventurers and visionaries. These were the words Stephen Austin had used when he wrote from Mexico City, according to Channing. Having so described the origins of the Texas revolution, Channing declared what he chose to call the real causes of the revolt.

The first cause of the Texas revolution was the avaricious greed of land speculators who sold their scrip to citizens of the United States. Second was Mexico's determination not to permit slavery. Third, American settlers were disappointed when they were denied the status of a separate state which they alone could control. Finally, the revolution had been successful because citizens of the United States, in violation of American neutrality laws, joined in the military effort while other American citizens gave financial aid. All of this was due to the restlessness of the American people and their impatience with the ordinary laws of progress.

To travel down this road of conquest would darken the country's future history. The annexation of Texas would almost certainly embroil the republic in a war with Mexico. There was in prospect another equally great evil. Annexation would fasten on the United States the menace of slavery. It would do so because in the older slave states the soil was exhausted. The owners of slaves in these states adhered to slavery, not on account of the wealth it extracted from the soil, but because it furnished men and women to be sold in newly settled southern districts.[14]

Channing's indictment of annexation and of slavery stirred a generation already endowed with a philanthropic spirit and an urge toward social reforms. It assured that the expansionist spirit in the northern states would face moral inquiries.

President Tyler was long convinced that Texas should be annexed, and Abel P. Upshur, secretary of state in 1843, was alarmed. Duff Green, Tyler's agent in Europe, reported, while in London, that Great Britain planned to prevent future annexation by causing Mexico to recognize the independence of Texas, and by extending a loan to Texas for the purpose of emancipating the slaves. A speech by Lord Brougham in Parliament denounced slavery. In November 1843, Upshur wrote a set of instructions to Edward Everett, the American minister, that epitomized the worst fears of the South.[15] To emancipate two million slaves and deprive the South of its labor force would bring disaster. The emancipated slaves would soon engage in a race war. Many would flee to the North and destroy the peace. Upshur's expressed fear of racial strife mounted as antislavery gained support in the North.

By the close of November 1843, it was generally known in Washington that President Tyler was about to propose the annexation of Texas in his message to Congress. At the first report, Daniel Webster observed that it would come to nothing because the entire North would oppose it. In a letter to Edward Everett in London, he predicted that at first it would be met with a general remonstrance throughout the North. All candidates would be interrogated on the issue, and if this failed to lead to excitement, then it would become a major issue in the election campaign of the next year. He noted with dismay: "A general election has come to be, on all sides, quite too much a matter of mass meetings, of commemorations and celebrations, of banners and trophies." There was, he feared, the danger that the Texas question would gain a high priority in the next election.[16]

The treaty was presented to the Senate late in April 1844. The opposition to annexation of Texas, the earnestness of that opposition and the character of it, was well expressed by Daniel Webster who wrote: "The Treaty is out here, and the accompanying papers make sensible people ashamed of their country. Never did I see such reprehensible sentiment, and unsurpassed nonsense, united. I am utterly astonished at Mr. Calhoun. What must he suppose this age will think of him, and us too, if we adopt his sentiments."[17]

Hitherto the explosive issue of Texas had been avoided by members of both parties because they were fully aware that once it was raised it would split both parties along sectional lines and greatly weaken them. The dramatic breakthrough of the Texas controversy in the winter of 1844 was only in part a product of political intrigue, a move to destroy Martin Van Buren, who was almost certain to be nominated for president at the coming Democratic convention. Cave Johnson, close political associate of James K. Polk in Tennessee, informed him of the plan to use annexation to wreck Van Buren's chances in the convention and Clay's hopes for election.[18] These two leaders would be confronted with the question of where they stood. If either favored annexation, the now-strong antislavery elements in the North would desert them. If they opposed annexation, they were certain to lose the support of the southern wings of their parties. In April 1844 both Clay and Van Buren faced the necessity of taking a public stand. Both men made ambiguous statements, but nevertheless it was clear they would oppose annexation at this time.

In sharp contrast, Daniel Webster, now retired from Tyler's cabinet and an onlooker in the race for president, took an uncompromising stand in opposition to annexation. He claimed that because no necessity required the annexation of Texas, we ought therefore to be content with the present boundaries. The nation has prospered and achieved strength within those boundaries, Webster said. The American people accepted that they had contractual obligations not to interfere with slavery in states where it already existed, but they would not consent to bring into the Union "a new, vastly extensive, and slaveholding country, large enough for a half dozen or a dozen States." Already a portion of the community was excited on the slavery question. It had not only attracted political attention, said Webster, "but it has struck a far deeper chord. It has arrested the religious feeling of the country; it has taken hold of the consciences of men." He warned: "But to coerce into silence, to endeavor to restrain its free expression, to seek to suppress and confine it, warm as it is, and more heated as such endeavors would inevitably render it, should this be attempted, I know nothing, even in the Constitution or in the Union itself, which would not be endangered by the explosion which might follow."[19]

Webster warned also against ardent speculations of extending the country either north or south. To be carried away by dreams of an ever greater empire would endanger the republic's stability and even its duration. These sober warnings were verified by developments following the

Mexican War that led eventually to Civil War, when the Union could only be held together by force.

At the opposite side of the political spectrum, the extreme annexationists entertained no fears. The independence of Texas had been recognized not only by the United States but by Great Britain and France. If the annexationists had any fear of war with Mexico they were not concerned. That weak and distraught nation was viewed with contempt. If war should come with Great Britain, let it come. The United States had been subservient to that grasping power.

Abraham Lincoln was to deny, although he was soon to become the champion of no extension of slavery, that annexation of Texas would have any effect on slavery.[20] There were New Englanders in the Democratic ranks who had no difficulty with the issue. They asked why should an annexation originating among the Texans be turned down? Why would anyone decline such a fortunate enrichment?[21]

The backdrop of this annexation movement was deeply rooted. It was one facet of the zest for rapid development and the pride and self-confidence that accompanied success. The feeling had no respect for the old ways of diplomacy. The United States was unique and guided by higher laws than the antiquated monarchies of Europe. Annexation fevers, at their extreme in 1844 and 1845, gave way to a recklessness that defied cautious diplomacy and negotiation.

John C. Calhoun tied annexation to the question of slavery. On December 26, 1843, Lord Aberdeen, the British foreign minister, sent instructions to Richard Pakenham, the new British minister in Washington, seeking to quiet the charges in the American press that Great Britain sought to promote emancipation in Texas. After Calhoun took Upshur's place as secretary of state, Pakenham conveyed Aberdeen's message that Great Britain would not interfere with either Texas or Mexico and that, while it was true that the British people were strongly opposed to slavery and hoped to see it abolished everywhere, Great Britain would not interfere.[22]

Annexationists exploited the popular distrust of the British for the purpose of promoting their cause. Southerners had already concluded that the future of slavery in the old states depended on access to the market for slaves in Texas. When Pakenham delivered Lord Aberdeen's message, Calhoun responded in a lengthy letter defending slavery, contending in belligerent terms that what happened in Texas was of vital concern to the United States, and that Texas was the safety valve for the preservation of the South's peculiar institution.[23] Given Aberdeen's repeated affirmations that Great Britain would not interfere, Calhoun's defense of the institution, looked upon as a shameful anachronism by western Europe, can hardly be viewed as a constructive act, but Calhoun distrusted the British and believed that they were plotting to interfere in the internal affairs of the United States. He sent a copy of his letter to the Senate, and Senator Tappan of Ohio released it to the *New York Evening Post,* and soon it was known across the country. This action tied annexation to the slavery issue.

The British were opposed to annexation for reasons of self-interest. The Gulf of Mexico was of major importance to British commerce, and Texas in the hands of the United States would create a situation dangerous to British shipping. Texas itself offered prospects of a free market and an independent source of cotton. Given the influence of British interests, and the powerful abolitionist movement in England that called for worldwide emancipation, the British government favored an independent Texas.

Aberdeen consulted with Thomas Murphy, Mexico's minister in London, and proposed that Mexico immediately recognize the independence of Texas and the boundaries of both Texas and Mexico. Should Mexico refuse, Great Britain could not oppose annexation. Two days later Aberdeen consulted Ashbel Smith, the minister of Texas, seeking assurance that Texas, if supported by

Great Britain and France, would not consent to annexation. Ashbel gave him a cautious answer.[24]

This came at a time when Great Britain was primarily concerned about relations with France and the danger of the collapse of her alliance with the French government. Aberdeen saw an opportunity to strengthen political ties by joining with France over the Texas issue and proposed to the French premier, Guizot, that the two countries commit themselves to defending Texas should the United States use force. This he undoubtedly viewed as only a very remote contingency. A firm stand by the two powers, he assumed, would be sufficient to restrain the United States. Both Guizot and Louis Philippe approved, but Guizot's lukewarm answer revealed a hesitancy clothed in suggestions for greater specificity. Aberdeen then amended his proposal with what became known as the "diplomatic act." Mexico was now required to become a party to the guarantee.

News from the United States that the Senate had refused to approve the treaty of annexation was accompanied by reports that the Tyler administration was ready to pursue a new approach. More important, Pakenham warned that any move by Great Britain would only strengthen the hands of the annexationists. Aberdeen now withdrew the "diplomatic act" and changed his evaluation of the situation.[25] Equally important, the British soon learned that Mexico was opposed to acknowledging Texas independence, believing that this would only lead to the United States seeking possession of California.

These diplomatic exchanges coincided with the march of American politics toward the elevation of James K. Polk to the presidency, an event that few others besides Polk himself would have predicted. The Whigs met at Baltimore first and nominated the popular and affable Henry Clay by a unanimous vote. The Democrats who met later in the same city gathered amid a series of violent political squalls. It appeared that Van Buren would be nominated, but he was no longer embraced with heartiness by southerners and his stand on the Texas question had turned indifference into hostility. It was certain that he would have the support of a majority, but the opposition was successful in renewing the two-thirds rule, first put in place in 1832. This eliminated Van Buren.[26] Waiting in the political corridors for the opportunity thus presented was James K. Polk of Tennessee.

Politics work in mysterious ways. The Democrats, beset with division had, in the words of Polk's biographer, bought a pig in a poke. He had suffered two successive defeats as a candidate for governor, but he was a weather-beaten politican of long experience who could readily believe that more favorable times would soon follow. His ambition, in the summer of 1843, was to be nominated for vice president on a ticket headed by Van Buren. Through the dark months following his defeat, he persisted in mending his political fences and carefully nurturing the powers in state politics in order to retain his leadership. At the same time he gave his public support to Van Buren, who would probably be the Democratic candidate in 1844.[27]

The rise of the Texas movement had Polk's approval from the beginning. He was an admirer of Andrew Jackson, and his hero had long been an advocate of annexation though he had moved with caution after the Texas revolution. Annexation posed no difficulties for Polk. It did not dawn on him that there was a moral dimension to the issue, nor did he fear that annexation could bring war with Mexico. National expansion was to Polk simply the inevitable growth of a free people.

He had learned from his mentor that the first rules of diplomacy were firmness and boldness. These qualities would assure success. Polk was possessed with a single-mindedness that was not easily affected by his immediate counselors. However, his limitations were balanced by an astuteness in politics that would carry him far toward the very ambitious goals that he privately entertained.

Tyler as president had alienated the ultra Whigs led by

Henry Clay and at the same time failed to win the support of the Democrats. He ventured to negotiate a treaty of annexation with Texas in the winter of 1844. After Polk's election victory Tyler sought to redeem his failure as president by annexing Texas by a joint resolution of Congress. This would require only a majority vote.

Once before Congress, the Texas question let loose a flood of debate and oratory. The constitutional issue served as a shelter to avoid more basic matters, and hour after hour of debate was devoted to it. Northern Democrats protested that they considered slavery a great evil and that they looked forward to emancipation, but then contended that slavery was not the issue. Not lacking in ingenuity, they argued that if Texas were annexed, the original southern states could be drained of their slaves and would be open to free labor. As for the slaves in Texas, they would have to compete with free labor and slavery would be found uneconomical. Many slaves would find it easy to flee to Mexico, where slavery was prohibited and where they would be easily assimilated because the difference in color would be less pronounced than in the United States.[28]

Partisans of any cause invariably spread their nets wide in the belief that different arguments would appeal to different people but no one argument will convince all. Others maintained that annexation did involve slavery. A representative from New Hampshire cited the fact that the state legislature, where there was feeling against slavery, favored annexation by a unanimous vote in the state senate, and by a more than two-to-one majority in the house of representatives.[29] Representative A. P. Stone of Ohio gave the debate a populist twist. Stone declared: "Agricultural interests are ground down to dust for want of a market. No sir, the whole system is one of robbery and oppression." The annexation of Texas, he said, would enable the middle-western farmer to extricate himself, and he hoped that God might speed the hour when the influence of Texas would be felt in the halls of Congress.

Should war come with England the war must continue until that country was driven from every foot of the soil on the North American continent.[30]

Debates in Congress give no clear indication why the joint resolution passed. In the Senate the vote was twenty-seven to twenty-five. Certainly both Tyler and Polk influenced the outcome. Party loyalty appears to have been a major factor, since the vote followed party lines. Another factor was the popular notion that the United States was not guilty of aggrandizement; it was doing no more than giving its consent to another country "uniting with us in government—and that country formed of one hundred thousand of our brethren, our kith and kin."[31]

Most significantly, the resolution only passed after some concessions were made to the opposition. Thomas Hart Benton tried to amend the resolution so that annexation would take place only after negotiation for a treaty with Mexico. This failed to gain majority support. Benton then introduced an amendment giving the president the option of appointing commissioners to negotiate with Texas the terms of annexation. Benton was led to believe that Polk would follow this course. It was only the adoption of the measure proposed by Benton that saved the resolution from defeat.

The new two-party system was now in operation. Polk and his supporters could not rest easily. He had won the election by the narrowest of margins. In the key state of New York the Liberty Party polled 15,814 votes, and it was Clay who was hurt by this third party vote. Polk carried New York by the narrow margin of 5,106 votes. The slim margin by which the annexation resolution passed was a second reminder to the newly elected president that he must proceed with caution.

Polk held privately an ambitious set of goals, however. He confided to George Bancroft, the historian and a member of his cabinet, that he would pursue great resolutions: settlement of the Oregon question, acquisition of California, reduction of the tariff to solely a revenue measure, and the establishment of an independent treasury. He had long been an advocate of the annexation of Texas and was prepared to carry it through.

Polk would preside over the transmutation of foreign relations into a crusade for national expansion. A series of factors moved the country toward this bold policy. The new two-party system promoted a rivalry that gave new life to the Democratic Party in the Middle West, where the depressed state of economy made it easy to muster support for territorial acquisitions. Mercantile and shipping interests took a new view of trade with the Orient, thanks to the British victory in the Opium War and a treaty opening five new ports in China.

The flood of immigrants into Texas directed attention to the Southwest, and the Texas revolution opened a vista of future acquisitions as immigrants made their way across the borderlands of Mexico. What had formerly appeared remote, now appeared within reach.

In the same period, technological advances in transportation made headway. The new phenomenon of steamships reduced the time of ocean crossings, and miles of railroad track were extended from the east coast to the Mississippi valley, initiating an enthusiasm for transcontinental railroads. As more and more produce from the Middle West was carried to eastern cities by rail, it threatened to bring decline to New Orleans as an ocean outlet. Faced with this, the city fathers pushed for a railroad from New Orleans to the Pacific, making their city the center for transcontinental trade. New Orleans likewise agitated for annexation of Cuba and a canal across the Isthmus of Panama facilitating speedy water transportation to the west coast.

As in the past, expansionism was an outgrowth of the limitless confidence gained by a people in a land of plenty. The nineteenth century was the American century, the century of phenomenal growth. Prudence had not wholly lost its hold, but given the fortuitous combination of economic and political forces at work, the way was open to the triumph of popular feelings and an adventurous bumptiousness in foreign affairs.

There were few restraints on this seemingly unlimited assertiveness, but President Polk recognized that he must tread his way with care or he would be overridden by Whig opposition. Convinced that he spoke for the whole people, whereas members of Congress spoke only for their own constituents, he was ready to be as firm as his hero Andrew Jackson. He also knew that he must not appear to be provoking war. Similarly, he felt that he must preserve the coalition of midwestern and southern Democrats who had elected him or he would become a president without a party.

Polk was a conscientious president, rising at five in the morning and working until late in the evening. He scrutinized every piece of paper that came across his desk and devoted himself to what he considered to be the best interests of the country.

He was not the leader of a plot. The twists and turns and the complexities of his first year in office defy a conspiratorial thesis. Polk did have a set of goals, but was lacking a prescribed plan for carrying them out. He hoped to achieve those goals by peace. Shortly after his inauguration, there were elements in Texas ready to embark on an aggressive campaign that would have resulted in war immediately, but Polk restrained the war makers.[32] There were other times when he explored the road to peace, but he never lost sight of his goals. These dictated his decisions.

He made no bold moves immediately after taking office. Mexico had broken off diplomatic relations after the passage of the resolution of annexation, thereby closing off, at least temporarily, the opportunity to negotiate. What Mexico might do was an open question. The reports from William Parrott, Polk's confidential agent in Mexico, and from John Black, the American consul in Mexico City, predicted that the country would not declare war. They both made reports of the public enmity toward the United States and described the paralysis of the government, but gave Polk no adequate estimate of the determination to resist. He readily concluded that the weakness of Mexico would eventually cause it to yield. In the meantime, Zachary Taylor and his forces had moved as far west in Texas as Corpus Christi and had orders to move all the way to the Rio Grande if the situation called for it. Taylor assumed that the area to his west was still in dispute, and he saw no signs of Mexican hostility that justified moving to the Rio Grande. Should war come, orders had already been issued for a prompt seizure of Santa Fe in New Mexico, and the ports of California.

The months of neither peace nor war in late 1845 and early 1846 were frustrating. In August 1845, Richard J. Coxe, an eminent Washington jurist, warned Secretary of State James Buchanan that to wait was to endanger the opportunity to gain California, which was of much greater importance than Texas.

Coxe represented the claimants against Mexico, and therefore he had a direct interest in American-Mexican relations. He wrote:

> You may rely upon it Sir, that the claims of our citizens upon Mexico furnish the government with a most potent lever with which to operate upon that nation. The annexation of Texas leaves open a most important question of boundary, which must be adjusted sooner or later. If this powerful lever is adroitly managed you may move this question as you will and adjust the boundary as you will. With a view to a satisfactory arrangement it would perhaps be desirable that Mexico should declare war. If she should not resort to that measure under the present feeling of excitement which exists in the country is it practicable to avoid hostilities long when you come to take possession of Texas, and to extend your authority to the lines upon which you mean to insist.[33]

Coxe held out no hope that the boundary could be extended to the Pacific by negotiations. Mexico should be faced with a demand for payment; if she refused, the United States should take the desired territory and then pay the claims. On the morning of September 5, Richard

Coxe called on Buchanan and warned that Mexico would not declare war but simply let matters drift. Buchanan asked him to draft a memorandum.

Similar ideas were stirring among American agents in Mexico. On July 26, Parrott spoke of the vexatious annoyances Americans had suffered and held that they would not come to an end without a vigorous chastisement. He thought it would be better if Mexico declared war than if it proposed negotiation because then the United States could secure the desired boundaries.[34] It is probable that Coxe's protestation merely served to confirm prevalent opinion.

While Polk contemplated the frustrations he faced, he received a report from General Robert Armstrong, one of his lifetime associates, who was now in London, that there were rumors that England held a mortgage on California.[35] With Polk's deep distrust of the British and his equally firm determination that Great Britain should never be permitted to acquire that territory, California came to occupy an even higher priority among his considerations.

It was a false rumor, but Aberdeen did view the anticipated annexation of California by the United States as unfortunate. He had urged Mexico to avoid war with the United States so that it would not happen. Mexico feared the loss of California above all else, but accepted that she could not defend it. Faced with this threat, the Mexican minister in London, on September 25, proposed to Aberdeen that if Great Britain would prevent annexation by the United States, Mexico was agreeable to any terms Great Britain might propose. Mexico had one goal, to keep California out of the hands of the United States.[36] Aberdeen carefully considered the Mexican proposal, but it appeared that it was unrealistic because the British had no investments in California, nor any treaty rights that would furnish legitimate grounds for opposition.

The proposal took on fresh interest, however, as his thoughts returned to the pressing problem he faced at home. Recent French actions had aroused a war scare, and it was feared that at some time in the not-too-distant future, should Louis Philippe be driven from the throne, the French would nourish their hatred of the British by launching an attack. No one feared this more than the Duke of Wellington, and he was leading a movement to prepare for war. Aberdeen held that the best way to prepare for war was to prepare for peace. War preparations invariably aroused a patriotic spirit so that the points of conflict became immersed in national honor.[37]

To block Wellington's strategy, Aberdeen looked for a way to strengthen the ties with France. This led him to consider uniting with France to oppose American annexation. Guizot had already denounced American expansion and had called for a balance of power in the New World, so Aberdeen approached him. The French statesman endorsed the project but raised questions about how it was to be effected. By this time Aberdeen had second thoughts, and he concluded that Guizot would not make a commitment. With enough doubts of his own, Aberdeen decided that he should not try to persuade France to enter upon what must become or could become a hazardous venture.[38]

Of this, of course, Polk knew nothing, but other developments served to convince him that British intrusion was a probability. He was meanwhile in correspondence with Thomas O. Larkin, the American consul in California, who warned that a British naval ship was off the coast and more vessels were expected.

Larkin raised a more interesting possibility. The Mexicans in California might revolt at any time, and these settlers professed kindly feelings toward the United States and offered vague promises that should war come, they would side with the Americans. When Polk met with Thomas Hart Benton the subject came up again. Benton's son-in-law, John C. Frémont, was in California leading a band of fifty men who planned to settle on the Sacramento River. The conversation apparently moved quickly to the possibility that Frémont could give the revolt a push and provide American leadership. A message was drafted at once and sent by a secret courier. Unfortunately, its contents have never been disclosed. But Polk quickly grasped that here was an opportunity to promote an uprising that would, as in the case of Texas, lead to annexation.[39]

Another hopeful note came as early as September when John Black informed Polk that the foreign minister of Mexico, Peñay Peña, was prepared to negotiate and would receive a commissioner. Peñay Peña added that he hoped that Parrott, who was distrusted in Mexico, would not be sent. Polk welcomed what appeared to be an opportunity to settle all questions by negotiation.

Here was a most delicate mission, one that called for much time to prepare, but the president and his cabinet decided everything at one brief session, including who should be sent. No one took note of the difficulties facing the Mexican authorities, no one suggested using caution because Mexico's proud people were about to be confronted with a loss of a major part of their territory, no one asked what inducements could be offered aside from a hasty estimate by the president regarding a financial grant. Instead, Polk and his associates were ready to take drastic action in the case of failure and would not hesitate once they had satisfied the public that they had peaceful intentions by going through the motions of diplomacy.

Secretary of State James Buchanan drafted the instructions to John Slidell. Because of the prospects of revolution in California that would establish a government independent of Mexico, the cession of California was no longer a sine qua non. The demands included the western border of Texas along the Rio Grande and that the boundary follow that river as far as Santa Fe. In return the United States would assume the payment of American claims. Mexico was offered $5 million for the cession of the western half of New Mexico and $25 million for California. Slidell was instructed to be bold in his demand for the payment of claims, an instruction that was scarcely necessary considering that gentleman's past career in Cuba, where he not only engaged in illegal activities on behalf of ship owners engaged in the slave trade, but also earned a reputation for highhandedness in dealing with Cubans. Slidell was also instructed to make it clear that should negotiations fail, the United States would employ energetic measures.

The government of Paredes was already on the verge of toppling and did so while Slidell was in Mexico. It was replaced by that of Herrera. Neither Paredes nor Herrera could do more than try to delay. The exchange of notes between the United States and Mexico in no way narrowed the gap between the positions of the two powers. The delay led Buchanan to warn that failure to receive Slidell would compel the United States to take redress into her own hands. The minister became increasingly peremptory in his appeals to be received, and finally, on March 15, 1846, after being told that he would not be received, Slidell asked for his passports and left.

The mission had been marred by bungling. Polk had depended upon the reports of William Parrott and John Black. Both were at best amateur diplomats with no training to analyze the forces at work, and consequently they led Polk to believe that peace was within reach. However, the mission failed also because of the extreme demands by the Polk administration and weakness on the part of the Mexican government. In such a revolutionary situation, any government that capitulated to American demands was doomed.

Polk too faced the necessity of living up to his commitment to firmness and to his promises at the time of the Democratic Convention that had nominated him in Baltimore in 1844. Nevertheless, he faced a weak and helpless power, and his belief, that should war come, it would bring a quick victory, contributed to his decisiveness.

The report of the failure of Slidell's mission did not reach Washington until April 8. In the meantime Polk, still holding out some hope that Slidell would be received, discussed with his cabinet and the leading members of the Senate, the possibility of appropriating $1 million to be used as a down payment. If this could be paid immediately, then possibly Paredes might agree to a treaty drawing new boundaries. The cabinet and several senators approved, but the proposal was dropped after Calhoun withdrew his support and Senator Allen of Ohio concluded that the Senate would not approve.[40]

Polk's final effort testifies to his desire for peace, but that hope was inextricably linked to his conviction that new boundaries must be drawn giving California to the United States. The president should have been, and apparently was, deeply concerned when told that a special appropriation could not pass the Senate. In this situation he could expect difficulties when he turned to Congress for a declaration of war. He was fearful that a combination of Whigs and dissident Democrats might defeat the measure, and he continued to envision that fear even on the day he delivered his fateful message.

This fear was more than counterbalanced by the assurances he received from Larkin on developments in California. To be sure, that letter may not have arrived until after war had been declared; but earlier reports of the activities of Frémont and the readiness of the local population to take up arms against Mexico, and Commodore Sloat's orders to seize the ports as soon as Mexico declared led to action. The orders to Sloat included the significant assurance that the ports were open and defenseless. California was ready to be taken, and faced with this priceless opportunity, restraint was not to be expected. The only reluctance was the possibility of war with Great Britain, and this did cause Polk to delay.

By May 6, with the concurrence of his cabinet, Polk decided to send a special message to Congress. That evening despatches arrived reporting that a party of General Taylor's dragoons had been engaged by a Mexican force. From the first, Polk had ruled that any crossing of the Rio Grande by Mexican troops would be resisted. The engagement took place in the disputed territory between the Nueces River and the Rio Grande, territory in which Texas had never exercised sovereign rights and to which Texas's only claim rested on a unilateral declaration.

Moreover, it had been the clear intention of Congress in its resolution annexing Texas that this area would be subject to negotiation. In the previous months General Taylor had blockaded the Rio Grande, thereby isolating Matamoras, where Mexican forces were stationed. Ignoring niceties, Polk announced that American blood had been spilt on American soil, and he called for a declaration of war and authority to recruit volunteers in support of Taylor.

The news gave rise to heated debate. All were willing to vote support, but many opposed a declaration of war. Calhoun sought delay and pleaded for "high, full, and dispassionate consideration." War did not exist, Calhoun maintained, because only Congress could declare it.[41] John Clayton of Delaware declared "that the whole conduct of the Executive in this case has been wholly unjustifiable."[42] Motions were introduced aimed at delay. They gathered twenty votes, but Polk's forces were sustained by twenty-five votes.

The committee on military affairs tied to the issue of declaring war a provision providing for the support of Taylor's troops. To vote against a declaration of war meant a vote against American troops. Many Whigs, including Robert C. Winthrop of Massachusetts, voted for the declaration with heavy hearts. Some may have recalled that the failure of the Federalists to support the War of 1812 had brought ruin to that party. Polk eventually had his way, but by the close of the year he faced violent opposition.

It is true that Polk would have preferred peace and that he had followed a zigzag course that at times gave evidence of peaceful intentions. On the other hand, he never swerved from his major objectives of the acquisition of California and a boundary that would permit a railroad to that state along the southern route. This firmness owed its strength to his faith that a rigorous policy of deterrence and funds to fill Mexico's empty treasury would lead that country, which he held in contempt, to come to terms. His policies were also bolstered by a belief that, should war come, it would be brief. His preference for peace was heavily outweighed by his expansionist ambitions.

As war with Mexico approached, relations with Great Britain also teetered on the edge of conflict. The Democratic party was committed to the annexation of Oregon all the way to latitude 54°40', the southern boundary of Alaska. Feelings that had been dormant burst forth in a crusade. Lewis Cass of Michigan, William Allen of Ohio (known as the Ohio Fog Horn), and Edward Hannegan of Indiana led the movement.

The election was not a national mandate for annexation. The country was sharply divided over both Texas and Oregon. No president can afford to divide his party without risking the failure of his administration. This was a danger that Polk faced, and he had to thread his way between diplomacy and politics. Party discord, so often an intruder in foreign relations, threatened to bring on a conflict with the world's greatest sea power, whose navy was capable of destroying the port cities and possibly taking all of Oregon. This did not dampen the spirits of the annexationists in the Middle West, who blamed the British for the economic depression that they were experiencing. The British appeared to them as imperious intruders, who had no rights to any part of the North American continent.

Across the sea a similar political situation limited the freedom of the British Foreign Office. The Whigs, the opposition party in England, attacked the recent Webster-Ashburton Treaty, as a surrender of national interests. Lord Palmerston denounced the treaty as capitulation and called for a strong program of national defense. The public's feelings toward the United States were also influenced by the thriving antislavery movement, which was particularly critical of the institution of slavery in the United States. Hostile Britons also believed that the energetic and ambitious republic, unrestrained by powerful neighbors and given to reckless conduct in foreign affairs, spelled trouble for the future. Edward Everett, after his return from serving as the American minister in London, warned that there were groups in England, including the military, who panted for an opportunity to put the upstart Americans in their place. The Tory government in London would have to tread carefully between its desire for peace and the challenges of the party in opposition.

The British foreign secretary, Lord Aberdeen, was a man of peace and had devoted himself to improving relations with the United States. He had hoped that the negotiations of Webster and Ashburton would settle the Oregon question, and he was distressed when they put the matter aside. His hope was that the boundary dispute could be resolved before it became a party conflict and a matter of national honor.

Unlike Texas, which had been severed from Mexico ten years earlier and gained recognition as a sovereign state, Oregon was a territory held jointly by Great Britain and the United States subject to terms mutually agreed upon in negotiations. Either country had the right to terminate joint occupancy after giving one year's notice. The status of Oregon had also been the subject of negotiations, and in the course of these each power had taken positions from which they could not retreat.

There were other distinctive disputes. Both nations could and did claim rights based on discovery; the Americans from the Columbia River north to the forty-ninth parallel and the British to Puget Sound and south to the Columbia River. What the rights covered in specific terms was never agreed upon. The conventions of 1816 and 1828 came about because of these competing claims.

Certain unforeseen developments occurred after the first convention was negotiated. Citizens of both nations were free to engage in the fur trade, but gradually the Hudson's Bay Company monopolized the trade north of the Columbia River and, through its control of numerous trading posts, served as a quasigovernment for its many employees.

The area destined to become the crux of the future controversy was the Oregon triangle, that part lying between the Columbia River and the forty-ninth parallel. Here were located the major operations of the Hudson's Bay Company, whose power and influence in London assured it of government protection. From the time of the earliest negotiations the United States consistently refused any compromise south of the forty-ninth parallel and the British had refused any compromise north of the Columbia River.

The British position was dictated by the interests of the Hudson's Bay Company. The United States commitment to the forty-ninth parallel rested on the consideration of contiguity, that this part of Oregon would adjoin the western part of the United States. Also, as early as 1826, the United States desired a west-coast port. The mouth of the Columbia River was blocked by sandbars, and the river itself was navigable for only a short distance inland. Possession to the forty-ninth parallel would provide fine harbors.

Both sides recognized that resolution of the Oregon question could not be delayed much longer. Lord Ashburton, before leaving for the United States in 1842, received instructions to seek an agreement to divide the territory at the Columbia River. Daniel Webster, was almost indifferent about Oregon, but he recognized that possession of a seaport on the Pacific was important. He suggested that, if it could be arranged to have Mexico sell northern California, including San Francisco with its fine harbor, then the British proposal might be acceptable. Lord Aberdeen believed that Ashburton had made a mistake in not exploring the question further. It should be settled before it became an issue in party politics, and before national honor became involved.[43]

Aberdeen and Edward Everett, the American minister in London, were anxious to settle the question. Secretary of State, Daniel Webster first proposed that Great Britain arrange for Mexico to sell northern California, but the

British promptly refused to have any part in this deal. The setback appeared temporary. Aberdeen was convinced that if Everett was granted authority to reach a settlement there would be no difficulty.[44] Webster was unhappy about his position as the lone remaining Whig in the Tyler cabinet, which made him the target of criticism within Whig ranks. To free himself, he proposed heading a special mission, but the British declined on the ground that, should it fail, the great attention it would receive would have unfortunate consequences. Aberdeen and Everett discussed the subject, and Aberdeen was anxious to have Everett receive instructions and be free to carry on the negotiations, but Webster professed that he did not see his way to draw up instructions that would lead to a treaty that could win Senate approval.[45] Since he had proposed a special mission and then assumed he could negotiate a treaty that would pass the Senate, his refusal to countenance Everett's authority to negotiate suggested that there were other reasons that he chose not to reveal. Everett, in later years, remained convinced that he and Aberdeen could have negotiated a treaty that would have been approved. When a treaty was negotiated three years later, it incorporated the very terms Everett and Aberdeen had discussed, and failure to give instructions to Everett appears to have been a serious mistake.

Late in 1843, after Webster had resigned and Abel P. Upshur had taken his place, Everett and Aberdeen hammered out prospective terms.[46] Finally, Everett apears to have convinced Upshur that a settlement was within reach, and the secretary of state authorized Everett to negotiate. By then Congress was engaged in heated debates on the Oregon question, and it had become a party issue. Everett believed that a treaty negotiated by him, the only remaining Whig in the administration, faced certain defeat. Therefore he proposed that the negotiations take place in Washington.

When Everett proposed that the boundary be drawn at the forty-ninth parallel. Aberdeen spoke of one difficulty.

His predecessors had twice rejected that boundary. The Peel ministry would need to be able to cite some concession. Reporting this to Upshur, Everett suggested that the difficulty could be resolved by giving to England the southern extremities of Quadra and Vancouver islands, both of which were south of the forty-ninth parallel in Puget Sound, on the condition that the Strait of Juan de Fuca be left open and free to American navigation.[47]

Everett's realistic approach found its way into a pamphlet written by the leading Boston merchant William Sturgis and soon reached London. There it gained the attention of the press and of the Foreign Office. Everett shortly found an opportunity to consult with a well-known British journalist, Nassau Senior.[48] After full explanations of the pros and cons, Senior wrote one article for a newspaper and one for the *Edinburgh Review* supporting the plan, but quickly came under fire from the leaders of the Whig opposition party, who charged that Senior was ready to surrender England itself to the Americans.

This was the situation as Polk took office in March 1845. He faced a party in which a most important and influential segment demanded a settlement at 54°40'. Meanwhile, Peel's Tory ministry in England faced an opposition that would reject any settlement that did not draw the boundary at the Columbia River.[49] The middle western expansionists would agree to nothing less than all of Oregon.

The Polk administration sought peace. Its newspaper, *The Union*, began to prepare the public for a compromise. Secretary of State James Buchanan assured Pakenham, the new British minister in Washington, that the administration sought a settlement by negotiation. Louis McLane, Everett's replacement in London, received instructions that called for him to find a settlement along the lines of the Everett-Aberdeen formula.[50] This was a carefully kept secret.

In the spring of 1845 the Peel ministry also sought conciliation. Aberdeen, in a letter to Pakenham on April 18, indicated that he was anxious to make peace. If Buchanan turned down the Columbia River as a boundary and, in turn, proposed the forty-ninth parallel, then he should propose a modification of that line "leaving us in possession of the whole of Vancouver's Island and free entrance into the Straits of Juan de Fuca." Aberdeen acknowledged that this did not quite meet with his wishes but "with some modifications it might be accepted."[51]

This proposal reflected the deep concerns of the Peel ministry at the time. On the one hand, Peel was pleased with the rumor that the Polk administration was prepared to lower the American tariff. On the other, the Peel ministry was deeply disturbed by a new rumor that France was considering an invasion of England. Also ominous was a report that the Americans were building iron steamers for service on the Great Lakes. This portended a possible American invasion of Canada. In the light of these instructions Pakenham should have been prepared to negotiate in a conciliatory spirit.[52]

The cautious treading in the waters of diplomacy came to an abrupt halt in July. Polk decided to offer to divide the territory at the forty-ninth parallel. He justified this action because his predecessors had made this offer. He termed it a concession.

At this point a radical turn took place. Pakenham rejected the proposal out of hand on the grounds that it had been presented as a concession and accompanied with the assertion that all of Oregon rightfully belong to the United States. It was certainly foolish to encumber the proposal with this unnecessary declaration of righteousness, but Pakenham had made a serious mistake. Aberdeen recognized it as such and declared that he had not followed his instructions.[53] However, it was the president who chose to exploit the error of Pakenham. Thereby he launched the country on one of its most trying periods. He did so deliberately. We cannot know what might have taken place if negotiations had not been broken off, but we also can assert that Pakenham's rejection extricated

Polk from a situation that was not to his liking, creating a great difficulty with the expansionists.

Polk conveyed to the British minister that negotiations were at an end. After delivering his message, Buchanan sadly observed at a cabinet meeting: "Well the deed is done, but he did not think it was the part of wise statesmanship to deliver such a paper in the existing state of our relations with Mexico."[54] Polk said he was glad it was delivered, "that it was right in itself, and he saw no reason for delaying it because of our relations with Mexico."[55] He took satisfaction in having withdrawn the offer to compromise and said that he was now free to return to a stronger demand. At a cabinet meeting on October 23, a despatch from McLane in London was discussed. It stated that Aberdeen "not only lamented, but censured the rejection of Pakenham," and that he would have seized upon the proposal and had little doubt that an agreement could have been reached. Aberdeen also said he would do so now if the president had not withdrawn the proposal. Polk said, "our proposition is withdrawn and no longer to be considered."[56] When Polk stated that the British were to be left in the dark, Buchanan warned that if left as it was the situation could lead to war.[57] Polk retorted that the British had no right to know what he would do.

Polk professed that he was pleased. He had now assumed a bold and firm position that accorded with his own inclination toward masculinity. He had also avoided losing the support of the extremists in his party and at the same time had not revealed his hand to southern Democrats who favored a conciliatory course.

He said that he did not expect the British to offer a proposition he could accept. The course he was following, he acknowledged, was "likely to create anxiety on both sides of the Atlantic lest peace be disturbed." Giving expression to his feelings, he stated: "It is however right in itself and I am fully satisfied with it. I have no doubt I shall be sustained in it by a large majority of the country. I do not believe there is any real danger of its leading to war, but if it is war I act upon Gen'l Jackson's maxim in conduction of our foreign affairs to ask nothing that is not right and to submit to nothing that is wrong."[58]

In his message to Congress in December, Polk outlined the course to be followed. He called on Congress to pass a resolution giving the required one-year notice of the termination of the treaty of joint occupation. He recommended that Congress pass legislation for the establishment of American jurisdiction in Oregon. Finally, he called for the establishment of blockhouses on the route in order to protect prospective settlers. He added that the United States stood by the Monroe Doctrine and warned Europe against interference in the New World. This pronouncement was directed against the British, who he believed were intent on taking California. The language was not flamboyant, but he once again repeated the American claims to all of Oregon. The claim to all of Oregon was, in fact, extremely flimsy, as many of those well acquainted with the history of the dispute had acknowledged.

The president was a hawk at home, but his secret instructions to the American minister, Louis McLane, focused on peace. The advocates of peace were left in the dark, and knowing the boldness of his course, they had reason to be concerned about what the president might do once the treaty of joint occupation was terminated.

A heated debate took place in the Senate. The opposition, led by Daniel Webster and John C. Calhoun, demanded to know what the president would do after termination. Webster called for adjustment and compromise. "Compromise I can understand, arbitration I can comprehend," he argued, "but negotiation, with a resolution to take and not to give—negotiation not to settle unless we obtain the whole, is what I do not comprehend in diplomacy or matters of government."[59] Calhoun asked, Was the amazing progress of civilization to be halted by a war for Oregon? The southern senator had warned the president that war with England over the Oregon question would be a disaster.[60] British naval superiority could take and hold Oregon until the United States achieved power on the seas. Polk could expect the New England Whigs to give him trouble. New England port cities had no defenses, and the merchants depended upon English credit. Thus the combination of Whigs and southern Democrats was to delay passing the resolution on termination for more than two months.

There were influential voices outside of Congress that dissented from the president. Edward Everett, recently returned from London, confided to a British friend, as the crisis mounted late in 1845, that he was haunted day and night by the prospect of an unnecessary war. Not only was he worried about what Polk might do, but also about the British, who might not understand that even the Whigs in the United States, who sought peace, would go no further in compromise than the modification of the line along the forty-ninth parallel—and Everett wrote this to Lord Aberdeen.[61]

Everett understood British politics and feared that the Peel ministry would be paralyzed by the Whigs, who were likely to denounce any reasonable compromise as capitulation. The British Whigs had opposed a settlement along the forty-ninth parallel before, and they might well feel called upon to adhere to the policy of their predecessors in the party. He first wrote to Lord Jeffrey, "I must, however, in candor say that I think your government was greatly to blame in 1818, 1824, and 1826 in refusing the offer which we made of the 49th degree North Latitude as the boundary, and this for no other reason than to gratify the desire of the Fur companies to monopolize the trade of the region west of the Rocky Mountains."[62] On December 28, 1845 Everett addressed a letter to Lord John Russell, leader of the British Whigs. He acknowledged that it was a delicate matter to write to the leader of the opposition, but he wrote because of his "feeling, that peace between the two countries is the greatest interest of the world, and that its preservation is wrapped up in the folds of your mantle." He stressed that the offer of the

49th had been altered and the modification would leave Great Britain with free ports on the southern tip of Vancouver Island. Whether his ministers would accept it was for them to decide, but if they chose to rally public opinion against it, it would be difficult for Peel's ministry to agree to it. Again Everett referred to the danger that the Whigs would reject it simply for the sake of consistency. If this should be the case, and they plunged into a war "for the sake of adhering to the worst traditions of Lord Liverpool and Lord Castlereagh," then they would have made war for the wrong reason.[63] Everett's letter may not have been a factor, but early in February, Lord Russell informed the Peel ministry that he would not oppose Lord Aberdeen should he choose not to adhere to the traditional demand that the boundary be at the Columbia River. At one point during the weeks of anxiety Everett, impatient with the British, expressed the opinion that perhaps, when dealing with the British, Polk's strategy was correct.

A political upheaval in London during late December and January of 1846 contributed to a change in the attitudes of the Peel ministry toward the United States. England faced a potato famine and a shortage of grain. This increased the agitation for a repeal of the corn laws that limited imports of grain. Faced with strong opposition within the Tory party, Peel resigned. However, he took office again when Lord Russell was unable to form a ministry. Peel then turned to assuring the governments on the continent that his ministry was dedicated to peace. He was also free to override the conservatives, who opposed repeal of the corn laws. The prospect of an opening of British markets appears to have had an influence in both the South and the North. An unrelenting demand for 54°40' possibly meant war, and that would mean the loss of what now appeared as an opportunity to improve economic conditions by an increase in exports.[64]

Aberdeen immediately became more conciliatory. Although he was still fearful that Polk might pursue a course that meant war, he was also encouraged by his discussions with McLane and by the reports in American correspondence that peace was within reach.

In that tortuous winter of 1846, when American opinion remained divided, Albert Gallatin, the aged Jeffersonian who had served the country so well as a diplomat under James Monroe and John Quincy Adams, published his "Letters on the Oregon Question" in the *National Intelligencer*. Gallatin paid for the thousands of the pamphlets that included his letters. They were widely distributed among clergymen and teachers; some 15,000 were distributed in Massachusetts. Most important, the letters were widely read by members of the Senate, where his great reputation carried weight. He sympathized with the hard-working farmers in the Middle West who were burdened by hard work and economic difficulties, but feelings rarely brought forth constructive solutions. The American claim to all of Oregon was an assertion unsupported by facts. Everett was delighted and wrote to Gallatin that he had rendered a service to the country "not inferior to any performed by you in the most active period of your life." Gallatin's letters were timely.[65]

There was now evidence that the British government was ready to come to terms. In late January, the London *Times* published an editorial advocating a settlement along the lines that Aberdeen and Everett had discussed. Everett wrote at once to Aberdeen inquiring if the views expressed were those of the ministry. Aberdeen could not acknowledge that this was so, but implied that it was. Everett, in turn, informed his old friend George Bancroft, who was a member of Polk's cabinet, stating that the editorial was the work of Aberdeen and that it should be viewed as the official British position.

By late February the earlier excitement receded before more sober thinking, and the tone of discussions changed. Gradually, attention focused on the wording of the notice of termination. It was at this point that Gallatin's influence made itself felt. After reading the original wording of the resolution, he pointed out what he considered to be a serious omission. He wrote: "The fundamental point

on which England has always insisted, for the maintenance of which she is fully committed, from which she
will not and cannot recede, is resistance to the exclusive
pretensions of the United States and protection of British interests in Oregon and of British subjects residing
therein, until the existing difficulties shall have been
definitely settled by an amicable arrangement."[66] Gallatin's influence cannot, of course, be measured, but the
editors of the *National Intelligencer* assured him that his
pamphlet carried weight with the senators who had co-
alesced into a party of peace, and who by the end of February appeared to have the upper hand.

Polk's position too had been changing since late December. He had consulted with his cabinet about whether
he should submit a British proposal to the Senate if it
were forthcoming. The cabinet agreed unanimously that
Polk should do so. However, he was determined not to
consult with members of the Senate. Should members of
the expansionist wing of his party learn of his leaning toward compromise the party would split. On January 4, in
a conversation with James G. Black of South Carolina, a
member of the House of Representatives, Black asked direct questions. Polk referred him to his annual message,
lectured him on the wisdom of a bold and firm course,
and concluded with his famous remark "the only way to
treat John Bull was to look him straight in the eye."[67] He
was equally curt with John C. Calhoun. On January 10,
Calhoun met with the president and pointed out that the
British claim to the valley of the Fraser River was as good
as the American claim to the Columbia River. A study by
the president of those demands would have confirmed
what Calhoun said, but Polk was as secretive as ever.

In late February, Senator William Haywood of North
Carolina, called the president. A friend of Polk's since
college days, Haywood deplored the course taken by Calhoun in criticizing the president, but stated that he favored drawing the boundary at the forty-ninth parallel.[68]
In his diary Polk did not reveal whether he gave Haywood
reason to believe that he too favored the forty-ninth, but

Haywood believed that Polk had agreed. On March 4, Haywood spoke at length in the Senate contending that the president's intentions were pacific. He did not refer to his conversation with Polk; instead he built his case on an interpretation of Polk's annual message.

The result was pandemonium. Haywood's friendship with the president was well known. Senators Allen and Hannegan leaped to the floor to castigate Haywood and to question the trustworthiness of Polk. If the president actually held the views attributed to him by Haywood, then roared Hannegan, Polk was "an infamous man—aye, an infamous man." If, as Haywood had argued, Polk had merely inserted some extreme phrases in his message to quiet the "ultras," then the president's conduct was "most vile and infamous."[69]

The fight in the Senate transferred itself to the president's mansion. Senators Cass and McDuffie called to talk about the violent debate. Referring to Haywood's speech, Polk declared that no one was authorized to speak for him, that he had made his own position clear in his message to Congress, and he urged Haywood to support the resolution. There was a series of meetings with senators, and each time Polk gave the same answer.

The debates in the Senate on the resolution were prolonged, but the peace advocates had gained control. Polk was compelled to accept that if the notice of termination was to pass, it would have to be accompanied by a friendly assurance that the United States was ready to make peace. Not until April 20 was agreement reached on the words to be used. The action came just in time to avert the danger that the British would learn that war had been declared against Mexico.

Aberdeen and McLane worked in harmony to prepare a treaty proposal. One issue caused additional delay. McLane sought to withhold navigation rights on the Columbia River from the British because he thought that Polk would raise strong objections, but the proposal as finally formulated did award these rights. It also recognized the property rights of British settlers.[70] The instructions to Pakenham that accompanied the treaty proposal called on him to refer any important changes to Aberdeen.

In Washington the annexationists were unhappy, and their sympathies were temporarily joined by Secretary of State Buchanan. Polk, however, overruled him in cabinet meetings and a draft of a treaty was sent to the Senate, where it obtained the two-thirds approval required.

In the background of the political labyrinth that had so postponed a settlement in the Senate was the influential good sense of men like Gallatin, Everett, Calhoun, and others. As Sir Robert Peel had suggested in January, it "would be disgraceful for two such nations to go to war." In the negotiations, the British claims were stronger than those of the United States. The near tragedy of an unnecessary war came about due to party rivalry on both sides, but the irresponsibility of the expansionists led by Cass, Allen, and Hannegan must be emphasized. Buchanan also had played a double game moving from opposition to support of the annexationists when he found that Polk's annual message to Congress in December was popular. Lastly, the president must bear a major responsibility for allowing himself to be used by the expansionists.

Expansionism moved the nation toward the final building of a continental empire. The road left no grounds for self-righteousness. Looking back at the close of the war with Mexico, Edward Everett wrote to his friend Robert Winthrop: "There is nothing novel in our present embarrassments; they belong to a career of conquest. Each step forward creates the necessity of taking another. Such was the history of Rome and Napoleon; such has been the history of the British government in India. Let us retrace our steps before we add another example to the list."[71]

A great transition had taken place. By 1850 the United States emerged from the war with Mexico as the dominant power in North America. At the same time the country experienced great industrial growth. At midcentury manufacturing establishments represented an investment of $500 million. A new transportation system had come into being. Railroads increased in mileage from 9,026 in 1850 to 30,626 in 1860, an increase of over 300 percent. By 1853 steam-driven ships numbered 1,390, and each year two hundred new ones were launched. This rapid economic growth was accompanied by the first great flood of immigrants and the prolific growth of cities.

Government became more and more important as these developments took place. Overseas trade created a demand for naval protection of sea lanes and of merchants residing abroad. A new drive centered in the South and among New York shipping interests for the annexation of Cuba, an interoceanic canal through Central America, control of a broad zone in northern Mexico for the development of mining interests, and the construction of a transcontinental railroad.

The new spirit found expression in the first issue of *Putnam's Monthly* in October 1853. Involvement in world affairs, wrote the editor, was inevitable. Government policy should be "based on our convictions of right and duty" and should be concerned "with something greater than petty selfish interests." There should be "prompt and full protection for every citizen, guiltless or wrong, whatever he may be." Europe must be excluded from the western hemisphere and there must be a willingness to receive new nations into the Union. There must be an "unreserved sympathy with people struggling for their emancipation" from despotism.[72]

This spirit led to the short-lived Young America movement, which enjoyed the support of Presidents Pierce and Buchanan. Although politics centered on the question of extending slavery into Kansas and Nebraska, Pierce and Buchanan pushed for the annexation of Cuba.

The inexorable process was temporarily interrupted by the Civil War and the high priority of the problems of Reconstruction. After the war Alaska was acquired, but the opposition was strong, and approval of the treaty was, it appears, only accomplished by the transfer of Russian funds into the pockets of some members of Congress. President Ulysses S. Grant supported the annexation of Santo Domingo, but his efforts came to naught. Foreign relations centered on the Alabama Claims dispute. The differences with the British were finally resolved by the Treaty of Washington in 1871.

4

Rethinking Foreign Policy: A New Ideology 1890–1917

IN his book *The Transformation of American Foreign Relations, 1865–1900,* Charles S. Campbell wrote, "As it was, seldom had a country not under duress experienced in so short a time, so radical a transformation of its relations with the rest of the world as did the United States in the Years between 1865 and 1900."[1] The decades following 1890 were to bring changes of equal significance.

Like most wars, the Spanish-American War in 1898 had unforeseen results. The conflict arose as a result of American determination to restore order in Cuba. President William McKinley did not want war but neither was he content to allow the disastrous conditions in Cuba to continue. Local rebellion against Cuba's Spanish masters had already gone on for four long years. McKinley, in his instructions to the new ambassador to Spain, made it clear that the United States could not tolerate the existing situation indefinitely. The pressures upon him from Democratic members of Congress were already great, and they mounted rapidly in the early months of 1898. Members of his own party warned that unless action was taken the Republicans would split and they would lose the fall election. No president could sit idly by confronting such a prospect.

McKinley also faced the dilemma that while Spain sought to be cooperative, the country would probably face revolution if Cuba was granted independence. On March 17, Senator Redfield Proctor of Vermont spoke after completing an inspection trip in Cuba. He was a highly respected man and widely trusted. His account portrayed appalling conditions. Perhaps no senator ever gave a speech that had more far-reaching results.[2] In April there was still no prospect of peace, but victory in Cuba came in less than five months. As the war gathered momentum, the comforting news arrived in May that Captain Dewey had destroyed the Spanish fleet in Manila in the Philippine Islands. In the meantime, the United States had acquired information that a far-superior Spanish fleet was on its way across the Pacific. Additional naval strength and army troops were sent to bolster Dewey's force. The reinforcements were under orders to hold Manila.[3]

After Spain's defeat, occupation troops remained in Cuba and were only withdrawn after Cuba, under protest, accepted the Platt amendment reducing Cuba to a protectorate. Debate began at once as to whether the Philippines should be held as a whole or in part. The president, in the months before the war, had faced a divided nation, and he was determined not to find himself in such difficulties again. He had not made up his own mind. He could see that once the glory of victory had subsided, difficulties would inevitably follow and he could suffer a backlash. McKinley was distinguished by his patience, and he was careful not to yield to the many inquirers. He was likewise determined that, whatever his final decision might be, it should have wide public support. With this as his guide he set out on a speaking tour in the Middle West to sound out opinion. As it soon appeared that the public favored annexation, he gradually turned toward this decision. His speeches made frequent references to the duty of the United States. In Chicago, on October 18, he added a new note. "My countrymen," he implored, "the currents of destiny flow through the hearts of people. Who will check them? Who will divert them? And the movements of men, planned and designed by the Master of men, will never be interrupted by the American people."[4] McKinley had made a decision that was based earnestly upon public opinion.

More earthly considerations than the "Divine Current" also came forward. Well before the war the Naval Board, led by Alfred Thayer Mahan, had called for a naval base in the Far East. Another consideration was the focus of attention on the threatened breakup of China that began late in 1897 and made headway early in 1898 as the major powers carved China into various spheres of influence. There was fear of a final partition that would leave the United States a lonely and helpless outsider. Annexation of the Philippines would safely plant the United States where it would have influence in the Pacific and be able to promote its trade.

The peace commission, dominated by proannexationists, was successful in negotiating a treaty that surrendered the islands to the United States. Annexation became a national issue. The newly founded Anti-Imperialist League promoted a campaign contending that annexation would betray the honored and long-held principle that people were entitled to self-government. One speaker, George Boutwell, in a speech before the Congregational Club in Boston in December 1898, pointed out that possession of the Philippines must of necessity catapult the United States into world politics. The islands would require a very large navy for protection against the separate or combined fleets of England, Russia, and Japan. China and Russia, he said, were already allied, and to take the Philippines meant that we "sit down under the shadow of this mighty power, knowing full well that our jurisdiction is a subordinate and tolerated jurisdiction, and that Russia is supreme." The British, he added, only approved of the United States's taking the islands because it would make the Americans dependent on Great Britain.

Senator John Daniel argued that it was impossible to transmit American ideals and institutions to the Philippines. We would not, said the senator, be tempted by the glitter of trade and empire because the mission of the United States was to set an example.[5] The liberal magazine the *Nation* expressed the opinion that self-government was a part of American constitutional principles and stood in the way of the United States becoming an empire.

In the Senate, Henry Cabot Lodge twisted the arguments of annexation opponents into a mistaken notion that the American people could not be trusted. Lodge maintained that to reject annexation was to repudiate the president. "The repudiation of the President in such a matter as this," said Lodge, "is to my mind, the humiliation of the United States in the eyes of civilized mankind and brands us as a people incapable of great affairs or of taking rank where we belong, as one of the greatest of the great world powers."[6] The Senate approved the treaty of annexation.

What followed annexation was a two-year war marked by cruelty and the death of ten times as many American soldiers as in the war with Spain. Time, and the emergence of a more realistic approach, led to a reevaluation of the decision of annexation. As early as 1907, Theodore Roosevelt acknowledged that the islands were America's Achilles heal because they could not be defended.

The acquisition of an empire gave to American foreign policy a higher priority than it had ever had before. Woodrow Wilson observed: "Much the most important change to be noticed is the result of the war with Spain upon the lodgment and exercise of power within the federal system." "When foreign affairs play a prominent part in the politics of a nation," Wilson wrote, "the Executive must of necessity be its guide: must utter every initial judgment, take every first step of action, supply the information upon which it is to act, suggest and in large measure control its conduct."[7] Wilson supported annexation. It was a question of whether the United States, Germany, or Russia would prevail. Theirs was the light of darkness, ours was the light of day. It was the duty of the United States to annex the island.[8]

The dramatic events of 1898 did not lead to further reckless adventure, but silent forces were in the process of altering the nineteenth-century alignment of powers. The rise of the United States, Germany, and Japan to great-power status and the increased strength of Italy, unified as a nation state in 1870, upset the old international order. Complicating relations still further were the promising beginnings of industrial development in Russia. Russia remained a largely backward society, but its immense territory, large population, and natural resources gave every indication that it would become a world power.

A global economic revolution was underway. The most dramatic growth took place in the United States. It already surpassed Great Britain as the world's workshop. By 1900 the American nation produced 26.5 million tons of steel a year.[9] This was greater than British and German production combined. The United States was also producing 455 million tons of coal, compared to Britain's 292 million and Germany's 277 million.[10] It was also the world's largest producer of oil. American energy consumption was equal to that of Great Britain, France, Russia, and Austria-Hungary combined.[11] America's impact on the world's commerce paralleled its industrial development. American exports increased from $334 million in 1860 to $1.896 billion in 1914.[12] The country had become the Hercules of the economic world.

Germany did not achieve unification of its numerous states until 1871. In the short lapse of time from then until the turn of the century this new nation climbed to first place in industrial production in Europe. By 1914 its steel production surpassed that of Great Britain, France, and Russia combined.[13] It also led the continent in the production of chemicals and electrical equipment.

Economic advances were also made in France and in Italy. Great Britain no longer led the world in industrial production, but it remained an imposing power in possession of the world's largest empire and a naval fleet equal to the combined strength of the next two naval powers, Germany and France.

Emerging from all of this was an increased rivalry for colonies and markets, together with an armament race. A mixture of fears and national ambitions intensified rivalries and elevated the importance of every nation's conduct of diplomacy and formulation of foreign policy. In this new scene of rising imperialisms it was inevitable that the United States too would give increasing attention to its relations with other nations. The change that took place has been ascribed to economic factors, to a psychic crisis accompanying the rapid changes in domestic life, and to threatening developments in the outside world. At the center of the change about to come were a new and friendly relationship with Great Britain and a subdued but nevertheless real distrust of Germany among those who were giving thought to the future position of the United States on the world scene.

Ever since the American Revolution, a distrust of England had permeated a large segment of the nation's public. Anglophobia was especially prevalent in the western states and had become a force that every administration either shared or accepted as a fact that had to be taken into consideration. However, it was not prevalent among business interests in the northeast and in the small band of intellectuals who looked to England as a kindred culture. American merchants had a close relationship with Britain and depended upon British credit. Their pro-British feelings paralleled those of the Whig party and its leaders such as Daniel Webster and Edward Everett.

The tradition of no entangling alliances remained in place. This policy originated in a wise acknowledgment that a commitment to a European power would leave the frail republic a puppet to be danced on the wires pulled by European statesmen. When the United States was a weak, thinly populated nation, isolationism had been realistic statesmanship, but had no place in the changed conditions.

American indifference toward the internal rivalries of Europe flourished in the absence of a major European war after 1815. The revolution of 1848 created a brief stir in favor of Hungarian independence and for a few months

Louis Kossuth was a hero, but the momentous unifica-
tions of Germany and Italy came as remote developments
and of no concern to the American people. The significance of the ascendance of these two nations to world
power in 1870 did not take hold until the 1890's when
Germany appeared as a threat in the Caribbean.

In 1823, John Quincy Adams' declaration of the Monroe
Doctrine served as a catapult that raised common American sentiments that Europe should not interfere in the
western hemisphere and that the United States should
not interfere in the internal affairs of Europe. Adding spice
to the pronouncement was Adams' dictum that the New
World was closed to further colonization. This blustering
note harmonized with national pride but not with any realistic assessment of power. It was the British command
of the seas that assured the republic of security and not
Adams' policy. Nevertheless, not until the turn of the
century did British naval power come to be viewed as
an ally.

The Monroe Doctrine did not immediately gain standing as national policy. President Polk gave it new life
when the Oregon question arose, and it was well on the
way to becoming an act of national faith during the Civil
War when France intervened with Mexico. By the turn of
the century, the Monroe Doctrine elicited emotions on a
par with references to the Declaration of Independence
and the Constitution. The Spanish scholar Salvador de
Madariaga pointedly said of the Monroe Doctrine: "I
know only two things about the Monroe Doctrine: one is
that no American I have met knows what it is; the other
is that no American I have met will consent to its being
tampered with . . . I conclude that the Monroe Doctrine
is not a doctrine but a dogma, . . . not one but two, to wit:
the dogma of the infallibility of the American President
and the dogma of the immaculate conception of American foreign policy."[14] The doctrine had no standing in
international law, it had no specificity as to exactly how
much of the Latin American world it covered, and it was
no more specific regarding what actions by European

powers it supposedly prohibited. But as a myth that had captured American thinking it was durable. It had behind it the force of American opinion.

Another myth that originated in the first decades of the republic, that the United States was a model for other nations to emulate, contributed to a sense of separateness. The founding fathers discovered it useful to puff up the importance of the republic while the Union was still in formative stages by equating it with a beacon light guiding the world to a more liberal order where reason and justice reigned. The hope for the future was in America because European monarchies were benighted. Thomas Jefferson, while minister to France, wrote to James Madison that "all monarchies aside from the British were governments of wolves over sheep. The French court," he wrote, "was nothing more than a school for inculcating corruption."[15] This was a common view, and it was easy to take the next step and conclude that the future of liberal government depended on the success of the American experiment.

This flattering self-image became more deeply engraved in national consciousness as the success of the "experiment" appeared to justify the faith. In 1824, Edward Everett, in his Phi Beta Kappa address at Harvard, called on his audience to accept the challenge to serve as a model for the future: "We are summoned to new energy and zeal, by the high nature of the experiment we are appointed to make, and the grandeur of the theater on which it is performed." It had "pleased Heaven to open this refuge of humanity." The experiment, said Everett, will tell the world "whether mankind can be trusted with a popular system of government." He, like his fellow citizens, saw success on all sides, and he exuded confidence: "Should our happy Union continue, this great continent, in no remote futurity, will be filled up with the mightiest kindred people known in history."[16]

In the land of plenty these attitudes and feelings were not challenged until late in the nineteenth century. The

United States was aggressive both in expansion and in soliciting foreign trade. The Mexican War and the crusade
of the Young America Party in the 1850's attest to the
bumptiousness of the new nation. New trade treaties
with countries around the world extended the sphere of
commercial relations. President Andrew Jackson eagerly
supported the promotion of trade, and he negotiated more
new treaties than any of the antebellum presidents. Americans were the epitome of activitism, and their energy
aroused fears that in the future this new colossus would
continue to be adventurous in international relations.

Older traditions gave way to a new look outward in the
1890's as depression and the Bryanite populist movement
accented feelings that the republic was undergoing rapid
change. Depression brought with it unemployment, labor
violence on an unprecedented scale, a farmers' revolt, and
general social unrest. Eugene Debs and members of the
American Railway Union did more than bring railroads
to a standstill, they questioned the capitalist system and
advanced the ideology of a class struggle. Amidst the fer-
ment, William Jennings Bryan sent tremors through the
established order with his attacks on the gold standard
and protests against social injustice. In the Protestant
churches the social gospel challenged the easy toleration
of social maladies. These developments suggested that
the United States was not a nation apart. It too was subject to the turmoil that accompanied the new industrialization in Europe.

Economic instability, business failures, and unemployment turned some merchants and manufacturers in a
new direction. To them it appeared that the heart of the
problem was overproduction and that the solution lay in
the expansion of overseas markets. In the course of the
decade China attracted attention as a country of major
interest. Here was a market, or so it appeared, of 400 million customers who, if they added one inch to their frock
coats, could keep the textile mills of America busy for
years to come. In New York City the prestigious *Journal*

of Commerce kept before its readers the picture of an emerging China and the importance of the government in promoting the China trade. Interested merchants and manufacturers organized the American Asiatic Association and lobbied in Washington for support.

Latin America also fell into line as a future market. In November 1906, Secretary of State Elihu Root, in an address before the Trans-Mississippi Commercial Congress, declared that the central question facing the United States was that of a surplus of capital and overproduction. Latin America had yet to embark on industrial development and needed both the surplus capital and American manufacturers.[17] Root entertained the faith that once the Latin-American countries introduced a modern economy and raised living standards, revolutionary disturbances would be replaced by stability and order.

A search for foreign markets ran as a continuing theme in the thinking of decision makers from the 1890's to the years before 1914. In the case of China the market proved to be largely a myth. The poverty in China, the fact that the market was in large part limited to the coastal areas, and the failure of American merchants and manufacturers to adapt to Chinese needs and tastes, plus the failure to provide credit, brought limited sales. Exports to China did not reach more than two percent of the total of American exports in this period. Investments there also remained at a low level. In 1914 the United States with an investment of $49.3 million dollars ranked far below other foreign powers.[18] However, the Department of State never ceased to champion treaty rights. In 1905, new Chinese regulations concerning the starting up of new enterprises, particularly in mining, drew strong protests from the American minister, W. W. Rockhill, on the ground that these rules contravened the 1903 American treaty of commerce. It is also true, that although exports to China did not increase significantly, optimism about a great China market did not dissipate.

In the Caribbean area, where American imperialism was most aggressive, evidence indicates that action was only minimally related to economic concerns. Dana G. Munro, author of *Intervention and Dollar Diplomacy in the Caribbean, 1900–1921,* concluded that security for the Panama Canal played a major role. Munro, upon completion of his monumental study, concluded that economic matters were occasionally given consideration, but wrote that he doubted "whether these considerations had any great influence in the formulation of policy."[19] Richard Challener, in his scholarly scrutiny of the navy, which played a major role in the agitation for bases in the Caribbean, states that many officers expressed little interest in trade.[20] However, concern for the security of the canal reflected the distrust of Germany, the nation that had so suddenly become an adventurous world power.

The outward thrust in the 1890's was something more than a need for markets. Within American society a new confidence had come that gave both American political views, and the moral and legal institutions that accounted for American success, universal validity. Americans flattered themselves that they were a moral nation and that the advances in science, medicine and education were the key to lifting the backward nations toward a higher level of enlightenment. Never before had the gap between western civilization and that of other societies appeared greater. Given this view of the world, the ancient Christian scriptural passage "Go ye into all the world, and preach the gospel to every creature" became the dictate for a large-scale crusade. In no other period did young people fling themselves so recklessly into the Christian crusade as after 1890. In colleges throughout the country chapters of the Student Volunteer Movement recruited candidates. Sherwood Eddy, one of the early members, noted: "China was the goal, the lodestar, the great magnet that drew us all in those days."[21]

The missionary spirit was not an isolated religious phenomenon; it was the religious aspect of the broader socioeconomic and political movement that looked beyond the limits of national boundaries. Missionary candidates were not religious ascetics. They reflected a normal excitement over an unusual career in an exotic corner of the world, free from the more prosaic patterns of the ministry or a position in business at home.

Compared to the modest success of the merchants in organizing, promoters of missions carried a large part of the church community with them and mobilized church-goers across the country into organizations that enlisted all age groups, male and female alike, into a crusade. Of these no one contributed more to the movement or had a greater influence than the Student Volunteers for Foreign Missions. Virtually every institution, from Yale to the most modest Church-related college across the conti-nent, had a local chapter. The exuberant confidence of the Student Volunteers was expressed in their motto: "The Evangelization of the World in this Generation."

Before the turn of the century missionaries had empha-sized individual salvation. Hudson Taylor of the orthodox China Inland Mission wrote dramatically: "The gospel must be preached to these people in a very short time, for they are passing away. Every day, every day, oh how they sweep over! . . . there is a great Niagara of souls passing into the dark in China. Every day, every week, every month they are passing away! A million a month are dying in China without God."[22]

Gradually, saving souls from eternal perdition became a humanitarian mission of uplift that would assist China to make the transition from its traditional Confucian culture into a modern enlightened state. The founding of schools and colleges and the establishment of hospitals now replaced the traditional street chapels as the focus of the movement. This broadening of action made possible the awakening of an interest in missions among a broad segment of the American Protestant public.

Eventually the growth of the missionary enterprise—which established hundreds of elementary schools, scores of hospitals, and thirteen colleges—demanded ever-in-creasing funding. Increased funding meant that the mis-sionary thrust at home must change from being only an esoteric activity within the churches to a broadscale campaign that enjoyed wide support. Women's and children's organizations flowered in the 1890's. In November 1906 the Laymen's Missionary Movement was organized. In the course of the next fifteen years the Laymen's Movement made foreign missions a matter of respectability, civic and Christian duty, and even patriotism. The general secretary, J. Campbell White, later president of the College of Wooster, called for investigation, agitation, and organization for the purpose of "enlisting the whole Church in the supreme work of saving the world."[23]

The Laymen's Movement sponsored the National Missionary Campaign in 1909 and 1910. Seventy-five conventions were held in cities throughout the country with a total attendance of seventy-one thousand registered delegates. The campaign reached its climax in a great convention in Chicago. "Here is a new sort of missionary meeting," wrote Lyman Abbott, editor of *The Outlook*. Leading businessmen in front and filling the ranks, observed Abbott, paid their traveling expenses and a five-dollar registration fee.[24]

What is the significance of the missionary movement in terms of foreign relations? Did missionaries shape American China policy? There is no evidence that leaders of missionary boards or that missionaries directly shaped China policy, but it is also true that the missionary movement and secular imperialism were wheels driven by the same explosive energy generated by a sense of superiority, moral duty, and ego satisfaction to be gained by activity in foreign countries.

Before 1900 missionaries looked to the American government for protection, but the time was to come when they would repudiate this. From the beginning of the movement, there was a deep Chinese hostility toward foreign missionaries, and at times there were riots aimed at driving them out. Government measures consistently involved the protection of Americans who were in China. There were times during the early 1890's when the American minister in Peking devoted much of his time to appeals from missionaries. The United States was a party to the unequal treaties imposed on China in the nineteenth century, and these treaties were backed up by force. Missionaries as well as business representatives were assured of protection.

The legal separation of church and state at home did not stand in the way of commonly held points of view and a sharing of both patriotism and nationalism. Both government officials and missionaries looked on China as a country in transition; both envisioned a China in need of medical benefits, modern transportation, and an effective government presiding over an orderly society. Alfred Thayer Mahan believed earnestly that China needed European culture as much as European technology. He combined his devout Episcopal faith with a firm belief that the United States must join with the British and preserve the balance of power in Asia. Mahan praised the work of the missionaries because he believed they were inculcating the moral principles of the West.[25] At one point he urged that the American minister should visit mission stations and present an annual report of their accomplishments. These should be publicized in the United States for the purpose of promoting greater support for missions.[26]

Missionaries, like diplomats, observed with disapproval the threatened partition of China at the turn of the century. The Methodist bishop Charles Henry Fowler saw the missionary effort in China as one aspect of a changing configuration of world powers, and that China would someday become a major power. The bishop told his listeners: "Her very numbers is God's promise of perpetuity. The Yellow Race will remain the menace of the world. It lies on the shores of Asia, a huge club, only waiting to be picked up by some Hercules. China is the world's problem for the twentieth century. Who will seize this club?[27]

The British shared the American interest in China missions, and this furnished a bond between the two countries. British crusaders for missions were frequent guests in the United States, and John R. Mott, the prestigious spokesman for American missions, was almost as well known in England as at home.

Concern with overseas markets and the outward thrust of foreign missions combined to turn the attention of the American people to a world order that was breaking down and suffering critical change. China was a power vacuum and the government in Peking could provide no defense against western aggrandizement. China appeared to be on the point of partition after the Sino-Japanese War of 1895. During 1897 and 1898, Russia moved into Manchuria, Germany into Shantung, and France into the southern Chinese border states. What Theodore Roosevelt was to say in 1905 had already been said innumerable times in America and elsewhere. China was the backyard of European politics. Roosevelt, the alert observer of the changing configuration of world powers, predicted that "our future history will be more determined by our position on the Pacific facing China than by our position on the Atlantic facing Europe."[28] China was more than a prospective outlet for the overproduction of the new industry that was changing the face of western civilization; control of China was, it appeared, to be the determinant in a world struggle for supremacy and security.

The spread of the industrial revolution in both the New World and on the continent of Europe, the resulting increase of interest in new markets, the tapering off of British dominance as the workshop of the world, and the growth of the European alliance system together with an immense expansion of the armaments race, sufficed to bring about a new awareness in the United States that the time had come for a reexamination of its foreign relations. Americans who were alert to the portentous world changes were greatly influenced by the experience of the Spanish-American War. Suddenly and unexpectedly the United States acquired the responsibilities of an overseas empire and with it responsibilities in the remote Philippine Islands.

The United States, in a mood of ebullience, entered a major sphere of European politics. Samuel Flagg Bemis, the highly respected diplomatic historian, described the decision as an aberration. Few people had any thought of the Philippines at the outbreak of war, but Roosevelt and Mahan had discussed the islands, and Mahan advised the president to see that the best admiral would command in the Pacific "for much more initiative may be thrown on him than can be on the Atlantic man." That the annexation was an aberration is not to assert that no one had any forethoughts of action in the Pacific, but few outside of the Naval Board did.

There is no way to determine how wide an impact the new economic and political transformations had on the public at large, but it led to the writing of articles and books that sought to change popular thinking. Editors of upper-class magazines sensed a new public interest in the state of the world, and their judgments were confirmed by the response of the reading public. The most influential of these writers, Alfred Thayer Mahan and Brooks Adams, did not so much create interest, they simply centered their articles on the issues that were already of public concern. The Spanish-American War lowered the curtain on domestic problems that had absorbed public attention during the Populist movement and Bryan's crusade, and set in perspective the dramatic sudden emergence of an American empire. Both Mahan and Adams offered explanations for the change and its crucial importance for the United States.

Mahan was already famous as the author of *The Influence Of Sea Power upon History, 1660–1783*. The book bore the imprint of the navy, which conceived its role as the high priest of the nation's security. The work became a classic, but from the historian's viewpoint it suffered from Mahan's failure to consider other than naval factors that entered into the making of war. Nevertheless, the book had an impact that made Mahan a celebrity in Europe as well as in the United States. After the coming of the Spanish-American War and the subsequent peace treaty, Mahan wrote for the best journals of the day. Almost invariably the articles were solicited by alert editors who were experts in discerning the public's interest.

A more effective propagandist for a change in foreign policy can scarcely be conceived. Mahan had no training in writing and, as Roosevelt was to say, he knew no history. Mahan himself was surprised by his sudden rise to fame. He thought it was due to "natural clear headedness, which has translated itself into style—to a habit of omnivorous though desultory reading, which has given me a large and pretty precise vocabulary—and finally, to the happy seizure of an idea to all intents original and unworked."[29] His ideas and the broad universal panorama in which he portrayed the position of the United States in the world were new, but it was the timeliness of what he had to say that arrested attention. As his biographer, William Livezey, assessed it: "His conversion was followed by a proselytism marked with moral earnestness of purpose, mystical certainty of mission, evangelical fervor and unrelenting effort in prosecution, yet tempered withal by a fair appreciation of the difficulties to be encountered and the obstacles to be overcome."[30]

Various segments of the public, depending on their profession and personal interests, accepted the new ideas for a variety of reasons. Mahan appealed to a sense of responsibility, to religion, to humanistic attachments to western culture, to economic interests, and to fears for the future security of the nation in a rapidly changing world. His writings did not ring with alarm; rather they were quiet appeals to reason. The articles were written with a note of authority that impressed large audiences who had given little or no thought to the complexities of international relations. The dual theme of responsibility for the nation's welfare and human welfare received repeated emphasis, as did his appeals to conscience. How he combined this array of diverse considerations is illustrated in his articles entitled "Motives to Imperial Federation" written in 1902. He claimed:

> Upon us has devolved, by an inevitable sequence of causes, responsibility to our conscience for an assemblage of peoples in moral and political childhood; and responsibility further to the world at large, and to history—supreme earthly judge of men's actions,—for our course in the emergency thrust upon us. As such the United States has accepted the burden. Its duties are not to be discharged by throwing them overboard, or by wrapping our political talent in a napkin for our own national security and ease.[31]

Such general ministrations accorded with the tastes of the middle class and were in tune with the moralism that had pervaded the discussions of Americans since colonial days. Clothed in these terms, which were almost identical to the terms of the missionary movement, the appeals for a new foreign policy were like a call to a nation of socially responsible citizens anxious to serve both God and country.

At the turn of the century, when China was the lodestar guiding public attention in foreign affairs, Mahan wrote a series of articles that were shortly published as a book entitled *The Problem of Asia*. He saw the missionary movement as an essential part of the Open Door policy. Contemporaries viewed the world as divided between the modern advanced nations—which enjoyed the benefits of advanced technology, science (including modern medicine), education, and Christian morals, together with democracy[32]—and undeveloped areas where superstition and backwardness of all kinds continued to dominate. China occupied the most prominent place among the backward nations, but it was also an area open to change where modernization was making inroads.

Mahan posed the question, would the new China become a giant power, devoid of the religious faith and the political ideals of the West or would it become a nation based on sound political and moral principles? He exemplified this view that it was as important for China to be as open to western thought as it was open to trade. "Christianity and Christian teaching are just as really factors," he wrote, "in the mental and moral equipment of European civilization, as any of the philosophical or scientific processes that have gone to build up the general result." He concluded that "From the purely political standpoint, Christian thought and teaching have just the same right—no less, if no more—to admission in China as any other form of European activity, commercial or intellectual."[33] This was Mahan, the devout Episcopalian, who saw the hand of God in the developments at the turn of the century.[34]

These appeals made it easier for the American community to give consideration to Mahan's tough and stark realism. The author firmly believed that self-interest was the driving force that motivated nations and that their success or failure in defending or asserting their interests depended on power. A wealthy nation such as the United States, if it chose to close its eyes to this fact, would eventually become prey to an aggressor or a combination of powers on the march for markets and other advantages. By Mahan's interpretation, the major instrument of power was the navy, and the American navy must be the equal of the navies of any two nations that posed a danger. Like other militarists, he acknowledged that war was a horror to be avoided, but the way to prevent it was to acquire a strength that would display such force that it would deter the aggressor.

An essential argument in favor of setting aside the traditional policy of isolationism was that the United States was vulnerable in both Asia and the Caribbean. American interests in China were threatened by European powers already effective there, who had demonstrated a determination to adhere to their slogans of God, glory, and profits. Only Great Britain had common aims with the United States. It was foreseeable, given the complexities of relations among European countries, that some combination of these nations would wish to achieve a predominant position in China enabling them to influence that country.

To Mahan the Open Door policy was intertwined with maintaining a balance of power in Asia.[35] Russia would dominate Manchuria, and Mahan was willing for Russia to have a sphere of influence in this border area. The vital territory that lay open was central China, in which new currents of thought were stirring and where there was promise of modern economic development. Therefore, China must be preserved as an entity where Chinese and foreigners cooperated in ushering in the future. This could only be achieved if there was a balance of power, and it was a responsibility of the United States to assist Great Britain in maintaining this equilibrium. Otherwise American self-interests would be lost.

The United States was equally vulnerable in the Caribbean. Mahan found no difficulty in convincing Americans that this area, close to home and identified with the hallowed Monroe Doctrine, was a vital national interest. And now that a canal was to be constructed across the isthmus there was a new danger. An extensive trade would mean that merchant ships of many nations would traverse the Caribbean and, with a history of disturbances in the small republics, there was the likelihood of incidents to provide a European power with reason to intervene. Should hostilities take place, a combination of European states might seek to intervene and establish a naval base or acquire territory. The United States had long adhered to a policy of ignoring the rivalries and combinations on the European continent, but the day had passed when that policy was of no concern. The European nation states would further find mutual interests in developing trade among the Latin-American countries and would inevitably seek an opportunity to strengthen their political position in that part of the world to protect and promote their trade.

Uneasiness about the developments on the continent centered on the rise of Germany into a great industrial state, and it was assumed that Germany would naturally become an aggressive competitor in world markets. She was also the strongest military power in Europe. Her predominance appeared even more assured after Japan's defeat of Russia in 1905. Mahan, as well as Roosevelt, John Hay, and Elihu Root, did not fear that Germany would pose an immediate danger, and relations remained friendly. The uneasiness was based not on hostility toward Germany but on the conjecture of future developments.

These aspects were prominent in Mahan's thinking. In July 1906 he wrote to Roosevelt stating what he had not said publicly. He noted that the Germans showed a great interest in establishing wartime rights for commerce to flow freely without seizure.[36] This, Mahan acknowledged, was of great importance to Germany, but he added, assure the trade of free passage "and you remove the strongest hook in the jaws of Germany that the English people have; a principal gage for peace." Great Britain and the British navy, he reminded the president, "lie right across Germany's carrying trade with the whole world. If you remove the hook then the English speaking peoples have lost a principal gage for peace." Mahan warned: "British interests are not American interests, no. But taking the constitution of the British Empire, and the trade interests of the British Islands, the United States has certainty of a very high order that the British Empire will stand substantially on the same lines of world policy as ourselves; that its strengths will be our strength, and the weakening of it injury to us."[37] Germany, he observed, is inevitably ambitious of transmarine development, and he did not grudge her that. However, there were dangers. "When to Germany are added the unsolved questions of the Pacific," he wrote in closing, "it may be said truly that the political future is without form and void. Darkness is upon the face of the deep. We will have to walk very warily in matters affecting the future ability to employ force."[38]

Underlying Mahan's realpolitik was a strong attachment to Great Britain, feelings that preceded the Spanish-American War and were strengthened by it. Before the war he had viewed Germany as the power that was likely to disturb the status quo. That nation, he believed, was likely to pursue colonial and commercial expansion abroad which might pose dangers to the Monroe Doctrine. British dominance of the seas did not endanger the United States. Equally important, he viewed Great Britain as a great "civilizing agency" and admired its "truly great work in India and Egypt."[39] These feelings also had been strengthened during his long visit in England in 1894. Everywhere he received a hero's welcome. He was dined by the queen, by the prime minister, and by the first lord of the admiralty. His history of sea power caught hold of the British as no other single volume did. The treatise awakened a renewed interest in the navy and a fresh appreciation of what the navy had done for the British. Three years after the visit he wrote to the historian James Ford Rhodes in words that fully reveal his pro-British feelings:

> I suppose my popularity in Great Britain, as an author profoundly in sympathy with their past history, and with the great part that they (in the main) are still playing in the redeeming the world from barbarism to civilization, from lawlessness to order, will always ensure me a hearing with them. You may be sure that I desire ever to use such influence—if I have it—to promote our mutual affection. I own, however, to thinking that so long as their ideal is world wide effort, and ours is isolation, either under the ideal of protection, or of non-interference, that there will be lacking that substantial identity of aims without which cordial esteem is unlikely.[40]

As a major figure in the transformation of American foreign policy, Mahan wrote didactic history that ventured to foresee the future. For all his ability and devotion, however, neither he nor anyone else during the first decade could predict what the century had in store.

There were other prominent men ready to embrace a sweeping new analysis of America's position. Roosevelt's old friend Henry Cabot Lodge pressed for what he called an enlarged policy, and Lodge managed to have inserted into the Republican platform of 1896 a call for Cuban independence. Lodge was one of the coterie of people who gathered at the home of Henry Adams on Lafayette Square to discuss the ills of the world.

Brooks Adams was also a member of this group, and his book *America's Economic Supremacy* inserted the needle to awaken the amiable public to current events and future dangers. He outlined the broad developments during the nineteenth century, the movement of the maritime and continental centers of trade westward toward the United States, the movement of continental centers of trade toward Berlin, and the slow but certain decline of England, beginning with the ruin of the sugar interests in the West Indies, due to the production of beet sugar and German monopoly of that trade. England had determined the fate of the modern century at Trafalgar, but now she was showing signs of age. Russia had long been moribund, but a revolution might free her from the past. She would almost inevitably attempt to conquer China and, with the aid of German capital, promote her interests there. Therein lay the great danger to the United States, for China was a storehouse of riches to be developed. Without England as an ally, America "must fight her own battle whether she wills it or not," Adams said. "The center of the economic system of civilization is in motion," he warned, "and until it once more comes to rest, tranquility cannot return." The United States must become armed, organized, and bold. With the decline of England and western Europe, Russia faced new opportunities and would strive for hegemony not only on the continent but in Asia. Germany, too, posed a more immediate threat. Brooks Adams was a close friend of Roosevelt, and both men shared similar fears for the future.[41]

The remarkable transition that took place in American foreign relations after 1908 was unique in that it was in considerable part the work of Theodore Roosevelt and a small cluster of his friends. This animated and dramatic leader exercised greater control of foreign affairs than had any previous president. He pressed with vigor against the outermost boundaries of the constitutional prerogatives of the executive and made commitments in the form of "understandings" with both Great Britain and Japan that he had to wrap in secrecy because they would not have been acceptable to the public.

Roosevelt believed very firmly that it was all important for English-speaking people to work together for the purpose of advancing civilization. This became his life purpose, transcending all other aims. There was in Roosevelt's crusade a strong moral element, and his moral convictions ruled out compromise and endowed him with the zeal and proselyting spirit of a crusader. Civilization was at the crossroads, as he saw it, betwixt the backwardness of half the world and the modern enlightened cultures replete with science, technology, and ideals of social justice.

Self-interest and ideals are usually seen as polarities, but in the case of Roosevelt these two opposites not only overlapped, they were simply sides of the same coin. The better world and the stronger nation he hoped to see established outweighed his interest in commerce and foreign investments. These economic interests, in Roosevelt's scheme of things, were means to the greater end and not ends in themselves.

There were in his approach to foreign affairs a series of postulates.[42] Above all, he was a nationalist who saw a contradiction between America leading the world in industrial development and its weakness in international affairs. The world was clearly at the edge of a transition in the balance of power that would inevitably threaten American interests in both the Caribbean and in the Pacific. He entertained no fear of invasion in the immediate future, but the rise of powerful industrial nations, interested of necessity in outlets for their goods, was already underway and portended a clash of imperialistic pursuits.

In this dangerous new world of international relations that was emerging, isolationism from Europe was irrelevant. Power would determine the future, and those who persisted in dreaming of peace were sentimentalists engaged in wishful thinking. An appearance of weakness in a nation like the United States, often the envy of the world, would be an invitation to the powerful to exploit their advantage. Therefore, the building of a strong navy ranked first among his priorities.[43] The way to preserve peace was to convince any nation that was on the move that the price of war was the destruction of its commerce and its port cities. An American fleet in foreign waters would be seen as a menace not to be taken lightly. Alfred Thayer Mahan's history of sea power bolstered his conviction that the navy was the first line of defense. As soon as Roosevelt became assistant secretary of the navy he and Mahan began to cooperate. He confided to Mahan, "to no one else excepting Lodge do I talk like this."[44] He assured the secretary that he spoke to him with the greatest freedom. Not only did Mahan help shape his views, he also built public support for Roosevelt's policy.

Roosevelt's concept of a civilized versus an uncivilized world came forth in his rhetoric as barbarity or savagery versus a civilization in which men abided by the virtues of honesty, responsibility, national honor, and a willingness to subordinate the self to social interests. Herein lay his justification of imperialism. Roosevelt adopted the "white man's burden" and assumed that he was a missionary-soldier of civilization.[45]

He wrote to his good friend Cecil Spring Rice, "It is a good thing for India that England should control it. And so it is a good thing, a very good thing, for Cuba and Panama and for the world that the United States has acted as it has acted during the last sixteen years."[46] To the expansionists it appeared that they were extending civilization. The futilities and tragedies that were ahead were not foreseen. Roosevelt's attitude toward native races took form early in his career and was set forth in his book *Winning of the West*. The warlike methods in expelling the Indians from their lands did not trouble him. It mattered little so long as the land was taken. Warfare was justified because it was for the benefit of civilization. This same attitude dominated his thinking in relation to the methods of the imperialists whether they were in Africa or Asia. He acknowledged that the wars against primitive men were the most cruel and brutal of all, but necessary in order to achieve the priority of white civilization. In addressing an assemblage of Methodists in Washington in 1909, Roosevelt declared, "it is of incalculable importance that America, Australia, and Siberia should pass out of the hands of their red, black, and yellow aboriginal owners, and become the heritage of the dominant world races."[47]

These perspectives enabled him to shoulder the burdens of imperialism. He was well informed about the horrors of war in the Philippines and the outrageous behavior of foreign troops including Americans, in China after the Boxer Revolt. As president he took prompt action to bring an end to the American atrocities in the Philippines. As Howard K. Beale explained, "His humanity deplored brutality. But his sense of history told him that brutality accompanied struggles with 'backward people,' that morality did not apply here, and that in the end civilization would be advanced and white domination of the world established; and this was desirable for mankind, including the backward folk."[48]

An equally important element in his foreign relations was Roosevelt's conviction that in the prospective war-torn world a close understanding with Great Britain was essential. His friendly feelings toward Great Britain began as he saw the friendship of the British immediately prior to the Spanish-American War and during the war. The British alone among the Europeans agreed that the United States was justified in its actions, and during the war they exhibited friendly feelings and then encouraged the annexation of the Philippines. Roosevelt's early change of attitude was soon accompanied by a recognition that in international politics no two nations shared so many common interests as did the United States and Great Britain. Both desired an equality of commercial opportunity in China and both had vital interests in preserving a balance of power in Asia.

A change in American thinking coincided with a crisis in British foreign relations and opened the door to collaboration. A turnabout in the British position in world affairs came after Japan administered a one-sided drubbing to the Chinese in the war of 1894–95. This alerted the world that China was powerless to defend herself. Japan began the dismantling of the ancient empire by detaching Formosa and would have added the Liaotung peninsula, had not France, Germany, and Russia stepped in to present Japan with a firm demand that she abstain. Those three powers then proceeded to do themselves what they had tried to prevent Japan from doing. In the autumn of 1897, Germany occupied Kiaochow on the Shantung peninsula and reduced that province to a German sphere of influence. Russia then acquired Port Arthur on the strategically important Liaotung peninsula. The right to build an extension of the Trans-Siberian Railway across Manchuria and down to North China had already been accorded by China in 1896. France joined in the scramble and gained China's consent to an area of French authority in southern China adjoining her acquisitions in Siam.

These sudden developments, in the words of William Langer, the historian of imperialism, posed "a problem of such magnitude that it came to overshadow all other issues and became the touchstone for European international relations."[49] China was of major importance to the British, who enjoyed 70 percent of China's foreign trade. Britain had become, in the years following the Opium War of 1840, the predominant power in the Chinese empire and long believed that her position was secure. Her nonintervention while Japan established herself on the continent and opened the way for Russia, Germany, and France to carve out markets and strengthen their economies, awakened concern in England that bordered on panic. A writer for the *Contemporary Review* expressed the general scare. He wrote: "Never before, in this century at least, has the British Empire been in such serious danger as today, despite the frequent boast that our means of defense are most efficient and the absolute certainty that our Government not only disposes of an over-whelming majority in Parliament, but has a united people outside at its beck and call, ready and even anxious to lend it every conceivable assistance."[50] During the next two years the British sought eagerly to work out arrangements with one or another of the major powers. A series of lengthy negotiations with Germany resulted in a treaty in July 1900, but it became subject to contradictory interpretations and did not meet the needs of the British. The second series of negotiations ended in failure. Whereas Germany had a vital interest in securing its eastern frontier by encouraging Russia to move into the Far East, Great Britain had equal reason to see in Russian expansion the greatest danger to her Far Eastern interests. Lord Salisbury was quite willing to concede economic priorities to Russia in Manchuria. He saw the division of China into economic spheres as inevitable, but he was uncompromising in his commitment to preserve the country's political unity. Count Witte of Russia was willing to agree to this because he favored a program of peaceful penetration. Witte thought that to dismember China would leave Russia empty-handed because she was not prepared to engage in war with the stronger nations. But Witte shortly lost control to more aggressive leaders.

The Boer War created even greater dangers. Great Britain was unpopular throughout Europe, and public opinion sided with the Boers. This posed the possibility of intervention by some combination of European powers.

One member of Lord Salisbury's cabinet reached the conclusion that the time had come for an alliance with the United States. Joseph Chamberlain, in a speech before the liberal union alliance on May 13, 1898, spoke of the common language, common culture, and common interests of the United States and Great Britain. He hoped for the day when the Stars and Stripes and the Union Jack should wave together.[51] Salisbury, however, preferred to wait for time to unfold an opportunity that would involve no risks. The big change came after Lord Lansdowne succeeded Salisbury as foreign secretary. Unlike his predecessor, Lansdowne believed that Great Britain faced a crisis, and he was anxious to explore new roads to security, including the establishment of ties with the United States. It was this conviction that the two countries had mutual interests that brought about the great transformation.

5

Implementation of the New Ideology 1898–1917

THE rhetoric at the turn of the century often took off on wings and was unrealistic. Propaganda was shaped to enlist different kinds of audiences, rather than sober analysis. Moralistic outpourings catered to public feelings. John Hay, shortly after the Boxer Revolt in China, dismissed as "mere flapdoodle" newspaper talk of the preeminent moral position of the United States authorizing it to dictate to the world. Hay, an ardent Anglophile, engaged in mere flapdoodle himself, but as secretary of state he more often kept his feet on the ground.

Policy changes were not a sudden break with the past. The clamor for markets was not born during the economic depression of the 1890's. The change in relations with England began in 1887 as a result of the settlement of the Venezuela affair. The agitation for a canal across the Panama Isthmus began in the 1850's. Had not the Civil War intervened, it is quite possible that Cuba would have been annexed much earlier. There were many foreshadowings of the dramatic events of 1898 and after.

There is no reason to play down the importance of prevailing ideology in explaining the decisions that added up to a transformation of policy, but careful attention must be paid to its background. Not every decision can be explained by ideology. The historian, like the statesman, must give attention to the interests at stake, the configuration of power that a decision will encounter, the readiness of the public to support a policy, and the balance between the power available and the power required to carry out a decision. Failure to take these into account, along with the character of the administrator, can lead to hasty conclusions that will not stand up under closer examination. We shall see the importance of this in explaining the coming of the Spanish-American War and the annexation of the Philippines.

Contemporaries bequeathed to us both wisdom and nonsense. Time and again the Monroe Doctrine served as shibboleth. Hard facts were often shrouded in philanthropic terms such as "duty" and "national responsibility." One contemporary writer wisely called for the modification of the Monroe Doctrine. He pointed out that it was a mistake to extend it to all of South America. It should be applied, he wrote, only "in the West Indies, in the Caribbean Sea, and Central America . . . Here the United States has the most important interests, everywhere recognized as vastly superior to those of other nations, due to God's arrangement of lands and waters, and to our determination to meet the world's need of a ship canal connecting the two great oceans." In South America, he wrote, other nations had greater interests and greater rights than the United States.[1]

This somewhat calm estimate stands as unique among the drivel put forth by many propagandists. At the other extreme was an article, entitled "America Mistress of the Seas," in which the writer contended that the American navy could hold the balance of power in the world "and cast the deciding vote in the councils of the nations where world policies are determined, where questions of war and peace are considered . . . It is hardly overstating the case to say that, with a dominating navy, the United States can dictate peace to the world and can wonderfully hasten the reign of beneficence in world politics."[2] Such inflated assumptions would more than once stand in the way of realism.

The rethinking of foreign policy brought with it far-reaching changes in relations of the United States to foreign countries. The two most significant developments were the conversion of the Caribbean into an American lake and the beginnings of a tacit "alliance" with Great Britain and Japan. Theodore Roosevelt, a bold master in the conduct of diplomacy, was a most energetic executive, but he was also mindful of the necessity of maintaining an equilibrium between the forces available to him and the projects he chose to support. His caution in Asia, where other powers could challenge any American intrusion into their spheres stayed his hand. In contrast he was bold in the Caribbean, confident that the public would support the Monroe Doctrine. William Howard Taft was equally forthright in Nicaragua. In the Far East his secretary of state, Philander C. Knox, a man without experience in foreign affairs, blundered in presenting the neutralization proposal. Wilson, like Roosevelt, was his own secretary of state, and he was aggressive in the Caribbean and stumbled into armed action in Mexico. Like Roosevelt, Wilson had a world view and was pro-British, but he was even more anti-German.

Roosevelt acted on the conviction that Great Britain and the United States had common interests. He also recognized that in dealing with the British he must be firm in upholding American enterprises or he would lose public support. During his two terms he developed a working relationship with London that was to have a permanent influence on world affairs.

Two questions blocked an uncluttered friendship with Great Britain. The Alaskan boundary question had been set to one side since the purchase of Alaska, because that remote country appeared of no great value, although the development of the seal industry and then the discovery of gold made it a pressing issue. Whether the line ran from the inlets of the many bays along the coast or from the headlands of the peninsulas would determine whether or not the Canadians would have an outlet to the sea and acquire part of the gold fields.

However, the Clayton-Bulwer Treaty, relating to the canal, was the more pressing matter at the time. The treaty negotiated in 1850 provided that any isthmian ca-

nal that might be built should be a joint enterprise of
Great Britain and the United States. At the time of negotiation overly eager agents of both countries stirred up a
heated controversy in Nicaragua. Great Britain appeared
as the expansionist power ready to grab control of the
strategic corridor, whose importance as a transit across
the isthmus was recognized by both parties. At the time
it was negotiated, the United States saw in the treaty a
bulwark against British aggression in Central America,
but in the years immediately following, the treaty became
the whipping boy of Southern Democrats in Congress
who charged that British activities among the Mosquito
Indians along the Atlantic shore of Nicaragua constituted
a violation of the treaty.[3] The British had long exercised a
kind of protectorate over this region, and they contended
that the treaty did not apply to long-existing arrangements. By 1854, thanks to a new understanding with England, concerning trade and fishing rights between Canada and the United States, relations between the two
countries improved, putting to rest the angry dispute
over the Clayton-Bulwer Treaty until the turn of the
century.

The Spanish-American War furnished a lesson about
the strategic importance of a canal. At the outbreak of
war the American naval ship *Oregon* was called from the
Pacific to join the Atlantic fleet. The time consumed in
sailing around South America raised the canal issue to a
high priority. By 1899 the building of the canal had won
enthusiastic support in Congress, and there was a determination to abrogate the Clayton-Bulwer Treaty. Secretary of State John Hay heard cries from angry members of
Congress of "Damn the treaty." At the same time the Foreign Office in London was being pressed by Canada to
assert alleged Canadian rights to a boundary in Alaska that
would give the gold-mining interests access to the sea. It
was the hope of the Foreign Office to use the Clayton-
Bulwer Treaty as a card in negotiations of both issues, but
the United States was successful in its insistence that the

canal was a separate matter and should be resolved first.[4] John Hay drafted a treaty that, if approved, would leave the United States free to build the canal, but it provided that there should be no fortifications constructed for its defense.

When the draft of the first Hay-Pauncefote Treaty found its way into the American press, the Senate promptly seized the initiative from the executive branch and insisted on amendments. Hay had been anxious to gain British approval of the treaty and had, in the eyes of Henry Cabot Lodge and Theodore Roosevelt, then governor of New York, failed to defend American interests. The key question was the right of the United States to defend the canal in time of war. The treaty would have left the canal open to all powers in time of war as well as in peacetime. Critics found the nonfortification part of Hay's draft to be the major fault of the treaty. Although, as British naval authorities said, it was in reality of minor importance, because the security of the canal would depend on the American navy and not on fortifications, it was inevitable that Americans should demand full rights to defend a canal that they were to build and for which they would pay. The British admiralty saw at once that defense of the canal would be in the hands of the American navy and raised no objections to this aspect of the Senate amendments, but the Foreign Office resisted because they saw no gains in the treaty for Great Britain.[5]

A new treaty was worked out in London between Ambassador Joseph H. Choate and Lodge, but only after lengthy exchanges. The British were not ready to yield on all points. In Washington, John Hay went over every article with members of the Senate. Finally, the treaty was approved by a vote of seventy-two to six.[6]

The Hay-Pauncefote Treaty was the first step in the friendly alignment of Great Britain and the United States. The British biographer of Lord Salisbury, J. A. S. Grenville, has written: "The Hay-Pauncefote is one of the great treaties of the twentieth century. . . . In concluding it," he states, "the British Cabinet had finally abandoned the attempt to bargain with the United States concessions to Canada in return for British concessions in Central America."[7]

It now remained for the United States to come to terms with the French canal company and Colombia. These arrangements were conducted in a bargaining atmosphere akin to that of an Oriental bazaar. Congress had already approved building the canal through Nicaragua, but to win congressional approval, it was necessary for the representative of the French company, Philippe Bunau-Varilla, and the company's American lawyer, William N. Cromwell, to align political support by contributing money to the Republican campaign chest and win influence with senators by shrewd use of their ample means. The rewards of these shady dealings resulted in an act of Congress stipulating that the canal should be built through Panama.

Having achieved that much, it remained for Secretary of State John Hay to open negotiations with the Colombian chargé in Washington for a treaty granting to the United States the right to build the canal through Panama, which was then a part of Colombia. The two negotiators were scarcely equal in bargaining powers, and the treaty they negotiated was one-sided. Hay was able to hold over the head of Herrán the threat that the United States could build the canal through Nicaragua. The new treaty provided that the United States was to obtain rights to a canal zone six miles wide and would pay Colombia $10 million dollars outright, and $250,000 annually. The grant was to be in perpetuity, thereby closing the door to Colombia for future revisions. The treaty gave the United States the right to establish tribunals in the canal zone, and American law was to apply. It was approved by the Senate on March 3.

In Colombia popular opinion called the treaty an outrage, and reports from there soon indicated that the legislature would not ratify it. In August the Colombian Senate refused its ratification. This was wholly within the country's rights, and the Colombian representatives pointed to the power of the American Senate to disapprove of treaties, but in Washington, Hay declared that for Colombia to refuse to abide by a contract was unacceptable.

In Columbia the citizens became embroiled in the political feuding that was going on in that country, where, for the first time, the public had an opportunity to weaken the hold of the dictatorship. Politics aside, the Colombians had good reasons for their objections. They were rightly disturbed by the prospect of American courts applying American law within the canal zone. This provision reduced to a sham the article stating that Colombia was to remain sovereign in the area. Likewise, the prospect that the most valuable territory in their possession was to fall into the hands of the powerful Yankee colossus injured their pride. Lastly, they were angry because, while the United States would pay the French canal company $40 million, Colombia would receive only $10 million.

The merits of Colombia's grievances were to matter little. Faced by its powerful neighbor and by Roosevelt, who saw in the delay a block to the march of civilization by a set of "unscrupulous monkeys" anxious to extort money, the action of Colombia would in the long run prove futile. Reports from Americans in Panama indicated that the storm of opposition would soon give way to approval, but Roosevelt was in no mood to wait.

The delay was causing leaders in Panama to fear that they were about to lose a great boon to the local economy. The French canal company saw that the intransigence of Colombia might well deprive it of the $40 million dollars. Extralegal dealings now led to short circuiting the government in Colombia by arranging a revolution in Panama. The company's headquarters in New York found funds for financing a coup which enabled the Panamanian leaders to raise a motley army of five hundred, hardly a formidable force if they should face Colombian troops.

Aware of this discrepancy of forces, Bunau-Varilla was forced to ask for American support. He met with Roosevelt and Hay, who did not commit themselves, but whose demeanor assured Bunau-Varilla that he could count on American assistance. Under a treaty with Colombia the United States did have the right to intervene to keep the Isthmus open, which it had done many times. The prospect of a revolution caused the authorities in Colombia to dispatch troops to Colón on the Atlantic side of the Isthmus. It was obviously no coincidence that the American cruiser *Nashville* arrived at the right time to disperse the Colombian troops and prevent them from putting down the revolution in Panama City, on the Pacific side. Panama declared its independence on November 4 and was promptly granted diplomatic recognition by the United States. On November 18 a treaty was signed allowing the United States the right to build a canal in accordance with the terms of the Hay-Herrán Treaty.

The actions taken deprived Colombia of its prize possession, and the protectorate that was established deprived the Panamanians of self-government. The United States gained the canal but also the ill will and distrust of Latin America.

Roosevelt could not be so bold in dealing with the British on the Alaska boundary controversy, but this time his mission was accomplished by a devious diplomacy that denigrated the claims of the Canadians. The boundary assumed importance with the discovery of gold in the disputed area. Roosevelt sent the first troops into the area in March 1902. At stake was whether the Canadians were to have a port giving them convenient access to the gold-mining area and whether some of the goldfields were within their jurisdiction. Roosevelt charged that the Canadians were engaged in blackmail. To the Canadians, it was no less clear that their claims were justified.

Roosevelt now carried out what the historian John Bartlett Brebner called a "discreditable coup."[8] He rejected arbitration on the ground that the procedure too often ended in compromise. In this case, he declared, the justice of American claims must be upheld as a matter of principle. After lengthy negotiations the procedure agreed upon, and provided for in the Hay-Herbert Convention, was establishment of a tribunal of six *impartial* jurists, three to be appointed by each side. Roosevelt then named Elihu Root, Henry Cabot Lodge, and Senator George Turner of the state of Washington, no one of them eminent jurists and two already well known as determined defenders of the American claims. Root was a man of distinction, but so closely associated with the president that he was not free to be impartial after accepting the appointment. Roosevelt, in making these appointments, was defying the convention.

Determined to achieve the decision he wanted, the president maneuvered to eliminate any possibility of matters going amiss. The disorder and violence in the disputed mining area offered him a plausible reason for sending armed reinforcements. At the same time he made it clear that if the commission failed to reach a favorable decision he would use force to draw the boundary.[9] This left the matter dependent on what Lord Alverstone would do as lord chief justice and the lone British appointee to the commission. Roosevelt believed that the boundary line was not of great interest to the British and that their only real concern was to get free of the Canadian supplicants. He therefore, in blunt terms, decided to offer the British a choice of either offending the Canadians or damaging good relations with the United States. To emphasize this to the British, he wrote to his long-term British friends and induced his loyal American associates in London to warn that it was the better part of wisdom to agree with the president.[10] Lord Alverstone was shortly under pressure to go along with his American colleagues on the commission, and so he did.[11]

British readiness to play Roosevelt's game continued. The Reciprocal Trade Treaty with Cuba of 1903, in return for opening the American market by reducing the duty on imports of Cuban sugar, provided for a 20 percent reduction of duties on American exports to Cuba. European nations had dominated the Cuban market, and this was intended to promote American exports. British merchants were quick to point out that this was inconsistent with the highly publicized American policy of equality of commercial opportunity. They protested to the Foreign Office only to find that it was not about to set aside its efforts to cultivate good relations with the United States in order to promote trade.[12]

At this same time, the United States turned toward converting the Caribbean into an American lake. In the Caribbean danger zone, with its unstable governments and revolutionary disturbances, dictators financed their governments with foreign loans. The creditors were beset with difficulties due to failure of the island governments to meet their financial obligations. Corruption and the readiness of local rulers to regard debts as something less than a sacred obligation plagued European bondholders, who inevitably looked to their governments for protection, if need be by threats of force. Given the jittery feelings of the times and rampant imperialism, there was the danger that some debt-collecting expedition would arrange a debt settlement by acquiring rights to establish a naval base in this region where their merchant ships were regular visitors.

The American navy was assigned the task of keeping watch on both foreign ships and native rulers.[13] Navy reports on the activities of Cipriano Castro, president of Venezuela, portrayed him as an unscrupulous dictator. Some of these reports found their way to the Department of State and to the president.[14]

In 1902 the repeated defaults of the Castro government on loans from investors led to an agreement by Great Britain, Germany, and Italy to bring pressure to bear on the unruly Castro by means of a joint naval demonstration. Two facts of importance deserve attention. There was to be no landing of troops and no sinking of Venezuelan ships, nor was there to be any seizure of territory; the blockade was to be peaceful. Secondly, aware of the sensitivity of the United States to any matters relating to the Monroe Doctrine, the European powers consulted the

United States before acting. Secretary of State Hay expressed regret that the governments should use force, but the United States "could not object to their taking steps to obtain redress for injuries suffered by their subjects, provided that no acquisition of territory was contemplated."[15]

During the preceding two years navy reports of German activity off the coast of Venezuela had aroused suspicions, and the intentions of Germany had become a matter of speculation. Among those who had cast a skeptical eye on Germany was Alfred Thayer Mahan, who deduced that Germany, with a rapidly growing industrial economy and the inclination for expansion, was likely to try its hand in the Caribbean. Of course, the German occupation of Kiaochow and the interest Germany had shown in the Philippines constituted hard evidence of German expansionist tendencies, but in part the fears expressed privately by both Roosevelt and Root were suspicions rather than conclusions based on hard evidence. Their deductions in a world where most western powers were on a search for new markets were not unreasonable. This was a period when fear and distrust permeated international relations and promoted speculations. It is not surprising that the American government watched German activity off Venezuela and occasionally showed a readiness to credit accusations on less than solid grounds.

In 1902, Great Britain and Germany had agreed on confronting Castro with force. "Naval policy makers," according to a leading scholar in the field, "worked themselves into a considerable frenzy over alleged German interests in the tiny island of Margarita" just off the coast of Venezuela. A navy commander assigned to watch over that area, Nathan Sargent, reported that their activities showed that Germany intended to acquire the island. A German naval vessel spent three months taking soundings and making surveys of many harbors. Sargent was concerned that Venezuela might be induced to offer Germany a base in return for Germany's canceling the sizable debt owed to German financial interests. Sargent's lengthy report found its way to Secretary of State Hay, who instructed the American chargé in Berlin to inquire. The Germans made an unqualified denial that satisfied Hay, and he dropped the inquiry. But Henry Cabot Lodge, the most prominent Republican senator on the Foreign Relations Committee, proposed to the navy that a vessel be sent to investigate. After that vessel failed to find any evidence of questionable German activity, a second vessel was sent. The General Board of the Navy reached no hard conclusions, but in drafting war plans the board did focus on Margarita.[16]

The distrust of Germany appears to have been quiescent at the time that Great Britain and Germany sounded out Washington about the plan for Venezuela. Nevertheless, a momentary flurry over the island of Margarita indicates a readiness to distrust Germany.

On December 13, 1902, a joint flotilla of British and German ships blockaded Venezuela. This measure clearly portended future incidents and went beyond what the United States had expected. Consequently, the United States promptly questioned the legality of the proclaimed pacific blockade. There was already criticism of the project in both England and the United States, but most significantly, Americans did not look upon British motives as sinister, while they distrusted Germany.[17] Instead, American criticism of Great Britain focused upon her having allied with Germany.

The episode entered upon a second stage when Castro offered to submit the question to arbitration by the Hague Court. The United States supported this step, and Henry White, the American ambassador in London, was instructed to urge the British to accept it.[18] The British Foreign Office, already under fire in Parliament, promptly agreed, subject to reservations. Germany delayed briefly, declaring that some of the claims were not arbitrable, but then accepted, also subject to reservations. The British, like the Germans, thought the reservations were important enough to show that both powers were intent on protecting their creditors.[19] As there was no subsequent agreement, it was necessary for the two powers to establish some common ground. Great Britain would have preferred to withdraw, but to do so would provoke distrust in Berlin, and this was to be avoided. Agreement on the reservations was reached on January 5, but there was further delay because Great Britain demanded assurance that Castro would agree to them.[20]

Meanwhile, the blockade continued in effect, and the delay proved costly. In mid-January, after Venezuelan forces had fired on a German ship at Fort San Carlos, the German commander destroyed the fort. This action created a wave of protest in both England and the United States.[21] The common feelings that burst forth in both countries caused the American public to feel that the two English-speaking peoples had much in common and promoted the tie between the two nations.

When the Hague Court rendered its decision, it upheld the claims of all foreign countries, but also ruled that the nations that had used force should have a priority in the payments. This ruling, which gave approval to the use of force, ran counter to Roosevelt's view of the Monroe Doctrine.

In the case of Panama, Theodore Roosevelt had been impetuous to the point of ruthlessness, and his bold actions aroused a storm of criticism. Roosevelt busied himself constructing rationalizations in defense, but these appear to have convinced no one. The response of the public caused him to be more cautious in the future, and he was reluctant to become involved in the turmoil of Santo Domingo, where internal rivalries set aside all efforts to establish orderly government and where foreign creditors pressed settlement of their claims.[22]

The office of the president in this small republic had become a turnstile through which rival leaders passed in rapid succession while the government's revenue, dependent wholly on the collection of import duties, fell far short of meeting the annual payments due on foreign debts and the minimum costs of internal administration. Because of the poverty of the Dominicans, the outrageous discount rates charged by foreign creditors, and the debility of the local government, Santo Domingo became what must have been one of the most insecure and most unhappy communities in the world.

Its dependence on foreign loans and on creditors who sometimes engaged in practices close to extortion, forced Dominicans to face a desperate situation that appeared destined to continue in perpetuity. Among the worst of these foreign claimants was the Santo Domingo Improvement Company of New York, which had acquired ownership of the major bank and a railroad. Of its loans, only 35 percent reached the Dominican treasury. The Improvement Company sold bonds through unscrupulous agents to unsuspecting small investors. The company's practices became fully known only in 1905, thanks to a study published then by the highly reputable economist Jacob Hollander, but the company did have a shady reputation, and Roosevelt knew enough about it not to come to its aid.

The company's representatives were removed from the custom houses in 1901, and the company, which was thoroughly hated in Santo Domingo, was confronted with the fact that other foreign creditors were to have first access to payments. It appealed to the United States, and Hay instructed the American representative in Santo Domingo to file a protest, although "unofficially" and not to exert pressure. Hay's action appears to have been no more than an adherence to routine procedure, but the representative of the American government, William F. Powell, pushed ahead with vigor, an action that caused Washington to rebuke him for his unwarranted aggressiveness.

In a showdown with the Dominican government, French, German, Italian, and British creditors called for what they deemed their equitable share of Dominican revenue. After violent arguments and in spite of prolonged opposition, the Dominicans finally agreed to submit the dispute with the Santo Domingo Improvement Company to arbitration, although the amount to be paid was not subject to arbitration, only the question of how it should be paid. The figure of $4.5 million had been set by the company, an amount the Dominicans had reason to believe was excessive. After further angry argument with the Dominican authorities, who refused to appoint a member to the board of arbitration because Congress refused to approve the proceedings, the zealous but radically indiscreet Powell broke off diplomatic relations. His actions were not only unauthorized but were in conflict with the administration in Washington, who did not favor drastic action.

Events shortly outran the preferences of Roosevelt for a hands-off policy. In Santo Domingo the irrepressible Powell, in spite of numerous rebukes from Washington, engaged in conversations with Dominican leaders about a treaty that would presumably include some features of the Platt Amendment that established an American protectorate in Cuba. The Dominican public was strongly opposed to American tutelage of any kind, but now its leaders, hard pressed by foreign creditors and finding no way to solve their financial difficulties, reluctantly concluded early in 1904 that only intervention by the United States could save them from an overthrow.

Roosevelt continued to hope that this would not be necessary. It was in February 1904 that he wrote his much-quoted letter stating: "I have been hoping and praying for three months that the Dominicans would behave so that I would not have to act in any way. I want to do nothing but what a policeman has to do in Santo Domingo. As for annexing the island, I have about the same desire to annex it as a gorged boa constrictor might have to swallow a porcupine wrong-end-to."[23] In the same letter he alleged that "the attitude of the Dominicans has become one of chaotic war toward us." However, after the situation appeared to improve, he called off negotiations.

After the close of the hostilities in the Dominican Republic in April, and after Morales occupied the presidency there, Roosevelt faced a situation that impelled him to take the initiative. There was no way that the Dominican government could meet its obligations. The distress mounted when the commission arbitrating the claims of the Santo Domingo Improvement Company decided that they should be paid in monthly installments of $37,500. Morales was already prepared to ask the United States to take over the customhouses. Foreign representatives, fearing that the award meant that their claims could not be met, pressed again and there was talk of intervention. By December 1904, Roosevelt was ready to act and assured Thomas C. Dawson, the new American representative, that he was prepared to accept an invitation to intervene. On January 20, 1905, the two governments signed an agreement establishing a fiscal protectorate. The protocol that was signed failed to muster the two-thirds vote necessary for approval in the Senate. This was due in large part to the opposition of the Democrats who charged that the action was taken to bail out foreign bondholders. Roosevelt then carried out the agreement as an executive measure.

In terms of improving the economic condition of Dominican Republic, American intervention was a success. The government received 45 percent of the revenue collected, and the foreign creditors were eventually paid. However, the intervention involved the United States in an ongoing struggle that led to sending in the marines and eventually to the brutal dictatorship of Trujillo.

In his annual message to Congress in December 1904, the president summed up his policy in the Caribbean, a policy that became known as the Roosevelt Corollary to the Monroe Doctrine. In it he asserted that whenever there was "wrong doing" in the western hemisphere it was the duty of the United States to use its police power. This amounted to an extension of the Monroe Doctrine changing it from an instrument of nonintervention to one of intervention, and arrogating to the United States the right to decide what constituted "wrong doing." This established the United States's power to police the area. Roosevelt justified his action with the pronouncement that, as the Monroe Doctrine prohibited intervention, it was the responsibility of the United States to put down wrong doing.

The opposition was in part politically motivated, but it also reflected a genuine distaste toward involvement, even in the Caribbean, unless there was in the eyes of the public a clear and present danger of foreign intervention. Economic interests played a part in the takeover of Santo Domingo's customhouses. The first moves were made in response to the unpaid claims of the Santo Domingo Company. Roosevelt appears not to have been greatly interested in that company's claims, and in the final arrangement they were treated in the same way as those of European creditors. The president's critics frequently questioned whether it was the responsibility of the American government to collect claims of creditors who had invested in a country where they knew there were great risks and where they often balanced those risks against heavy interest charges. For Roosevelt, who was determined to eliminate and prevent foreign intrusion and to make of the Caribbean an American lake, the answer to that question was self-evident.

In the Caribbean the United States entertained no fears of involvement with a major power in establishing an American sphere of influence there. East Asia presented American presidents with a radically different situation. It was remote and American interests were minor in terms of security and economic investment. However, a significant segment of the American community viewed China either as a potentially great market or as a kind of ward of American goodwill. It was expected that the American government would play a major role in protecting China from imperialism and in facilitating the work of missionaries, and at the same time protect its markets from being closed to American foreign trade. Between the government in Washington and Americans who exalted the importance of China there existed much room for misunderstanding. American China policy, based on national interests, was a world apart from the interest in and friendship for the country itself. Commenting on the official American attitude toward China, Akira Iriye, an authority in the field of diplomacy, renders this view: "It becomes evident at once that the official policy of the United States, in spite of the promptings by business, naval, and missionary circles, remained on the whole passive and at times even negative."[24]

The philanthropic public magnified China's importance, saw her on the threshhold of a great awakening from an unchanging past, and calculated her presumed future greatness in western terms. Their picture of China was derived from early traders and travelers and more recently from the writings of hundreds of missionaries who, when home on leave every seven years, travelled across the country speaking to church audiences. Arthur Smith, an author of popular books on China, reduced the ancient and great Chinese civilization to the level of a Sunday-supplement human-interest story. He had much to say about the daily lives of the Chinese, but he specialized in picking out what he deemed to be all-pervading Chinese traits, such as "The Disregard for Accuracy," "The Talent for Misunderstanding," "The Talent for Indirection," "Intellectual Turbidity," and "Absence of Sincerity." He, like many others, exhibited the racism common among arrogant westerners.

An uneducated Chinese, said Smith, found any ideas a surprise, and they usually caught him so unprepared that it took him "an appreciable time to get such intellectual forces as he has into a position to be used at all." His stress on unfavorable characteristics might be amusing to a smug westerner, but they gave no hint of the richness of Chinese culture or the high level of Confucian ethics.

As a missionary out to win support for missions, it was necessary to portray a bright side too, and Smith admired the Chinese industry, perseverance, patience, and good humor. Other missionary accounts described foot-binding, infanticide, and the sale of girls into slavery. But always these tales conveyed that there were great needs in China that were waiting to be filled. Unfortunately, what westerners saw as needs did not accord with what the Chinese saw as their needs.

A series of myths about China also enlivened the public's interest: China was a great future market; the celestial empire was looking to the United States as a trustworthy friend; the American Open Door notes and the friendship of the United States had saved China from partition. At the close of the Boxer Rebellion a sizable segment of the American public had come to the conclusion that China was entering a period of tutelage and that it was duty of the United States to undertake the task. Hay dismissed this as mere flapdoodle, but in succeeding years the myths gained an ever stronger hold. An attitude of paternalism held sway.[25]

No presidential administration could afford to ignore these myths, but faced with realities, those responsible for foreign relations had to take national rivalries into account. Asia was an arena where any challenge to the powerful European network of interests by philanthropic adventurism was ruled out. The European alliance system functioned in China as it did in Europe. At the convention of the foreign powers in Peking after the Boxer Rebellion, William Woodville Rockhill, the American representative, found that the European diplomats had one eye on the interests of their allies and that the combinations ruled out recognizing the primary interests of China. Large indemnities and territory seemed infinitely more valuable than a strong China, and wherever three or more Europeans were gathered together, there was the inevitable consideration given to alignments in Europe. Rockhill observed, "The French Minister is apparently willing to do anything which puts the Germans in a false position, and the British is willing to do the same as regards Russian."[26]

The Open Door myth came to imply much more than equality of commercial opportunity. The original notes of 1899 did no more than propose that the powers agree to abide by the principle of equality in commercial opportunity. The second set of notes on July 3, 1900, committed the United States to respect China's independence and territorial integrity. Those notes did not commit the United States to upholding China, and even though Roosevelt distrusted Russia and confided privately that he would like to counter her aggressive moves in Manchuria, he also admitted that the American public would not support strong action. Thus, no action was taken other than a mild and futile protest in favor of equality of commercial opportunity. Eventually the phrase "Open Door" lost all specific meaning. Originally it was little more than a statement of the long-avowed policy calling for equality for commercial opportunity. In popular usage, it came to imply something like an American shield protecting China from its enemies. Myth though it was, it was deeply lodged in the minds of a large part of the American public. Its meaning swelled in tandem with the crusade for missions. It was generally assumed that the good work of the missionaries and the government's China policy were both part of the philanthropic outreach of the United States. So blurred was the sharp distinction between the two in popular thinking that every administration from Roosevelt through Wilson found it politic never to speak in more realistic terms on the China question.

During his second administration, Theodore Roosevelt was primarily concerned about China insofar as it might influence the balance of power. Since China was hopelessly weak, he did not respect her as he did Japan, which won his respect as a force that could contribute to establishing a balance of power.

Roosevelt's success in mediating the Russo-Japanese War was an outstanding achievement.[27] Bringing together the Russians and the Japanese required infinite patience with both sides and a shrewdness in appealing to the self-interest of both belligerents. He was anxious to prevent mediation by any of the European powers because he was certain that they would exploit the situation to gain advantages for themselves. Roosevelt sought peace, but he also sought to contribute to the establishment of a lasting balance of power in the Far East.[28] China, however, paid a price. Roosevelt agreed to Japan's taking Korea, the

Liaotung peninsula, including Port Arthur, and part of southern Manchuria. He instructed Rockhill, now minister in Peking, to advise the Chinese to sign a treaty with Japan agreeing to these settlements and not to make a fuss about it.

In the summer of 1905 he became impatient with China. Chinese merchants launched a boycott of American goods in protest against the restrictions on Chinese immigrants. The movement was a limited success, for a brief time, in the larger ports. Roosevelt was also upset by the Chinese cancellation of the American China Development Company's contract to build a railway from Canton to Hankow, which reflected unfavorably upon the integrity of American business. At an early stage the company had sold a majority of its stock to French and Belgian capitalists. Late in 1904 the stock changed hands again, and this time a group of New York capitalists took control. In 1905, after an expenditure of $3 million dollars, only twenty-seven miles of track had been completed. By this time the first stages of Chinese nationalism had appeared, and the Chinese were anxious to eliminate foreign control of their railways. Rockhill was highly critical of the company and recited the facts to Roosevelt. It was revealed that the American company had taken the initiative in the sale and had been sold at the high price of $6,750,000. Roosevelt still blamed the Chinese, and he wired Rockhill: "The President does not see how we can submit to such a blow, especially as the concession was largely obtained through the action of the government. . . ."[29]

Rockhill, a distinguished scholar in Oriental history and an explorer of Tibet, wrote a vigorous reply attacking the company, but he was obligated to try to make China reverse its course. He was not successful, and these developments, of course, did not endear China to the strong-willed president.

That same year, 1905, Taft went on an extended tour of East Asia, finally visiting Japan, where he entered into an agreement with the prime minister, Taro Katsura.

The prime minister acknowledged that the United States could not enter into an alliance, but he proposed "a good understanding or an alliance in practice." Taft explained that even this presented difficulties, but he encouraged just such an agreement. The exchange of cables between Roosevelt and Taft did not become known until 1924. Their contents revealed that an understanding had been reached with Roosevelt's approval and that if Japan should be attacked by a third party the United States would come to her support.

Not all Americans went along with the policy of restraint in regard to China. Among these was Willard Straight, who had witnessed Japan's takeover of Korea during the Russo-Japanese War and who, after the war, was stationed in Mukden, in Manchuria. Straight developed a strong hostility to the Japanese, and he was the first to contend that the Japanese in Manchuria were discriminating against the Americans in violation of the Open Door policy. His efforts came to naught in the first year after the war thanks in part to Rockhill, who believed that Straight exaggerated the difficulties and still had hope that the Japanese would accord Americans fair treatment. He attributed these disputes to the unsettled conditions following the war.

The whole range of American policy in Manchuria came under close examination in 1908. The establishment of a municipal government in Harbin in northern Manchuria by the Russian company that owned the Chinese Eastern Railway led to a review of policy. Harbin could scarcely arouse serious concern. The only American in the city of some ninety thousand was the American consul, and Americans had no business interests there. The town was the railroad center for the Russian company and suffered from the presence of disorderly elements, remnants of bonanza seekers, criminals, and brothels. In response to complaints from some of the sixty thousand Russian inhabitants, the railroad company established a municipal government.[30]

The American consul, Fred Fisher, in December 1907,

wrote to the Department of State calling attention to the fact that here was a city in China governed by a foreign power. Willard Straight endorsed the letter and warned that if the Russians could do this in northern Manchuria then the Japanese would do the same in the railroad towns along the South Manchuria Railroad. William Phillips, third assistant secretary, analyzed the problem and presented his conclusions. To yield would mean that the United States must give up its extraterritorial rights in the city. China would have good cause to complain that the United States was contributing to its losses in Manchuria. And, finally, Phillips pointed out, "Japan is undoubtedly waiting for the moment to enforce a similar proposition in Southern Manchuria."

Phillips was supported by American consuls, and their protests and activities in Manchuria aroused excitement in both Tokyo and St. Petersburg, and reports from both capitals reached the American secretary of state. Elihu Root was content to limit his protest by agreeing that the establishment of the municipal government by the Chinese Eastern Railway meant a loss of American extraterritorial rights. He realized that to challenge both Russia and Japan would probably drive those two powers together. The continuing controversy called for closer examination. Root finally instructed Alvey A. Adee to prepare a polite but firm answer, and added a forthright estimate of the long-term course to be followed. His memorandum closed by putting the dispute into the perspective of the actual interests at stake:

> On the other hand we do not wish to be bumptious or disputatious or unfriendly in the assertion of our rights, or to become a protagonist in Manchuria, taking the responsibility of carrying on a vexatious controversy with Russia. A quiet, firm, maintenance of our position is our true policy and in that the interests to be preserved are the future interests of the open door and there is no present interest which would justify us in ehibiting undue excitement in this quiet and firm maintenance of our position.[31]

This was not a new position. The limited interests of the United States did not justify boldness.

That the United States had the good judgment not to become a protagonist in a part of the world where a strong posture was likely to lead to serious difficulties was further illustrated in the Root-Takahira Agreement. This vague agreement, which has often troubled historians, aimed at smoothing over American Japanese rivalry. It made clear that the United States did not propose to challenge Japan in Manchuria where the Japanese had developed important interests at the expense of the Open Door policy. As one historian put it: "The exchange, rather, was just in air clearing joint declaration of policy designed to smooth over the ill will which had been generated during the school segregation and immigration crisis of 1906 and war scare of 1907."[32]

The boldness of the United States was limited to a constant pressure on China to abide by the unequal treaties that were negotiated in the midnineteenth century. As a party to those treaties, the United States was also a party to western imperialism. China was subject to abiding by import duties set by treaty and not by the Chinese government. These duties were collected by the Imperial Maritime Customs Service, which was dominated by foreigners. The treaties included extraterritoriality whereby foreigners in China, including Americans and American corporations, were not subject to Chinese law or to Chinese police jurisdiction. During the Taiping Rebellion, Great Britain had created the International Settlement of Shanghai, and that major city was a state within a state governed by foreigners. Such intrusions were wholly inconsistent with China's independence and territorial integrity. The American treaty with China negotiated in 1903 stipulated a series of rights of American business interests that were likewise inconsistent with Chinese sovereignty.

The United States held China to strict observance of the treaties. This confrontation with China posed no dangers. Only on the basis of treaty rights did the United States act in response to developments within the spheres of influence of the other powers. This policy approached what Akira Iriye has described as passivity.

Large-scale economic penetration was taking place in China, and the United States was left behind. This was not a result of government policy, although the United States also followed a cautious path in that respect. It was willing to forward to the Chinese government proposals of new enterprises, but did not support the projects or in any way permit its legation to vouch for the good faith of American companies or the merits of their proposals. Only if China appeared to be acting in violation of treaty rights did the representatives of the United States protest. Intercession of the American government in the case of the American China Development Company was an exception.

Shortly after Rockhill arrived in Peking, the legation was asked to transmit to the Chinese government a letter from A. W. Bash of the China Investment and Construction Company requesting participation in a railway loan. Rockhill declined to do so and wrote to the secretary of state for further instructions. He explained: "If the legation is duty bound to do what Mr. Bash requests it to, then in the eyes of the Chinese all his communications would have official support. This I hardly think is what the Department of State wishes." Alvey Adee acknowledged that other foreign governments in China had represented corporations of their own country and China had always looked upon such requests as requests by the foreign government. "Our position," wrote Adee, "has been the opposite of this, for we expect our agents to be scrupulous in avoiding any appearance of soliciting favors for Americans or American corporations."[33] Adee thought that this policy had worked to the disadvantage of American citizens. Only if an American corporation in China was denied rights stipulated by the treaties would the United States intervene.

The Open Door policy, especially after 1905, lacked a

firm mooring with regard to the realities of Asia. When the danger was partition of China, the policy had more relevance, but that was no longer the situation. The race for territory and spheres of influence was over. Consequently, all nations willingly professed their adherence to the Open Door. In so doing, they proclaimed that they were no longer interested in territorial concessions and their lust was now directed to more practical matters. Railway contracts, mining rights, and other enterprises absorbed their attention, rather than territory. The capitalists of Europe spearheaded the drive, and their Governments supported them. This support was restrained only by the political concerns of the home governments. Prospective contracts for enterprises in the political bailiwick of an ally could only be supported at the risk of losing the allied nation's cooperation in the maintenance of more important interests. For example, London firmly refused to support a British corporation that secured a contract to construct the Fakumen Railway within Japan's sphere in southern Manchuria.[34] The British government, whose primary concern in Asia was the security of India, could not offend her ally. Other governments operated under similar restraints in supporting their business interests, however, politics did not seriously hamper their business classes. Investments in China doubled from 1900 to 1914.[35] The Open Door policy provided no protection to either Chinese or American interests in this new situation.

If the United States was to take the lead in the Far East, then it too would presumably have to lead the way in investments, which were the measure of a nation's influence in China. Equally important, only a large stake in China could justify a strong policy, vigorously implemented, by Washington. The United States sought to compete with wealthy shareholders in the total China economy while holding almost no shares itself.

The Department of State, compared to the leading foreign offices in Europe, stood guard over only minor economic interests. In 1914, British business investments totaled $607.5 million, or 37.7 percent of all foreign investments in China. Russia with $269.3 million, Germany with $263.6 million, Japan with $219.6 million, and France with $171.4 million ranked next to order. American business interests amounted to $49.3 million, only 3.1 percent of the total.[36]

With investments went control over railways, mines, and other enterprises, the very basis of the new economy emerging in China. The British gained an early lead in the railroad field, and the investors invariably demanded guarantees that meant control. The most important of the British railway agreements specified that the chief engineer, the fiscal officer, and the majority of the board of directors should be British. These arrangements could be justified on grounds that the Chinese lacked experience in managing large transportation systems, but thereby a precedent was set that was adhered to long after the Chinese were competent to run railways themselves.

Foreigners demanded guarantees that went well beyond reasonable assurance of security for their investments. The British and Chinese Corporation, financiers of the railway from Peking to Newchwang, held a first mortgage on both the property and the earnings of the line. This adequate protection of the British investment was further buttressed by a provision that the Imperial Government of China "unconditionally guaranteed and declared itself responsible for the payment of the principal and interest." The loan agreement also stipulated that the chief engineer should be British and the principal members of the staff European. Consequently, the Chinese, although they owned almost as many shares of stock as the value of the British loan, had no control. In addition to controlling the railway, the British also dominated the car and locomotive works at Tongshan and the Shanhaikwan Works associated with the railway company.[37] These, in turn, manufactured equipment according to British design, thereby giving British manufacturers of similar types of equipment an advantage in selling to other railways in China.

At least technically, business arrangements of this sort did not conflict with the U.S. policy of the Open Door. To have countered this movement, Americans would have had to pursue a similar course of eagerly promoting investments. This was precisely what they did not do. The result, as J. Newton Nind, an American trade journalist, wrote after a tour of China, was that Great Britain had come to dominate the Orient.[38] The absence of American investment had its counterpart in a lack of any serious interest in the China market on the part of American manufacturers. A writer for the *Far Eastern Review* observed: "With the complete indifference of American manufacturers to this great field, and their refusal to look the situation square in the face, there is only one termination to the unequal contest." Whatever "progress has been made to date with American cars and rolling stock in China," this writer reported, "is largely due to the push and hustle of the Japanese." The sale of American locomotives and railway cars in China was due to the enterprising spirit of the Japanese Mitsui Company and not to the efforts of the American manufacturers.[39]

Speaking before the American Manufacturers' Export Association in September, 1911, William C. Redfield, business executive, member of Congress and the secretary of commerce under Woodrow Wilson, explained how manufacturers in England and Germany were aggressive because these two countries must export or die because of the limitations of their home markets. "Here in America," said Redfield, "the reverse is true." American industries developed "with a proper and sole regard to our domestic needs. Out of this same background, has grown the peculiar outlook of the American manufacturer upon the foreign field. To him it is not or has not been the chief market he seeks, but rather an incidental one."[40] To be sure, Redfield now saw a need for foreign markets and urged their importance, but the whole burden of his address was the lack of interest and failure of American manufacturers to develop markets abroad.

In a situation where influence depended to a consid-

erable degree on investment and commercial ties, the
weakness of the United States obviously was that its
China policy had no substantial economic undergirding.
With no economic roots in China sufficient to nourish a
strong will, the United States found it difficult to rise
above the ranks of the onlookers.

The Taft administration set out to invade the field of
investments in China. This new approach was a bold departure from the original Open Door policy by which Hay
had limited his policy to equality of commercial opportunity. Willard Straight and younger diplomats promoted
the new approach. During his last weeks as minister in
Peking, Rockhill received instructions to take a strong
stand for American participation in the financing and
construction of the Hukuang railways in central China.
At home the Department of State took the initiative
in the organization of a group of American bankers, including J. P. Morgan, Kuhn Loeb and Company, the First
National Bank of New York, and Edward H. Harriman.
Straight left the Department of State to become the agent
of the group. The European bankers were about to reach
an agreement when Straight came forth with his proposal. It shortly became apparent that while the bankers
were willing to include the United States, the foreign
governments held out for their own national interests.
There was also strong Chinese opposition. The cry in
China was now "Who owns China?" Across the country
there was violent opposition to foreign ownership of railways. Not until two years later did the hard-pressed Chinese officials come to terms.[41]

By October 1909, Secretary of State Philander C. Knox
had put together a bolder proposal, a plan for neutralizing
the railroads in Manchuria. Knox believed that in all
cases where the imperial credit of China was pledged for
railway construction, the powers that had pledged themselves to the Open Door policy should have equal participation. Knox counted on the support of Great Britain and
France. He overlooked the British ties with Japan and the
French alliance with Russia. Both powers chose not to

offend their allies who saw in their possession of the Chinese Eastern Railway and the South Manchuria Railway the levers which would increase their influence. For those two powers control of the railroads was a political question of first importance. Alexander Isvolsky, the Russian foreign minister, was decidedly hostile. He declared that the proposal would seriously injure Russian interests. Japan, in consultation with Russia, was warned not to accept. At the same time Japan proposed that the two countries enter into an alliance. Knox's ill-advised proposal came to naught.

Defeated in this first effort, Knox next embarked on a currency loan to China that would enable her to develop Manchuria. Rockhill, now ambassador to Russia, warned that no other western power had as great interests in that part of Asia as Russia and that Russia would never surrender its gains in Manchuria and Mongolia.[42] He also advised the secretary of state that Japan had "an almost immediate need of expansion upon the mainland of Asia."[43]

Neither economic affairs nor security interests of the United States in Asia were vital. The failure of the Taft administration to perceive these facts led it into this diplomatic blunder.

The Taft administration also failed to recognize that a new wave of nationalism was sweeping China. Had officials consulted reports from the American legation, carefully prepared by Secretary Charles Tenney, their obsession with investments in Chinese railroads would have cooled. Tenney described the new movement to regain control of foreign-owned enterprises. The Department of State disregarded these reports as part of the traditional Chinese hostility to foreigners. In October 1911 the era of Chinese revolutions began, and the currency scheme died with the overthrow of the Manchus.

The election of Woodrow Wilson in 1912 brought into office a man who, like Roosevelt, elevated the presidency to an office of leadership and high standing. Wilson was to carry forward the Progressive program for a positive state that met the needs of a new day. Rightfully known as a Progressive, in many respects he was a conservative who reflected the enduring influence of Edmund Burke. He distrusted the passions of men when they led to crusades characterized by emotion rather than careful judgment. He was deliberate, cautious, and patient, qualities that gave him an independence that even his closest associates found difficult to penetrate. He was not easily influenced. As Colonel Edward House and Robert Lansing were soon to learn, Wilson was "his own man." It was a trait that became ever more pronounced and contributed to his failure at winning the peace in 1919 and 1920.

During his first term in office he achieved more in the way of Progressive reforms than had been achieved in the preceding twelve years. These measures were long overdue. As John Blum said in his biography of Wilson, "The entire program perhaps satisfied the yearnings of the past better than it anticipated the needs of the future." However, as Blum also stated, "His was incontestably a magnificent performance." At this stage, he was the shrewd politician who concentrated on what was realistic and could be achieved.

Wilson was better schooled in domestic affairs than he was in international politics, but he did not come to the presidency without convictions in regard to foreign affairs. Like Roosevelt, he was both an internationalist in his world view and a dedicated nationalist who took pride in American legal institutions and technological achievements. His ideas in foreign relations were not original. They were those of a generation of Americans who entertained ideals of a new world free of imperialism. He shared the popular analysis of financial ills that reduced the difficulties of the country's economy to overproduction and found a prospective solution in the development of foreign markets. He paid his respects to this doctrine many times.[44] Together with this view was a distrust of business interests which intruded on the sovereignty of weaker nations. Shortly after taking office President Wilson denied government support to American bankers who sought to impose on China a contract that would seriously impinge on China's sovereign right to be master of its own economy. His distrust of business found expression again when he suspected that foreign business interests, both British and American, were supporting Huerta in Mexico. Wilson opposed economic imperialism, but he was also ready to play a major role in world affairs. The overproduction tenet was only one side of Wilson's world view.

It was Wilson's hope that a general reduction of tariffs and a freer exchange of the world's goods would improve the international economy and promote peace. Freer trade would weaken imperialism. He was opposed to spheres of influence, to investments in foreign countries on terms that deprived the native government of control, and to colonies.[45]

John Wilson Cooper, Jr., in his book entitled *The Warrior and the Priest: Woodrow Wilson and Theodore Roosevelt*, published in 1983, presents a clear portrayal of the commonalities and the differences between these two men. They became bitter antagonists, but they also shared similar views. Both had a sense of mission, a comprehensive world view, and a belief that the United States must participate in world affairs. The two men were also ardent American nationalists at the same time that they were admirers of the British form of government. Roosevelt first spoke in terms of an international organization; Wilson soon after became the promoter of a league of nations.

The differences between the two presidents centered on their respective attitudes toward war and the use of force. Roosevelt saw glory in a military struggle and often said that it was in warfare that men achieved a nobility of spirit and escaped from inborn self-centeredness. He gloried in his days as a fighting man in Cuba, and upon American entry into World War I he anxiously sought to join the military.

In contrast, Wilson dreaded war because it let loose the worst of human passions and set back sober thinking and hindered social improvements. This deeply fixed conviction stayed with him even after the break of diplomatic relations with Germany. His final decision that the United States must join the First World War came only after a traumatic reflection, in which he thought much about the horrors of warfare and the inevitable crippling effect it would have on liberal thinking at home. These attitudes caused him to delay a preparedness campaign early in the war, and it was on this issue that Roosevelt first split with him. Roosevelt saw weakness and indecision in Wilson's failure to make prompt preparations, and a failure to grasp that only a nation ready to make war would have any influence on the belligerents.

It took Wilson almost three years to reconcile himself to actual military participation. For a time, Roosevelt held his judgment of the belligerents in abeyance, but the German violation of Belgium's neutrality carried him over into the Allied camp. The sinking of the *Lusitania* in May, 1915 was a final turning point. He confided that, had he been president, he would have called for war the next day. As a man not in office he was, of course, freer to call the tune, but the feelings Roosevelt displayed were compatible with his earlier efforts to build a tacit alliance with the British.

During his tenure in office Roosevelt pushed his program, including his foreign policy views, with great energy, but he never campaigned for action unless he was certain that he could win. He worked under the restraints placed upon him as the leader of the conservative Republican Party. Consequently, he left untouched the need for tariff reform, for a drastic reorganization of the banking system, and for legislation assuring to labor the right of collective bargaining. In an age when the evils of child labor were glaring, Roosevelt did nothing to improve conditions. It was not until he had left office and embarked on his program of the "New Nationalism" that he embraced more far-reaching reforms.

Much the same was true in the area of foreign relations. Roosevelt knew what the public would accept and carefully avoided confrontation on policy questions where tradition stood in the way of public acceptance.

However, when he left office, he had not publicized his basic foreign policy, and traditional attitudes in large part persisted.

Woodrow Wilson too moved cautiously on domestic affairs, but he exhibited greater skill than Roosevelt in educating the public to the need for reforms and he went well beyond Roosevelt in his achievements. He was able to build a new Democratic Party that eschewed populism but also mobilized the support of the more conscrvativc elements in the party.

From the first days of the war Wilson was not neutral. In a conversation with Colonel House on August 30, 1914, he condemned Germany's part in the war. According to Spring Rice, the British ambassador, he told him on September 2: "Everything that I love most in the world is at stake."[46] A few days later he confided: "If they [the Germans] succeed, we shall be forced to take such measures of defense here as would be fatal to our form of government and American ideals."[47]

Of greater importance than these private feelings was Wilson's stance on British rulings concerning neutral trade. The Declaration of London of 1909 had been rejected by the British but had won the approval of the United States Senate in 1912. The debate in England continued virtually down to the eve of the war. Division on the question hinged on whether, should war come with Germany, England's navy would play a major role, or would the British become a major participant in land warfare on the continent. Opponents of the new legislation argued that it would be necessary to blockade the Netherlands and Belgium. Advocates of more lenient rules to be directed against Germany contended that the navy could bring Germany to terms and that to offend neutrals was unnecessary.[48] Until the outbreak of war the British admiralty adhered to the view that it would suffice to capture German ships and to blockade the north coast of Germany.

War had scarcely begun when the British reached the decision that it must fight a continental war because the

Germans had overrun Belgium. On August 20 the British cabinet approved an order-in-council authorizing detention of neutral vessels bound for a Dutch port and specifically included food as contraband. By August 30 fifty-two ships had been detained in British ports. By September, British orders included the seizure of shipments not only of oil but also of a long list of minerals. Various British government officials recognized that the orders were a violation of international law, cutting off all American trade with Germany.[49]

The United States was now caught between defending its rights as a neutral and at the same time maintaining friendly relations with Great Britain. Acting Secretary of State Lansing at first took a purely legal view of the question, but he quickly changed his approach. In a conversation with Spring Rice he implied that the United States would not interfere with British economic warfare. John W. Coogan, in his scholarly study entitled *The End of Neutrality,* attributes Lansing's change to the influence of Wilson. Mindful of the situation that had prevailed before the War of 1812, Wilson was anxious not to arouse the feelings of the public in opposition to England. That could lead to war. At this time there had been no controversy with Germany so that the only danger of becoming involved in the war was through the American relationship with Great Britain. John Coogan states: "Yet to Woodrow Wilson, struggling in the last months of 1914, with the normal duties of his office, the extraordinary demands created by the war, and the personal trauma of his wife's death on August 6th, these same assumptions appeared to offer the surest, safest guidelines to true neutrality. The president believed passionately that the United States must remain above the madness and carnage that had engulfed Europe."[50]

The sparring was not over in spite of Wilson's pro-British feelings. Negotiations at times reached the danger point, and protests from private interests compelled the Wilson administration to take a firmer course. This, in turn, so disturbed the British, who were facing a life-

and-death struggle, that on one occasion they foolishly charged the Americans with being influenced by pro-German feelings.

Wilson was determined to remain neutral, and he believed that he was as neutral as it was possible to be. Neutrality for a powerful and proud nation was an ideal that was unattainable in any perfect sense. Almost any action had an effect on the belligerents, and taking no action was likewise favorable or unfavorable for one of the two sides that were at war. A weak nation had no choice but to accept humiliation or be destroyed, but the United States was a major power. As a neutral, Wilson sought to mediate, but neither side was ready to compromise after paying the high price of men and money that the war had already cost. In taking an uncompromising stand on submarine warfare Wilson was on less certain ground. Nations in danger are willing to reach for the most frightful of weapons, but Wilson had to consider that unlimited submarine warfare would almost inevitably result in the loss of American ships, and then the American public would demand war. But once having held Germany to strict accountability and taken the position that if Germany resumed unrestricted submarine warfare, then the United States would sever diplomatic relations, it remained for Germany to decide Wilson's future course. After this step the only hope of staying out of the war lay in its coming to an end.

Wilson was pro-British and willing to overlook British violations of neutral rights, but when these violations reached a new high in 1916, Wilson said that if Germany were not the "scourge of the world" he would be ready to face the British in a showdown. Wilson saw the British as imperialists and denounced what he called their "commercial slavery." He affirmed that when the war was over he would call for the building of a navy strong enough to counter British aggressiveness. Germany's conduct during the war convinced him that British infractions were the lesser of two evils.[51]

Broader historical forces than the submarine question

brought about the American entry into the war. Wilson's speech calling for a declaration of war has been criticized on the ground that he raised false hopes that led to disillusion. This raises the question why disillusion after the war was as great in Europe as it was in the United States. Speeches summoning people to great sacrifices are inevitably clothed in high aims. Wilson's speech was not so different from the later Atlantic Charter.

Although Wilson's aims for a world free of imperialism was not realized, it was, to quote one of Wilson's more severe critics, a "masterpiece." Seen from another perspective, Wilson "recognized the central problem of his time and of twentieth-century European politics, that no peace structure could endure that did not encompass both German and Russian ambitions and energies."[52] The road to peace, as he saw it, was not to return to the balance-of-power system, but to establish an economic marketplace open to all alike, in an integrated political order of self-governing states.

Wilson's world was not to be. The Europe of pre-1914 was destroyed. Austria-Hungary was no more. The Great War had made possible the revolution in Russia. Japan gained a greater hold over China, and the war planted the seeds of totalitarianism in Italy and Germany. The horrors and hatreds of war had "burned themselves into the minds of ten millions of people."[53] Thus the peace was lost before the Paris Peace Conference.

By the time Wilson returned to the United States he had become a tragic figure. He could have compromised on Article 10, and he was wrong in not doing so. His egotism descended into stubbornness and he was wholly unrealistic. Here, as Robert Ferrell states, he made his greatest mistakes. Wilson, who "possessed one of the keenest intellects to ponder affairs of state could behold neither the country's best interests nor his own."[54]

The decision to enter World War I owed much to an inexorable historical process. The renewal of unrestricted German submarine warfare was the immediate cause.

Viewed in the broader context, it was rooted in the same causes that had brought about the rethinking of American foreign policy.

Central in promoting the rethinking was the rise of a powerful Germany that posed a threat to British control of the seas and to American control of the Caribbean. The American response was part of the larger picture of dollar diplomacy, including concern for the Panama Canal, Roosevelt's tacit "alliance" with Great Britain and Japan, Wilson's adventurous policy in Mexico, the burgeoning national industry, the increased interest in world markets, and the self-confidence born in the aftermath of the Spanish-American War.

The American empire was not something bestowed upon an energetic people. It had come about by hard bargaining, by conquest, by eager grasping of opportunities, and expansionist fevers. There had always been enthusiastic support of national interests. The United States had established a bold posture, and as the war eroded neutrality and national interests, and honor appeared to be at stake, it was to be expected that, short of the war coming to an end or Germany agreeing not to use submarines, the United States would enter the conflict in the same spirit that she had exhibited so often before.

The two months between the German resumption of unrestricted submarine warfare and Wilson's call for a declaration of war inflicted great agony on the president. He asked the question: "Is the present war a struggle for a just and secure peace, or only for a new balance of power? If it be only a struggle for a new balance of power, who will guarantee the stable equilibrium of the new arrangement? . . . There must be, not a balance of power, but a community of power; not organized rivalries, but an organized common peace." When he called on Congress to declare war, Wilson closed by saying of the United States, "God helping her, she can do no other."[55]

Early on, Wilson had recognized that the best hope of the country for staying out of the war lay in efforts of mediation. His efforts failed. From the beginning he had believed that a German victory and the destruction of British sea power would have tragic consequences, and he bent American neutrality into a benevolent force partly because of his private leanings and partly because of the nation's economic ties with Great Britain. He could not tolerate German submarine attacks on passenger ships, not only because of his own basic humaneness but also because he knew that once German submarines sank American ships he would be forced into war. Wilson, the moralist and ardent opponent of war, was like other statesmen caught in a coil of dilemma. His first responsibility, however, was to the nation.

6

The Coming of a Revolution
in American Foreign Policy
1932–1941

As the world's most serious depression brought into question the validity of a laissez-faire economy, and widespread unemployment plunged millions into despair, the international order fell into disarray. No one in 1932 or 1933 could foresee that the first challenges to that order would end in a global struggle that would terminate in the ascendancy of the United States and the Soviet Union as the two major world powers.

In the United States during the 1920's there was an aggressive policy of promoting foreign investments. It appeared that by means of its financial strength the United States could promote a stable world order. By 1929, American foreign investments totalled $15 billion dollars, and the country's foreign trade was four and one-half times as great as it had been at the turn of the century. In 1925, Herbert Feis, a member of the Department of State, called attention to the dilemma in an article in the distinguished journal *Foreign Affairs*. There were, said Feis, important political implications. The United States was investing heavily in countries whose security depended upon the success of the League of Nations, yet Americans had rejected membership in the League. This dilemma became ever greater. The United States disapproved of the Geneva Protocol that would have strengthened the League, refused to join the World Court, and in the economic realm adopted a high-tariff policy culminating, in 1931, in the highest tariff in American history. In 1927 it promoted the Kellog-Briand Pact outlawing war as an instrument of national policy. Senator Reed of Missouri rightly labeled it as no more binding than an international kiss.

Disillusion gave birth to a peace movement. Ernest Hemingway, who had seen the First World War firsthand in Italy, said that he was sickened by talk of glory and honor; what he had seen on the battlefields reminded him of the Chicago stockyards. Both the peace movement and political isolationism ignored human history. The orderly status quo that coincided with American interests was temporary.

By 1931 that order faced challenges. Adolf Hitler was rising to power in Germany. The Mukden Incident on the evening of September 18, was quickly followed by the Japanese takeover of Manchuria in defiance of the existing treaty system. Here were the beginnings of an international upheaval that culminated in World War II.

Great Britain and France were no better prepared than the United States to face the tests ahead. All three were to follow a policy of appeasement in hopes of avoiding a general war. The United States stood to one side, and without its leadership there could be no effective unity among the democracies.

The transition that took place in foreign relations between 1931 and 1941 was the more unsettling because of its great dimensions. What was not visible in 1931 was that if the United States remained committed to its vital interests in an orderly world based on the existing treaty structure, and if it adhered to the firm belief that it was a rightful participant in European affairs and in East Asia, then there was a likelihood of war with two powerful nations, Germany and Japan. Germany was determined to control American participation in Europe and to limit American participation in East Asia to Japanese dictates. No way was found to preserve the peace that did not surrender these basic American interests.

This chapter analyzes the painful transition up to World War II. The course zigzagged between appeasement and firmness, becoming a tortuous experience. The alternatives were not clearly perceived at the time. The hope persisted that some peaceful solution could be found. Caution thrived on the memories of World War I and the understandable distrust between states and between political parties within states.

No longer were national economies isolated phenomena independent of one another. All nations were intertwined in a world economy, swept together into a global depression that began in 1929. As their economics collapsed, nations resorted to measures to shield themselves from the worst of the decline. An extreme economic nationalism took hold as countries raised tariffs, set up quotas on imports, juggled their currencies to gain an advantage in the foreign markets, and some eventually reduced their foreign trade to a barter system in which the exchange of commodities took place without any exchange of currencies. In a world of great interdependence, economic nationalism led to militarism and to totalitarian governments that defied the human values that had slowly become the core of western civilization during preceding centuries. A crisis ensued that reached beyond the economic sphere and undermined public confidence in the rule of law, in traditional ethical teaching, and human rights.

Herein lay the basic causes of World War II. A study of the diplomacy of the 1930's reveals not only the breakdown of collective security under the League of Nations but also negotiations rendered futile by the rise of totalitarian states determined to achieve prosperity and hegemony by conquest. The conflict between the supporters of the status quo and the promoters of a new world order was too far-reaching to be readily settled by negotiation. The so-called "have" nations cherished the existing order based on free trade and parliamentary government. Other powers, sustained by an extreme nationalism, were determined to carry out their aims by war if necessary.

At the center of the economic collapse was the decline of international trade. All nations were affected by the depression, but Germany and Japan were the hardest hit. Both were heavily dependent on foreign trade and on a healthy world economy.

Germany labored under heavy reparation payments in the 1920's, but had made a substantial recovery. In 1929 there remained the grievances against the Treaty of Versailles, and there persisted the feeling that Germany was entitled to a stronger position. The industrious and efficient German people understandably believed that given their great industrial machine, the most successful in Europe, and given that the German population was equal to that of England and France combined and their country must export to remain prosperous, Germany was entitled to a dominant position on the continent.

Throughout the 1920's, Americans were friendly to Germany and invested large sums that enabled her to grow industrially. There was a sympathetic response to her grievances and an even friendlier feeling toward Germany than toward either England or France.[1] This attitude was held by each of the three American presidents and many members of the foreign service. Hugh Wilson, the acting chairman of the American delegation to the disarmament conference of 1933, wrote to Secretary of State Cordell Hull in 1935: "Let me say that the attempt to prolong indefinitely the subjugation of Germany has always seemed an effort to maintain the abnormal. In their policies the Foreign Offices were opposing the inevitable normal development of a powerful people." The Treaty of Versailles failed to recognize the rightful position of Germany in Europe and was, Wilson wrote, "not a peace in the real sense of the word. It was rather a continuation in another form, of conflict with Germany."[2] Readiness to correct this injustice came too late, and the depression years brought with them the rise of Hitler.

The first omen of a breakdown came with the failure of the Austrian Creditanstalt on May 11, 1931. The failure of this bank, which supposedly controlled two-thirds of the industry in Austria, created uncertainty about the entire banking structure in Europe. Almost at once, anxious foreign investors began to withdraw their money.[3] Germany warned that it would not be able to meet the payments on reparations. A neutral commission of financial experts, after studying the German situation, verified the German protest that it was not able to pay. Again, confidence in investments in Germany plunged and led to a further withdrawal of funds.

Reparation payments were linked to the $10 billion war debts owed to the United States by England and France. Germany's inability to pay reparation payments made it highly improbable that England and France would meet their obligations. The prospect of this breakdown threatened to bring further disaster. In 1931, President Hoover, convinced that the causes of the depression were international, tried to avoid the final collapse by declaring a one-year moratorium on the payment of international debts. Other governments and bankers tried temporarily to aid Germany, but these attempts were short-lived.

The debacle was accompanied by a general decline in world trade. The export trade of the United States diminished by 21 percent in 1930 and 1931 and by another 18 percent in the first four months of 1932. The twenty-four nations that supported about 75 percent of the international export trade suffered a loss of about 12 percent in world trade in 1931. Along with the decline, and in considerable part because of it, nations suffered the most severe economic reversals in history. Germany and Japan were the most deeply affected.

Hitler exploited German bitterness over the Treaty of Versailles, holding that Germany had not been defeated but had been tricked into peace and that the wrongs of that treaty must be corrected. He appealed to German national feelings with his speeches about a mystical German state that had its origins in the remote past, a state that was more than a political institution, that embraced all generations past and future. Germany, as he portrayed it, was the holy land of the pure and superior Aryan race. The great Germanic peoples supposedly had been defiled by the Jews and the debilitating doctrines of Christianity. The Jews were made to serve as the scapegoat for all the nation's tribulations. Hitler urged Germans to march with their heads high. To labor, he promised employment and glory as the servant of the state. To the industrialist, he promised the suppression of Communism and a speedy recovery built on the creation of a great armaments industry. To the soldiers, he promised a heroic role in the service of the people. To many depressed by unemployment and victimized by defeatism, Hitler promised a new day and meaningful lives in the service of the state.

Hitler and his party never won a majority in an election before his takeover of power. He became chancellor in January 1933 after a small group of advisors convinced President Hindenburg that a coalition including Hitler was consistent with the Weimar constitution. Thereupon parliamentary government came to an end in Germany. Within two years Hitler had created a powerful army and a gigantic armament industry. In 1936 he occupied the Rhineland in violation of the Treaty of Versailles, and no effective action was taken against him.

Only in 1933, when it appeared possible that Hitler might be chancellor, did the western world take him seriously. Earlier his extreme behavior more often reduced him to a subject of caricature. Today it is clear that the rise to power of this perplexing and frightening personage was a direct product of the world depression and the many crosscurrents of intellectual, spiritual, and psychological upheaval between the years 1929 and 1933. Germany, the country of Immanuel Kant and Goethe, had lost its moorings.

In 1932 Emil Lengyel's study of Hitler appeared in the United States. The book depicted the danger that the Nazis represented. Lengyel portrayed Hitler as a madman, but did not minimize his appeal. Hitler, he wrote, had no program; his propelling force was the will to power. Lengyel saw Hitler in the context of the Germany tragedy. He gave meaning to a depressed and lost people by giving them something and someone to hate. Hitler substituted hatred of the Jews for the distrust of the upper-class economic hierarchy, and replaced the defeatism of postwar Germany with faith in the future achievement of hegemony. In place of unemployment there was to be full service in the war industries. Bolstering Hitler's confidence was his conviction that the English and French were decadent. Lengyel's was among the first of many books about Hitler that were presented to the American public, but it remained for Hitler, by his own expansionist program, to convince them that eventually he would be their hated enemy.

In Japan a transition brought an end to party government in May 1932. Throughout the 1920's, under the leadership of Hamaguchi and Shidehara, Japan had pursued a conciliatory diplomacy. Isolated members of the two major parties disagreed with the policy, and the military services were restless and potentially powerful. A vision of the future domination of Asia was present, but the time had not yet come to challenge the powerful western states in the Pacific.

The adoption of western technology, the growth of industry, the achievement of a high literacy rate, and the cabinet system of government gave to Japan the appearance of full modernization. However, there continued to exist, and even grow stronger, authoritarian schools of thought and values that had deep roots in the nation's history. Japan's political structure was not democratic. The governments that came to power did not represent election returns or political parties. The ministers of war and the navy were, by constitutional mandate, members of the armed services. A prospective new administration could be prevented from taking power by the refusal of the armed services to permit one of their members to serve. There was no tradition that curbed the military from participating in politics. The populace at large believed in the emperor's divinity, and he was a useful symbol of power for the reigning elite. He consulted with the appointed Privy Council. Before advising the emperor, however, the council reached the final decision that the emperor then approved.

In terms of foreign policy, Japan was not a monolithic structure. There was general agreement that someday the nation would dominate East Asia and that neighboring states would follow the imperial design in their own self-interest. The major difference among the ruling groups was in tactics and not on policy or goals. Among the elite it was believed that the extension of the empire should take place at a moderate pace that would not bring on a dangerous confrontation. In contrast, the army and the navy demanded that there be no backing down in the ongoing penetration of China.

Professor Akira Iriye, who has helped us to understand Japan's perspective on its international position, has commented concerning the Manchurian Incident of 1931 that it can be viewed as a result of part of the military going against the established authority. As to its historical significance, he states: "It marked the return of national security considerations as the basic framework of national policy, and it also signalled the emergence of Pan-Asianism as an official ideology."[4] Control of Manchuria and North China now became, in the minds of the Japanese, essential to their security. The rise of nationalism in China posed a threat to which the Japanese were increasingly sensitive.

On September 18, 1931, the Japanese Army in Manchuria exploited an incident outside of Mukden on the South Manchuria Railway as an excuse to go to war and to seize control of all of Manchuria within a few months. The incident resulted from the Chinese boycott of Japanese enterprises and goods, the killing of a Japanese army officer, and the fervent campaign in Chinese schools in Manchuria calling for recovery of Chinese control. The government in Tokyo only learned of the army's action a day later.

China appealed to the League of Nations. Secretary of State Stimson cooperated with the League to the extent of instructing Charles Gates Daws to sit with the League Council, and issued the nonrecognition note stating that the United States would not recognize any agreement brought about by the use of force. The United States also agreed to be represented on the League Commission of Inquiry.

The causes for the Japanese invasion were complex. Japan had acquired extensive interests in Manchuria, and these appeared threatened by the awakening of Chinese nationalism. Manchuria was largely at the mercy of local bandits, and Chinese officials were unable to maintain order. The Lytton Commission of the League of Nations, on which the United States was represented, investigated the situation and heard testimony from both sides. The commission concluded that the invasion was unwarranted, but it also agreed: "This is not a case in which one country has declared war on another country without previously exhausting the opportunities for conciliation provided for in the Convenant of the League of Nations. Neither is it a simple case of the violation of the frontier of one country by the armed forces of a neighboring country, because in Manchuria there are many features without an exact parallel in other parts of the world."[5] As to the creation of a new government, known as Manchukuo, the commission implied that it was a puppet of Japan and did not represent the people of Manchuria.

The situation in China, where a weak government presided over an impoverished peasantry and could not undertake a program of reconstruction without foreign capital, concerned not only the United States but the world at large. China was not able to defend itself, and a situation existed that was responsible for the instability of East Asia and that could undermine the peace. Under the leadership of the new minister of finance, T. V. Soong, China turned to the League of Nations and to the United States for the assistance of experts and to acquire capital. From the scope of planning and the cooperation of the League, it appeared that it was possible to launch a large-scale program for the strengthening of China. In 1933, however, the program was still in its early stages and largely confined to plans rather than to carrying forward reconstruction.[6]

The plan for strengthening China aroused deep concern in Japan. Because the United States Reconstruction Corporation, independent of the League, had advanced a $50 million loan to China in the form of saleable surplus cotton and wheat, the Japanese ambassador in Washington questioned Secretary of State Cordell Hull and made clear that Japan was opposed to the United States and the League program for reconstruction. The American loan had been extended independently of the Department of State. Faced with the inevitability of Japanese opposition, the question soon turned on the importance of China, on whether the plans drawn were practical, and whether the Nationalist government in Nanking was strong enough to carry the plans through. Reports from the American ambassador in Nanking, Nelson T. Johnson, portrayed a dismal and almost hopeless situation. Preferring to avoid difficulties with Japan and pessimistic about the ability of the Chinese to carry out the plans discussed by the League commission, the Department of State chose not to become a participant.

Japan's hostility mounted when the League sent Ludwig Rajchman to China as a technical expert, a man well known for his strong sympathies with Chinese opposition to Japan. The commission of the League did not restrict itself to projects for building roads and railroads. It concerned itself with broad political and social reforms. The Japanese were also well informed of Chiang's plans for building an air force and strengthening the army. These anxieties led to an announcement at a news conference by a representative of the Foreign Office, Eiji Amau. Speaking with the approval of the Foreign Office, Amau stated: "We think our guiding principle should be generally to defeat foreign activities in China at present, not only those of a joint nature but those conducted individually, in view of the fact that China is still trying to tie Japan's hands through using the influence of foreign powers."[7] The Amau statement immediately provoked serious discussion in Washington, but was only one of many assistance projects under discussion in the nation's capital and in the League of Nations.

The question for Washington was, Should it go ahead with help for China, thereby endangering relations with Japan, or should it desist? Consultations revealed that there was an unwillingness to challenge the Japanese stand. No one in the Department of State at this time was moved by concern for China. The dominant tone was that the United States would be unwise to "stick its neck out." Stanley K. Hornbeck, chief of the Far Eastern Division of the Department of State, told the British ambassador that the United States "did not intend to be placed in a position of leadership in initiating proposals for joint or concurrent action."[8] Maxwell Hamilton, in the Far Eastern Division, believed that American interests in China were no more important than were the interests of other powers, "if as important."[9] It was believed that a statement should be made for domestic consumption, but that it must be an innocuous expression of opinion and bear no note of protest. More important, Hornbeck killed a report from a treasury official who had studied China's needs and advised modes of assistance that would help promote unification in China. What emerged was a policy of hands off that the United States was to maintain until late in 1938.

American officials could keep their eyes closed, but the Amau statement was too important to relegate to a basket of forgotten items. The future course of Japan had been bluntly stated, and that course ran counter not only to treaties but also to an underlying friendly disposition toward China. Ambassador Joseph Grew, no more inclined than his friends in Washington to take a stand, and less concerned about China, had no further doubts about the future course of Japan. And the Far Eastern Division had resolved that there must be no further financial aid for China.[10]

Shortly after Hull's response to the Amau statement,

the Japanese ambassador, Hiroshi Saito, called on Hull and expressed the wish, on his own responsibility, for a proposal between the United States and Japan that would at least indicate a tacit agreement to work together in the years ahead. What Hull said in his quiet and friendly manner told more about the differences that divided the two powers than the note that he had sent to Japan. He observed how the world had changed, how the development of aircraft was reducing distances between nations, and that it was now necessary for nations to live in peace with their neighbors. He would welcome the United States and Japan becoming partners in promoting peace. The two men met three times. At the final session Saito presented a written proposal calling for a joint public declaration. When Hull looked back on the proposal after some years, he observed that such an agreement would have made the United States a partner in Japanese aggressions.

As Dorothy Borg has written, Hull was anxious to be conciliatory, but there was a point beyond which he would not go. A firm American policy had yet to take form and would depend on future developments.[11]

In 1933 and 1934 the Japanese military established a hold on the northern provinces of China and stationed troops in Peking. The Japanese met increasing resistance, and by 1936, as Grew put it, they were thunderstruck "by the sudden and unexpected determination of China to yield no more to Japanese pressure." There appeared to be an increasing unity in China.

On December 1, 1936, Chiang Kai-shek was kidnapped by the Communists in Sian. Foreign service officers had given only slight attention to the Communists after their Long March and the establishment of their headquarters at Yenan. In Sian, Chiang had no choice but to come to terms with the Communists and to agree that his Nationalists and the Communists would present a united front against Japan. This development, together with Edgar Snow's recent book, *Red Star Over China*, had a dramatic effect on western opinion, and, of course, future results of the Sian coup were to go beyond any west-erner's imaginings.

The Communists were determined to resist, and they saw greater opportunities for strengthening their position in China if war took place. More important, hosts of young people in China were shame-faced by the failure of the Nationalists to stand up to the Japanese. The Chinese turnabout brought a pause in Japanese aggression during which it appeared that the truculent policy that had been pursued was a failure, and it was time to search for a different direction.

Japanese leaders favoring this new approach were members of the Foreign Office, the foreign service, industrialists, and financiers.[12] In their view, a war with China would be immensely costly, long drawn out, and would isolate Japan in the international order. The appointment of Naotake Sato as foreign minister early in 1937 heralded a change from what Ambassador Grew saw as "blustering, sabre-rattling of the days since the Manchurian incident," to a liberal diplomacy.[13] Sato was outspoken in his criticism of the old policy. He proposed to deal with China on the basis of equality and a recognition of China's interests. There was great political risk in taking such a firm position. The army was subdued for a time, but remained a controlling force. Sato's term in office lasted for only five months.

On July 7, 1937, the Marco Polo Bridge incident occurred outside of Peking. This was a minor affair involving Japanese and Chinese troops in the vicinity, but it set off a period of indecision in Japan. No large-scale Japanese troops movements occurred such as those in 1931. Japanese and Chinese negotiations continued for several weeks in an effort to localize the conflict. In the meantime, more clashes took place. A new spirit arose among the Chinese. There was a determination not to enter into any agreement that would perpetuate Japanese control in North China. The Japanese did not retreat from their position. However, a month after the Marco Polo incident Grew informed the State Department that, although

the Japanese public were in full support of their government, he also observed that there "was no discernable enthusiasm for war."[14]

The pause raised important questions for the western
powers. Could the United States and Great Britain offer
to mediate the conflict? The British Ambassador, Sir
Robert Craigie, believed that joint action by the British
and the Americans would only serve to strengthen the
hands of the military in Japan. A week after the Marco
Polo incident Grew advised against mediation because it
would not be accepted by Japan. The Japanese, Grew
stated, were committed to driving the western powers
out of Asia and they contended that the occidentals had
no moral right to be participants in relations between the
Asiatic nations. For Japan to agree to mediation by the
western powers would be to surrender this basic position.[15] Craigie favored a strong joint statement by the
Americans and the British. It would be useful to show
that the two stood together.

In the summer of 1937 the question was still open regarding what course the United States should pursue.
Grew was a diplomat of long experience and accepted
that it was the role of an ambassador to carry out policy
and not to make it, but he was a worried man and nothing
concerned him more than the possibility that the United
States might repeat what he called the disastrous errors
of former Secretary of State Stimson in 1931. On August
27, Grew dispatched a lengthy message giving his views
as to the proper course for the United States. He held that
the United States enjoyed better relations with Japan
than had been true for many years, and ascribed this
to the impartial policy pursued by the United States
since 1933. The conflict between China and Japan was inevitable and had been in the making for years. Japan had
preferred to contain the conflict after the Marco Polo
Bridge incident. This had failed either because of uncon-
trollable conditions or because of Japan's inept tactics.
The United States, Grew believed, should not seek to in-

fluence either China or Japan. The fundamental objectives of the United States should be to avoid involvement, protect American rights, and at the same time adhere to complete neutrality. "Looking at these considerations from a purely material point of view we believe that they constitute a practical asset to American interests and that the importance of this asset will increase in direct ratio to our continuance of the policy and methods which we are now following," he wrote. But he also made clear that he was not in favor of winning Japanese friendship at the expense of China.[16]

On September 2, 1937, Secretary of State Hull responded. He explained that the policy of impartiality had been adhered to in the hope that it would encourage Japan and China to develop cooperativeness, but that hope was now gone. Hull acknowledged that for the United States to stand on legal or moral grounds was highly unlikely to bring hostilities to an end. Then Hull made an important point:

> In shaping our course, it is necessary for us to have constantly in mind not only the possible serving of that objective, not only the possible effects of the possible steps, upon Japan and upon China or upon both of those countries, but the attitude and the wishes of our own people, the principles in which this country believes, the courses pursued by other countries, and various general and ultimate as well as immediate and particular objectives.[17]

He added:

> I feel it desirable that you overlook no opportunity to impress upon Japanese officialdom the importance which we attach to the principles laid down in my statement of July 16 and the significance of my statement of August 23, and to suggest to them that by the course which she is pursuing Japan is destroying the world's good will and laying up for herself among the peoples of the world a liability of suspicion, distrust, popular antipathy and potential ostracism which it would take many, many years of benevolent endeavor on her part to liquidate.[18]

Hull's response was a moral response, and it was that of the American public. There was a deep sympathy for China among Americans that had its origins in the missionary movement at the turn of the century. By 1912 a myth had come into being that John Hay and the Open Door policy had saved China from partition. Woodrow Wilson believed in that myth.[19] It found expression again in 1919 in opposition in the Treaty of Versailles when the concessions to Japan at China's expense provoked strong criticism. Public-opinion polls after the outbreak of the Sino-Japanese War in 1937 confirmed it.

The outburst of American condemnation of Japan was followed by the president's speech at the dedication of a bridge in Chicago on October 5, 1937, proposing a quarantine on aggressors. Thus the United States served notice to Japan that it no longer adhered to the course of impartiality. The Japanese were also alarmed by the Brussels Conference, which they mistakenly believed had been called by the United States. On November 16, 1937, after five months of war in China, Yakashiro Suma, the Japanese ambassador in Washington, called on Hugh Wilson, assistant secretary of state, asking about the change in policy. Wilson said the change was inevitable in view of the Japanese invasion of China. It would not, he said, have been compatible with the nation's dignity to remain silent on what was taking place.[20] By 1940 friends of China and critics of Japan sought to halt trade with Japan, denouncing the fact that the Chinese were being killed with material from America.

There could be no hope of peace with the increasingly rigid state of affairs between the United States and Japan. The United States repudiated any and all changes in East Asia that were in violation of the Nine Power Treaty of the Washington Conference. Japan, because of the internal situation and her deep conviction of the necessity for change, objected strenuously to the United States adhering to a treaty negotiated in 1921. That treaty was, from the Japanese point of view, not relevant to the changed conditions of 1938. Early in 1938 the president of the Japan-Soviet Oil Company met with Hornbeck and Sumner Welles. During their conversation Welles, an advisor to Roosevelt, reiterated that any action taken by the United States must "be on the basis of terms consistent with the Nine Power Treaty." The company's representative, Mr. Matsukata, "appeared disconcerted" at this remark. Hornbeck's memorandum recorded: "He said that if the American government felt that it must fall back on 'historical' ground and insist on applying the Nine Power Treaty the whole problem was very difficult."[21] Any settlement that was in accord with the terms of the Nine Power Treaty would be tantamount to Japan's acknowledgement of defeat. Opinions voiced by the United States along this line weakened the position of the moderates in Japan who were desirous of avoiding war with the United States.

Moderates in Japan suggested that mediation under the good offices of the United States would be accepted. A British proposal, which did not receive final endorsement, resulted in the drafting of an American memorandum that began with the enlightening foreword that it "probably sheds more light on the thinking in the Department of State in 1938 than any other."[22] The British peace terms proposed that Shanghai be returned to China, that Manchukuo be recognized, and that Japan be guaranteed investment rights in North China. To this the American memorandum responded: "There is room for doubt whether recognition of Manchukuo by China really would remove one of the irritants that tend to disturb international relations generally."[23] It would not go to the root of the conflict. "Its one assured effect would be to confirm the confidence of the Japanese in the efficacy of the method which they have been following, that of using armed force, in pursuance of objectives of policy."[24] The Department of State assumed that the United States would not wish to take, participate in, or be associated with any initiative to persuade the Chinese to accord the recognition of Manchukuo. The State Department was likewise opposed to granting Japan a preferred position in North China. This American response spelled out in specific terms why the United States was unwilling to be a party to mediation. The alternative was to wait until both China and Japan were exhausted and therefore prepared to make concessions.

Hull had been determined to avoid any action that would place the United States in the forefront as leader of the opposition to Japan. During the Brussels Conference of 1937 he resisted being placed in that position with a firmness that European leaders found disgusting. Policy changed in 1938.

Hull's caution did not stand in the way of his sending a vigorous protest in October 1938. The note recited at length Japan's continuing violations of the Open Door policy and implied a hint of retaliatory action. Hull charged that the Japanese had instituted discriminatory exchange controls in areas under their control in China, had established monopolies that would deprive Americans of the right to undertake trade and industry, had interfered with American property and other rights, to the point of censorship of mail and telegrams, and had interfered with Americans' rights of residence and travel.[25] This protest arrived in Japan in the midst of internal political struggle in which Konoye was spending all his energy to prevent the army from taking over control of the recently enacted mobilization program.

Foreign Minister Hachiro Arita went beyond denying each of the complaints. He now uncompromisingly informed the United States that Japan was establishing a new order in Asia. His note contributed in a major sense to the confrontation that was emerging.

> Japan at present is devoting her energy to the establishment of a new order based on genuine international justice throughout East Asia, the attainment of which end is not only an indispensable condition of the very existence of Japan, but also constitutes the very foundation of the enduring peace and stability of East Asia.

It is the firm conviction of the Japanese Government that in the face of the new situation, fast developing in East Asia, any attempt to apply to the conditions of today and tomorrow inapplicable ideas and principles of the past neither would contribute toward the establishment of a real peace in East Asia nor solve the immediate issues.

However, as long as these points are understood, Japan has not the slightest inclination to oppose the participation of the United States and other powers in the great work of reconstructing East Asia along all lines of industry and trade; and I believe that the new regimes now being formed in China are prepared to welcome such foreign participation.[26]

This view was shared by the prime minister and all elements in Japan. As they saw the situation, Japan must draw upon Manchukuo and North China, welding them into an economic unit that would secure that degree of economic self-sufficiency that would give her security in the event of war. These convictions would not be altered by diplomatic notes.

Nor did the strength of those Japanese convictions change the views of Hull or his associates that these aims were being advanced by use of force and in disregard of the rights of other nations, rights established by treaties to which Japan was a signatory. This was the essence of Hull's response: Japan was bound by treaties and was not free to embark upon a course directed toward the arbitrary creation of a new order in Asia. American adherence to the Nine Power Treaty and Japanese determination to carry the war in China through to final success presented the danger of a final resort to arms. Arita's new plans for Asia were a major factor in promoting in Washington a discussion of economic sanctions.

The war in China promoted a momentum that brought repeated political crisis in Japan. The army gained additional leverage. Early in 1938, Admiral Nobumassa Suetsugu was appointed minister of Home Affairs. This was the first time that an army officer who had been a party to the long series of revolts within the army, and the series of assassinations that had taken place, was included in the cabinet. Ambassador Grew referred to him as a "military firebrand," one of those soldier-statesmen, soldier-politicians, who was an extremist.[27] The admiral, as it turned out, was soon replaced, but the central question of domination of the government by civilians or by the army remained. Early in the year plans were underway to establish full-scale mobilization of industry, trade, the press, and other aspects of life. Grew acknowledged that such mobilization was inevitable in any nation that was at war. How the war should be carried out was the pressing question. Extremists of the army preferred to have decisions made wholly on the basis of military considerations. Civilians, including Prime Minister Konoye, stood firmly for carrying on the war, but with due regard to diplomatic, financial, and economic realities. The army demanded that the mobilization plan should be carried out by Imperial Headquarters and put into effect immediately.[28]

Ambassador Grew was well informed, thanks to his close associations with other diplomats and with several Japanese civilian leaders. He had a high regard for Konoye and particularly for the lord keeper of the privy seal, Kido Kóichi, who he described as extremely well informed and a definite realist.[29] At the same time he was fearful of the great influences of Admiral Suetsugu, whom he considered "a visionary and an active advocate of totalitarian doctrine." The great danger was that the army would achieve complete control. Throughout 1938, Konoye managed to avoid this, but as Grew reported, Konoye would remain in office only so long "as it may please the Army to have him there."[30]

It remained an open question what kind of government would emerge and whether the proclaimed New Order in Asia would eventually lead to a closed economic unit including control of all foreign trade throughout East Asia. Grew could only guess about the future. He expected mobilization to be permanent, but he did not expect a dictatorship or totalitarian state along German lines.

By the close of 1938 relations between the United

States and Japan were becoming strained, but they were not as yet locked into a collision course. Much would depend on not only what happened in Europe but also future developments in Japan. The increasing power of the army and its resolve that nothing in the way of diplomacy or other considerations must stand in the way of victory in China boded ill for the future. At the same time the United States edged closer to a course from which it would be difficult to retreat. In December it met China's plea for assistance with a $25 million grant. It was supposedly a commercial deal whereby the United States would receive Chinese tung oil. Although the secretary of the treasury promoted it, Hull was strongly opposed, stating that Japan would see through this ill-camouflaged grant in aid and judge it for what it was. Since there was no way that tung oil could be delivered from the interior of China, this was true. Further dangers mounted in January, when Japan cut off all negotiations with the government of Chiang Kai-shek.

Also at the close of 1938 the United States faced the question whether Japan's New Order in Asia was to be countered with notes protesting on grounds of treaties and international law, or to be met by economic sanctions. The former had failed to deter the Japanese. The latter entailed risks that Japan would respond with measures that would make her inviolate to sanctions if they were imposed. She might go to war in the Dutch East Indies. Both Hull and Grew, long oriented to traditional diplomacy, opposed sanctions. They would wait it out until such a time as Japan took overt action directly against the United States.

Grew stated that economic sanctions "would simply result in making the Japanese more intransigent than ever." He added that it would be "extremely hazardous to assume that the program which Japan is carrying out at such enormous costs would be allowed to collapse upon their being brought about precisely that which that program was intended to meet."[31] The Japanese were deeply aware that they were dependent upon the United States. It was to free themselves of this dependence that they were instituting the New Order in Asia.

Akira Iriye believes that Americans saw Japan as inferior to the United States, both economically and militarily, and concluded that they had little to fear. He states: "There is no question that here was an element of complacency. American military leaders as well as American policy makers wanted to believe that the measures they were taking would suffice to hold Japan in check."[32] Hornbeck in the Division of Far Eastern Affairs exemplified this overconfidence. He remained assured that Japan would not attack until the strike actually occurred on Pearl Harbor.

The escalation of difficulties in relations with Japan neared a crisis just as the Munich Conference brought developments to a head in Europe. The American public was well informed from the day that Hitler rose to power of the radical changes taking place in Germany. The media told the story of the curtailment of civil liberties, of the reorganization of the public school system into an agency for instilling in youth military virtues and faith in the future German Aryan state free of Jews and other non-German people, and the leader principle with its exaltation of the Führer. Control of the press extended beyond censorship and established government scrutiny of books sold in every bookstore, even the shops in railway stations. National socialism was to become the new religion undermining the flabby teachings of Judaic Christianity. The traditional "Guten Morgen" was replaced with the greeting "Heil Hitler." What was underway was more than a new political organization; there was to be a new society in which individuals had no rights and only duties to the state.

Americans looked on the new conditions in Germany as unbelievable, and Hitler was portrayed in caricature. Their response was a combination of contempt, ridicule, thorough dislike, and fear, and reaction to the Nazis was well-nigh universal. "By the autumn of 1937," according to Langer and Gleason, historians of those momentous years, "hardly a trace of intellectual or spiritual neutrality remained."[33]

Gallup polls reported the American attitude. The caricature of the Führer that prevailed earlier had gradually changed into one of a powerful warlike leader who threatened world peace. In May 1936 the following question was asked of those interviewed: "If England and France have a war with Germany and Italy, which side do you support?" Sixty-five percent agreed to support England and France, and only three percent favored the totalitarian states.

The German regime was well aware of Roosevelt's strong feelings and of the possibility of having to fight not only England and France but also the United States. The German chargé d'affaires in Washington, in September 1938, wrote a lengthy report for the Foreign Office in Berlin commenting on American hostility. He stated that the causes went deeper than merely ideological aversion to totalitarian states. American participation in the First World War, he said, "came to pass in order to prevent a threatening shifting of the balance of power in Europe, which would have had a serious effect upon American political and economic importance in the world." He warned that "the relations between America and England were close. If England is involved in a life-and-death struggle," he predicted, "America will, as in 1917, seek by every possible means to prevent the defeat of England, because this would result in shifting of the balance of power in Europe and Asia, which would directly affect America. Therein lies America's vital interest, which she already feels to be threatened by the urge toward expansion and the desire for power of the totalitarian states."[34] This perspective statement was to prove correct, but the reality expressed therein had not yet been widely accepted by Americans.

American foreign policy in 1935 was directed at staying out of any future war. Roosevelt, as well as his closest advisors, remained opposed to involvement in Europe. Between war and peace, there was only one choice: Americans chose appeasement. The immediate prospect of Mussolini going to war in Ethiopia brought to a head plans that had been discussed but put aside. With war almost a certainty, Congress enacted neutrality legislation that provided that, whenever the president recognized the existence of war, he could forbid the sale or transportation of munitions to the belligerents and could also warn American citizens that if they travelled on ships belonging to a belligerent they did so at their own risk. The momentum that carried this legislation through in a great hurry owed its force to the current phobia, drummed up by the Nye Committee in the Senate, that America had entered the First World War only through the machinations of bankers and munition makers. In the planning stage both the president and the Department of State supported the measure, but sought to insert into the bill a provision leaving the president free to apply it to aggressors alone. This proposal raised a cry that, if enacted, it would leave the decision of war or peace in the hands of the executive. Critics of the president added the lurid charge that it would make Roosevelt a dictator. Roosevelt compromised on this feature. Senator Tom Connally of Texas denounced the bill as it finally passed, stating: "That is a form of declaration which announces that the United States will take the side of the strong and powerful against the weak, unprepared, and the defenseless. . . . The surest way to involve this country in war is to let the rest of the world believe that we will fight under no circumstances at all. . . . It is the President's function to conduct our foreign affairs." It was, he said, "to put ourselves in a plaster cast internationally, and give up whatever international influence America possesses toward peace and toward the pacification of disputes through all the world."[35]

Connally was soon to be proven right. With the outbreak of the Italo-Ethiopian War and the invocation of the law, its effect was to aid Italy. Exports to Italy increased from a monthly average of $25,403 during 1934 to $367,785 in October 1936, and $583,735 in November. Crude-oil exports rose from 61,708 to 417,474 barrels.[36] Faced with these unsavory facts, the president called for a moral embargo and defended it as consistent with the spirit of the neutrality law. By this ploy he redressed some of the ill-effects of the law. But the neutrality legislation remained on the books and was extended to the civil war that broke out in Spain in the summer of 1936.

The British and French were no more ready to confront Italy with an effective deterrent. The League of Nations imposed sanctions, but these did not include oil. Italy had no need of arms, but it did need oil. Members of the League acknowledged that they had failed to meet the stern test of protecting its members. Anthony Eden, in a speech before the Council of the League, gave reasons for the failure. There were, he said, certain risks that sanctions could lead to war, and these risks were so great to their own interests that they were not taken. The risk, not named by Eden, lay next door, where Hitler appeared ready for war. Roosevelt did include oil on the list he drew up under the moral embargo, an act that gave the democracies some faint hope that he would not submit to the isolationists.

Fear of a general European war not only governed the policies of England and France, but influenced Roosevelt when the Franco revolt broke out in Spain. The president recognized that the neutrality policy, by cutting off trade with the established Republican government, had the effect of favoring Franco, who received considerable aid from both Italy and Germany. Faced with the danger of a general war, England led the way in establishing the Non-Intervention Committee, which met in London on a regular basis. Hitler and Mussolini had nothing to fear. The highest priority of the committee was to prevent war from spreading. Regarding the large-scale interventions in Spain, on behalf of Franco the committee closed its eyes and made his victory possible. There was no love for the Spanish Republic. The American ambassador in Madrid alone found reason to admire that government, and he reported that the British diplomats showed contempt for the established Spanish government. What all feared was a general war, because Hitler would probably win it and in the process destroy Paris.

Events reached a dramatic crisis in September 1938. Since March the Nazi party in the Sudeten area of Czechoslovakia had been demanding autonomy. During the last week in September, Hitler took up their cause. In a speech broadcast to the world, he screamed defiance and threatened war unless his demands were met. The army in Czechoslovakia was mobilized, and the army in France partly mobilized. The American ambassador, William C. Bullitt, sent his family away from Paris in anticipation of German bombing. The French minister for air confided to Bullitt how ill prepared his country was to meet an attack. The French had 600 planes. French intelligence stated that the Germans had 6,500. The minister believed that the Germans could bomb Paris at will. The French had only very inadequate antiaircraft artillery. He predicted that the destruction in Paris would surpass all imagination and warned that the safest place for the next two years in France would be a trench, provided that one was equipped with a gas mask. Bullitt reported these sad facts to Roosevelt.[37]

In the background, Chamberlain was certain that he alone had established rapport with Hitler, and he sent him a private letter to be delivered by the French without their seeing its contents. In it he stated that if German troops crossed the boundary of Czechoslovakia, the French army would attack Germany at once and the British would support them. Edouard Daladier, French foreign minister, told Bullitt that nothing would stop Hitler. He was determined to humiliate every nation on earth, and thereby "to make his wish law in Europe."[38] In a statement on September 27, Chamberlain assured Hitler that the British government would guarantee that the plan he proposed would be carried out. Bullitt doubted that this would satisfy Hitler, and he thought there would be war within twenty-four hours. Then came news that Hitler had invited Chamberlain, Daladier, and Mussolini to meet him in Munich the next day. Bullitt's anxiety was not due to his having any great concern for Czechoslovakia. He viewed the demise with indifference. Moreover, Daladier stated that his policy of appeasement had the support of the United States.[39]

The crisis came to an end at the Munich Conference on September 29 and 30. The final session continued until 2:30 in the morning. The Sudeten area was to be delivered to Germany at once. In return Chamberlain gained only Hitler's promise to preserve peace, which he accepted in good faith. Roosevelt too was relieved that war was avoided and he was optimistic.

In October, Bullitt returned from Paris and called on both the president and Henry Morgenthau. He reported that Daladier was certain that Hitler's promise meant nothing. War could come at any time. The alarm caused Roosevelt to spring into action. The aircraft industry must go into high gear, and every effort must be made to arrange for sales of aircraft to France. He ordered the immediate release of the new Douglas bomber, despite the objections of Secretary Harry Hines Woodring, who said that the plane incorporated certain items that were secret and that it had been built partly at government expense. Bullitt pleaded that both the British and French must have immediate help.[40]

The meeting with Roosevelt had immediate results. Bullitt relayed to him Daladier's proposal for a French mission to come to the United States to gain the assistance of the American aviation industry. Roosevelt agreed at once. From this meeting between the president and Bullitt came the first assistance that went to the Allies. Here was a major turning point in relations with the beleaguered Allies. The president had never sympathized with appeasement, and he thoroughly disliked Chamberlain, who was described by banker Thomas Lamont, as the most dedicated of all the anti-American Britishers. After the Munich Conference, Roosevelt's primary aim was to prevent Hitler's victory.

The United States was scarcely better prepared than the French. The army consisted of 183,447, less than half of whom were equipped for immediate service. In May 1940 the country had only 160 pursuit planes and 52 bombers. Aircraft production had yet to get underway. Even had the country at large shared the president's views, the United States could have done little to change the military situation, although signs of forthcoming help from the United States might give the opponents of Germany the courage to continue.

Americans, as had the British and French, lived with the conviction that war was to be avoided at all costs. Equally important, there was a general feeling that it could be avoided. Now suddenly came the prospect of war. American critics of Roosevelt stood on vigilant guard against aid to the British and French, fought against the revision of neutrality laws, and assured themselves that what might happen in Europe was of no serious concern to the United States. As the controversy became more heated during the next two years, isolationism was rekindled by reminders of the horrors of war, and leaders employed every possible argument that could gain support from some group somewhere. The president's popularity did not protect him from charges of villainy. He was distrusted and hated by many as the man who had carried through a program of reforms that had transformed the country into a welfare state.

The years between 1938 and the attack on Pearl Harbor were years of honest anxiety and distrust. The president stood firm in his efforts to render aid to the Allies, although the opposition occasionally led him to be something less than frank and given to what his most friendly biographer has called "machinations."

The details of the debates, the criticism of the president, the many differences among isolationists' motives, and their forceful arguments, as well as slander, could not reverse the course of events. Opinions changed in step with the new developments in Europe.

The isolationists represented a wide spectrum of political views. There were a scattering of German Bund adherents, some Communists, liberals of a near-pacifist persuasion, and individuals with ties to the countries from which they had migrated. The majority were conservatives. The most influential of the groups, America First, organized in 1940, represented a cross section of the community who were conscientious in their belief that America's vital interests were not at stake in the European conflict.[41] Business people were divided, as were the clergy. The eminent Reverend Harry Emerson Fosdick, who had served as a chaplain in World War I, devoted most of his popular Sunday-afternoon radio sermons to denouncing war. His colleague at Union Theological Seminary, Reinhold Niebuhr, who had a large following among college students, called for realism. Neibuhr, a dedicated interventionist, was left of center and had been a member of the Socialist Party.

The isolationists did not lack funds, their message was in harmony with long-established attitudes, and it was easier to portray the horrors of war than it was to explain why a victory for Hitler and German hegemony would undermine America's position in the world. Except for a brief period in the early summer of 1940 after the fall of France, when it appeared that England would fall too, no danger appeared of a German invasion of the United States. Indeed, there was no danger of invasion; it was not in Hitler's plans.

The fall of France turned American opinion around. Overage destroyers were sent to England. Revisions of the neutrality legislation, decisively defeated again and again, now passed in October 1940 by votes of 63 to 30 in the Senate, and 243 to 181 in the House. In March 1941, Congress passed the Lend-Lease Bill by a vote of 60 to 31 in the Senate and a vote of 317 to 71 in the House. By the spring of 1941, there was strong support for all-out aid to the Allies, and many interventionists criticized Roosevelt for delaying action.

The debate over the implications of a Hitler victory continued. There was no danger of a German invasion in America, but a German triumph in Europe would, argued the interventionists, enable Germany to weaken the United States by economic measures that were already a part of German policy. Ever since 1933 the National Socialists had embarked on full control of all foreign trade and established a barter system. Central to this policy was a strong armament industry and a self-sufficient economy. The world faced the prospect of a German-dominated Europe that would apply this system to all territory under its direct control. Hitler did not plan to absorb all of Europe into his realm, but weaker powers would become client states and their foreign trade would be under German control. Freedom to trade wherever and whatever was profitable for private enterprise would be abolished. Only a totalitarian state could impose such close control over the economy.

The barter system had already been applied with considerable success in the markets of South America and in smaller states in Central Europe, with the result that American trade with those countries had been sharply reduced. That system could be extended further once Hitler was victorious. Japan was proceeding along the same lines, and the subordination of Manchuria enabled Japan to move in the direction of a self-sufficient economy.

Existing relations between the American government and separate corporations and entrepreneurs would be threatened. Separate enterprises would be permitted to engage in trade with Europe only when the trade served German interests. Only if the United States revolutionized its economy and established some form of totalitarian control could there be a degree of equal bargaining power. Not only would the private-enterprise system have to be curtailed or abandoned, it also would have to adopt totalitarian methods of subordinating all aspects of life to central government control.

Fear of this taking place was expressed by many members of Congress during the debates on the Lend-Lease Bill. The subject was given primary attention by various speakers from government departments, and was forcefully set forth by well-informed journalists whose audiences were the better-educated segments of the community.[42]

The American Adolf Berle, assistant secretary of state, warned that the world was rapidly being divided into two camps. The totalitarian countries were bent on achieving economic self-sufficiency either by barter agreements or conquest. Democratic countries must therefore create a democratic world where there was freedom of trade.

It remained for Douglas Miller, after fifteen years' service as the commercial attaché in the Berlin embassy, to convince the business community of the danger it faced. In direct language enriched by his own firsthand experience, Miller drove home the futility of dealing with Hitler and described in stark terms what would happen if Hitler should win. His book, entitled *You Can't Do Business with Hitler*, warned that, in a world dominated by Hitler, the United States, with its free enterprise economy, would be in a weak position to bargain. The central power in Berlin, in full control of all business activity, would set the terms. For the United States to compete it would be necessary to "upset our whole economy as we know it now."[43] There would be no alternative but to convert to a planned economy wholly under government control.

The political and economic arguments were intertwined and inseparable. How important both were was demonstrated in the long debates over the Lend-Lease Bill in Congress, passage of which effectively brought to a close the United States' neutral status. It was soon followed by convoys on the Atlantic, and the beginning of a shooting war before war was officially declared in December 1941.

Relations with Japan became inseparable from the war in Europe. Hitler's defeat of France and the fall of the Low Countries in the spring of 1940 created unprecedented excitement in the United States and hastened the first steps toward war. The near-collapse of Great Britain further endangered the balance of power in the Pacific and opened the way for Japan to launch its campaign to drive the western powers out of East Asia. In January 1941, Roosevelt wrote to Grew, "As to your very natural request for an indication of my view as to certain aspects of our future attitude toward developments in the Far East, I believe that the fundamental proposition is that we must recognize that the hostilities in Europe, in Africa, and in Asia are all parts of a single world conflict."[44]

The conflict in Europe provided the momentum for an all-out effort to mobilize the raw materials that the United States would require if war came. Especially after the German victories in Europe, the dominant concerns in Washington were the mobilization of raw materials and services on which the United States was dependent, especially imports, the aircraft industry, and the armed services. Roosevelt and Morgenthau would tolerate no dragging of feet by members of the administration. It was decided that Charles Edison and Woodring, secretaries of the army and navy, must go. They lacked the force to meet the rapid pace and did not share the sense of emergency that now gripped the administration. Government corporations were already engaged in buying up rubber and other materials that were in short supply. Cabinet meetings were almost scenes of panic in which the president made short shrift of any objections. Hap Arnold of the air force was carrying on a separate campaign against furnishing the British and French with aircraft. Roosevelt instructed the secretary of war to tell him in no uncertain terms to shut up.[45]

Oil inevitably came up for discussion. British, Dutch, and American interests controlled virtually all of the world's oil, except for Russian, Romanian, and Mexican supplies. If Germany and Japan could be deprived of oil, it would be a great step forward. There was further lengthy discussion over methods of conserving the supply.

It was in this setting that attention was given to cutting off oil exports to Japan. In 1939 the United States had exported 28 million barrels of oil to Japan, an amount that came within 3 million barrels of Japan's total imports of oil. Japan was storing oil and at the same time consuming 25 million barrels a year. An interoffice memo from the Treasury Department carried these conclusions:

> If the United States—alone or together with Great Britain—is willing to spend $25 to $35 million a month on an oil conservation program, and if the Dutch and the British will either destroy their wells in Dutch East Indies, or embargo oil exports except to British areas, and if Russia could be induced to take over the Rumanian wells, and if England would concentrate and extend her bombing attacks on German oil producing centers: then Japan will have to sue for peace with the Chiang Kai-shek Government in the very near future inasmuch as without oil reserves her military operations would be greatly hampered, etc.[46]

There were frantic efforts to take some actions that would be effective when the United States' hands were tied as far as offering immediate assistance to England and France, and it appeared to the most influential leaders that the time had come to put in place an embargo on oil and other shipments to Japan. Under the National Defense Act passed early in the summer, the Treasury Department was granted the authority to control exports. As Herbert Feis stated in his book *The Road to Pearl Harbor*, "There, of all places in the American Government, the sense of crisis was most alive; the feeling that Hitler must not be allowed to win, the most ardent; and the will to act upon feeling, the most bold."[47] Morgenthau was a dynamo. There was concern in the State Department that

Morgenthau was rash and after a bureaucratic struggle, the president placed the authority to control oil imports into the hands of an army officer.

In the meantime, Ambassador Grew stuck to his view that sanctions would drive the Japanese further toward war, and now he feared that they would drive the Japanese into an alliance with Germany. But among men of the character of Morgenthau and Stimson, any concern about what Japan might do received slight weight. To them and to the president the proposal to embargo oil offered a release from the frustrations induced by the fact that there was so little they could do.

After interdepartmental meetings two plans went forward to the president, one drafted by Sumner Welles and one by Morgenthau. Welles's plan, reflecting the fears that prevailed in the State Department, provided for a limited embargo. In the exchanges the Treasury demanded a complete embargo on all kinds of oil and scrap metals. Roosevelt was left to decide. While he was reflecting, a message reached him from San Francisco that the Japanese were building up supplies by large purchases and before long the American army and navy would face shortages. Welles was successful in modifying the Treasury plan. This placed an embargo on aviation oil and number-one-grade heavy melting iron and steel scrap. As the Japanese could transform lower octane gasoline into aviation fuel, and did, Morgenthau harried members of the State Department with the question of when would they extend the ban to all oil except what was useful in automobiles.

From an American perspective the embargo on oil was a major turn toward deterring Japan. From a Japanese perspective, it confirmed their worst fears. However, we now know that it was not decisive in altering Japan's course. The new government had already decided to push the war to the south, and the Japanese had occupied the northern third of French Indo-China by early August. Japan was firmly committed to its course and that course was not to be changed. Ambassador Grew, so long the patient and cautious observer, was convinced by September that now there was no turning back.

Germany pressed Japan for an alliance in 1939, but was refused. New negotiations between the two countries began early in the summer of 1940. There were those in the Japanese councils who distrusted Germany, but on September 27, 1940, Germany, Italy, and Japan signed the Tri-Partite Pact. If any of the three powers became involved in war with a power not then engaged in war, the other two signatories would declare war against that power. The Tri-Partite Pact was clearly directed against the United States. Both the Germans and the Japanese thought it would deter the Americans from declaring war. Japan had also considered the danger that Germany would take over the East Indies once the European colonial powers were finally defeated.

In response, the United States, after the Tri-Partite Pact, placed a full-scale embargo on oil and scrap iron to Japan. What Japan might do remained uncertain, but the hope was to deter her from launching an attack. Stanley Hornbeck seemed more certain than others that Japan would not go to war. He greatly underestimated Japan's strength. The Americans based their policy of deterrence on their mistaken perception that Japan would retreat in the face of American power. Ambassador Grew knew better. He warned that Japan was not to be deterred unless she could reach a settlement with the United States that in no way compromised Japan's long-term aims. The authorities in Washington also misjudged the situation.

The kaleidoscopic events of late 1940 and developments in early 1941 promoted a feeling of encirclement in Japan. The United States was increasing its help to China, strengthening its position in the Philippines, and working closely with the British and Dutch. On the other hand, it was anxious to postpone a possible war with Japan and to be free to devote all its energies to Europe, although it appeared in Washington that the only hope of postponing the war was to deter Japan.

Early in 1941, Japan took the initiative in seeking a settlement. Two American missionaries, Fathers James N. Drought and James E. Walsh, provided the occasion when they placed in the hands of Postmaster General Frank C. Walker a draft for an agreement that they believed acceptable to Japan. Secretary of State Hull, early in April, agreed to meet with Ambassador Nomura to discuss the proposal. Discussions took place several times each week. The Japanese ambassador was assisted by Minister Wakasizi, minister-counselor of the embassy. Hull relied heavily on Joseph Ballantine, a foreign service officer who spoke Japanese, and Maxwell Hamilton, both of the Far Eastern Division of the State Department. President Roosevelt was kept well informed and met from time to time with Nomura.

Nomura did not represent the views of the belligerent elements who were in control in Japan. He sometimes agreed with Hull on points that his superiors at home would have contested. Hull and Ballantine repeatedly reminded Nomura that his friendly statements contrasted sharply with the pronouncements of Foreign Minister Matsuoka. Nomura sought to explain Matsuoka's statements as those of a politician who quite irresponsibly sought public favor.

In the prolonged negotiations, Japan was asked to make a 180-degree turn, rejecting military expansion, intervention in neighboring countries, and economic nationalism. In July, Japan sent its armed forces into southern Indo-China. Its actions there and in China added to American skepticism.

The negotiations centered on the Tri-Partite Pact, Japanese occupation of China, and the application of the principle of equality of commercial opportunity throughout the Pacific area. Japan was not asked to renounce the pact, but to provide assurance that if the United States became involved in the European war in self-defense, Japan would not declare war against the United States. Hull's earlier definition of self-defense meant that should the United States enter the war with Germany, the reason would ipso facto be self-defense, since Germany was attacking the vital interests of the United States. Therefore, the Japanese saw in Hull's demand a request for a blank check. Nor did the United States call for immediate withdrawal of Japanese troops from China, but it did seek a firm commitment that Japan would withdraw in a reasonable period. The United States did hold that Japan should commit itself to the principle of equality of commercial opportunity.

Throughout Southeast Asia the western powers reinforced their defenses and the United States made preparations to reinforce the Philippines. The Japanese feared that these measures were aimed at it, since it had occupied Indo-China. Both the United States and Japan were locked into a situation where neither was free to negotiate purely in terms of its national interest.

The most difficult question for Japan was the American insistence that it withdraw its troops from China. Important leaders, among them the lord keeper of the privy seal, Kido, were prepared to make such an agreement—reluctantly to be sure—if Japan was permitted a reasonable time to get out. Kido had concluded that Japan was bogged down in a quagmire and that to continue the war was hopeless and only served to weaken the country. Tojo, the minister of war, would not admit to this. To make such a move would discredit the army and also result in a reduction of its budget.

Negotiations entered upon a new stage in late August when Premier Konoye secretly proposed a meeting with Roosevelt. The president welcomed the meeting, but observed that, should it end in failure, the results would be catastrophic. The message from Konoye was accompanied by a series of proposals. These were carefully examined in the State Department, and all those consulted agreed that they could not be accepted. Ambassador Grew in Tokyo differed. He did not believe that the Japanese position was hardening, and he warned that time was running out. As he saw it, the Konoye-Toyoda government sought peace and represented the forces of moderation. However, he acknowledged that the action of Japan was also subject to other interpretations, and that she was only seeking to postpone a war until her economy was stronger. The meeting never took place.

It could be said that officials in Washington misread the Japanese proposals; however, we know now that Nomura sent a message in which he held that the proposals were a step backward and narrowed the possibilities of reaching agreement.

American officials were also influenced by their fear that if the government in Japan did make peace, it would be overthrown by the army, the same fear that prevailed in Tokyo.

Fear and uncertainty were also felt in the councils of the Japanese. In July the chief of the naval general staff, Osami Nagano, advised the emperor that Japan should try as much as possible to avert war. The supply of oil, in event of war, would only be sufficient for one and a half years. When the emperor asked him if it would be possible to win a sweeping victory as in the Russo-Japanese War, Nagano replied that it was doubtful if the Japanese could even win.[48] The lord keeper of the privy seal, the emperor's closest advisor, reached a similar conclusion. A war with the United States, he thought, if naval estimates were correct, would be a hopeless one.[49] On October 11, Chief Oka of the Naval Affairs Bureau met with Kido and stated that with the exception of the naval general staff, "the brains of the Navy didn't want war with the United States." On the following day the cabinet met and several members expressed hope that negotiations with the United States would prove successful. Admiral Toyoda, minister of foreign affairs, said agreement was within reach on the Tri-Partite Pact and on the economic question and the only difficult problem remaining was the American insistence on removal of Japanese troops from China.[50] Tojo rejected evacuation of troops, dismissed the negotiations as futile and insisted on war if agreements had not been completed by a specific date.

There was equal reluctance on the American side. No

decision had been taken about what should be done if negotiations failed. Since September 1940, Hull had warned
that the major concern of the United States was "in not
China—repeat not China"—but the South Pacific. Hull
repeatedly stated that the policy of the United States embraced French Indo-China, Thailand, and the Dutch East
Indies.[51] But in the final negotiations a major consideration was that no agreement was acceptable that could be
seen as selling China down the river. Not only would this
have been highly unpopular with the American public,
but also in the critical international situation in the summer and fall of 1941 it would have sent signals to those
fighting Hitler that the United States had adopted a course
of appeasement. No one had a keener sense of the sym-
bolic significance of China for the American public than
Roosevelt, and at this time the president was intent on
unifying the country before entering the war against Germany. Appeasement of Japan at China's expense would
only have divided the country further.

By 1941 there could be no peace unless the United
States accepted terms that permitted Japan to go ahead
with establishing her New Order in Asia. This the United
States would not do. The days of appeasement before the
Munich Conference were now past. The world was not
only involved in a global war, it was immersed in a political and social revolution. The American people remained
opposed to war, but had approved aid to the Allies. The
United States had gone beyond neutrality and was already convoying ships in the Atlantic, vessels that had
orders to shoot if attacked. The United States and Japan
confronted each other and were committed to programs
that clashed. Although Japanese leadership was not made
up of warmongers, they were convinced that for reasons
of national security they must establish the New Order
in Asia. Once Japanese policy became committed to the
belief that the nation's security was at stake, it was next
to impossible to reverse the course. Kido, lord keeper of
the privy seal, advised the emperor that it would be wiser
to wait until Japan achieved greater strength, but the mo-

mentum that had taken hold prevented this option. The military was in control. All that remained by late September was for an incident to take place. The Japanese provided the incident.

Important questions have been raised concerning the position adopted by the United States. Was it realistic to insist that Japan abide by the Nine Power Treaty to maintain the Open Door of 1922?[52] The international treaty structure had been subject to change many times. Time and again the final determinant had not been treaties but the forces of superior power. In the course of time nations lost or gained in relative strength and brought with those changes alterations in the political configuration.

Did American interests in China justify that, as a condition of peace, Japan must withdraw her forces? American trade with Japan was approximately double the trade with China. Investments in China surpassed those in Japan, but they were not great enough to be accorded a high priority. Nor was the door closed to American investments in Manchuria. Japan favored foreign investment in Manchuria, and this included the Japanese army, which had given its approval to a project.[53]

The question has also been raised whether or not a truce proposal might not have been worked out in November 1941 if the United States had not rejected the Japanese proposal for a meeting between Roosevelt and Konoye. Ambassador Grew had advocated that the meeting take place.

Final answers cannot be given, but these questions were viewed in a broader perspective in the closing months of negotiations. The prominence of the Nine Power Treaty in the many exchanges can be misleading. The broader question was, could Japan be induced to reverse its course? Could the government of Japan, long under the ultimate control of the military, once again be controlled by the moderates in Japan? There was every reason to arrive at a negative answer based upon the history of the previous ten years.

Was the central question whether or not American interests in China justified an uncompromising stand? Not only China mattered, but all of East Asia. Japan's occupation of French Indo-China testified to Japan's determination to incorporate all of East Asia, including the Philippines, into the New Order of Asia. China was important, in part because of the friendly sentiment for that country, feelings deeply rooted in the United States and reinforced by the history of China since 1897. Ambassador Grew, who had consistently maintained that China was of no great importance to the United States, also firmly believed that concessions to Japan should not be made at the expense of China. No administration in Washington was inclined to make such concessions, and if it had, it would have divided the country and crippled the conduct of foreign relations. Yet, short of such concessions, there could be no arrangement that could have met Japan's demands.

Finally, the conflict with Japan had become inseparably intertwined with America's sympathy for Europe, where a German victory appeared within reach. Appeasement of Japan, allied to Germany, would have undermined confidence in the United States and probably strengthened Germany's authority. The United States, regarded as the strongest power in the world, offered the hope that she would continue the course she was pursuing and that it would inevitably lead to American entry into the war.

7

Origins of the Cold War
1940–1945

THE World War II alliance of the United States and the Soviet Union was based on their common interest in defeating Hitler. It was a marriage of convenience that was to come to an end with the defeat of Germany. Before that victory, the interdependence of the two powers tied them together in an uneasy relationship. David Eisenhower, in the biography of his grandfather, *Eisenhower at War, 1943–1945*, stresses the mutual dependence of the eastern and western fronts. Not to recognize this, he writes, "is to overlook the fact that without a resurgent Russian front an Allied invasion of Europe would have been impossible, and without the pledge of cooperation in the form of a simultaneous offensive on the eastern front, the Allied landings in northwest France could not have been undertaken when they were. To overlook this interdependence . . . entails the risk of misunderstanding the nature of Allied-Soviet wartime cooperation, and the evolution of the wartime settlement."[1] Military considerations necessarily held the highest priority throughout the war.

The long-range aims of the United States were held in abeyance during the early years of the war. The United States stood committed by the Atlantic Charter to a world of free states, noninterference in the affairs of other states, no recognition of territorial conquests, and freedom for the people of the world to govern themselves. Central to this policy was the long-cherished program of the Open Door calling for equality of commercial opportunity in foreign markets, a feature that led Franklin D. Roosevelt and Secretary of State Cordell Hull to insist that the British abandon the imperial-preference system when the leaders of the two powers met for the Atlantic Conference in Placentia Bay off of Argentia, Newfoundland, in August 1941. From the perspective of domestic politics these points could only be applauded. They were deeply rooted in Wilsonianism, and they were of a nature that did not arouse opposition among the many conflicting interests in the electorate. They did not always jibe with the interests, legitimate or illegitimate, of the other members of the family of nations.

Equally important in American foreign policy was firm opposition to spheres of influence. Roosevelt was opposed to these areas of foreign authority, and Hull was convinced that there must be no spheres of influence in the future. Each and every nation must be free to choose its form of government, and once established, that government must be truly independent and free from foreign interference. It was commitment to this principle that foredoomed friendly relations with the Soviet government once Germany had been defeated.

The clash over spheres of interest brought an end to the Nazi-Soviet Pact of 1939, causing Germany to go to war with the Soviet Union. German dependence on Romania for oil and on Finland for nickel, together with its need for food supplies from eastern Europe, caused Hitler to extend his ambitions during the first year of the war. Before the war he had no intention of extending his rule over the Balkan States.[2] He had hoped to maintain peace in the Balkans, but Hungary and Romania, thanks to the territorial settlements after World War I, were at swords' points. War between them was only avoided because Germany mediated. Mediation and military considerations shortly involved Germany in Yugoslavia as well. And when Italy extended the war to Albania and threatened Greece, Great Britain sent armed forces to Greece, its treaty ally. If the British had gained military ascendancy in Greece, they would have been within easy reach of the Ploesti oil fields in Romania. Again Germany moved to the south.

The Nazi-Soviet Pact did not eliminate or modify the long-term goals of the Soviet Union. It seized Basarabia, a part of Romania, without abiding by the agreed-upon stipulation providing for consultation before taking action.[3] It disregarded the limits set by the pact in the Baltic States and seized territory in Lithuania that was on Germany's borders.[4] Soviet activities in Bulgaria signalled Soviet ambitions on the Dardanelles and in Iran.

On September 3, 1940, the German foreign minister protested. Ribbentrop cited Soviet actions in both Romania and Hungary that were taken without consultation. He stressed the Soviet action in Lithuania, adjacent to Germany, where the Soviet government had agreed to consult if it took any actions.[5] In November, Molotov declared that the Soviet Union "would have to have effective guarantees of her security." The Soviet foreign minister explained that the question that interested the Soviet Union in the near East "concerned not only Turkey, but Bulgaria, for instance." The Soviet Union was also interested in the fate of Romania and Hungary, together with Poland, Yugoslavia, and Greece; and Molotov asked for an explanation of Germany's position in those countries.[6] The tension mounted, and in mid-November the gulf between the two imperialist powers was wide enough for all to see. The German ambassador in the Soviet Union reported the conditions laid down by Molotov for agreement with the German position on Romania. The first called for immediate withdrawal of German troops from Finland, a country within the Soviet sphere of influence. The second provision read:

> Provided that within the next few months the security of the Soviet Union in the Straits is assured by the conclusion of a mutual assistance pact between the Soviet Union and Bulgaria, which geographically is situated inside the security zone of the Black Sea boundaries of the Soviet Union, and by the establishment of a base for land and sea forces of the USSR within the range of the Bosporus and the Dardanelles by means of a long term lease.

Also required was recognition that "the area south of Batum and Baku in the general direction of the Persian Gulf is recognized as the center of the aspirations of the Soviet Union." The agreement on Romania was also to be subject to Japan's renouncing her rights to concessions for coal and oil in northern Sakhalin.[7]

The ambitions of the Soviet Union preceded American entry into the war. They were in direct conflict with the policy of the United States, and when the Soviet Union set out to establish spheres of influence after it was able to repulse the Germans, the stage was set for future difficulties between the two major world powers. Soviet aspirations only became known to the United States beginning in 1943.

In December 1940, Hitler reached his decision to attack the Soviet Union, and in June 1941, Germany invaded. Hitler was confident that the Russians could be defeated before winter arrived in 1941. During the first six months a German victory appeared probable. The Germans laid siege to Leningrad and moved far into Russia.

Pressing military considerations made it necessary to postpone discussions of postwar arrangements, but Stalin expressed distrust of the Atlantic Charter even while the German armies laid siege to Leningrad and advanced into Russia. When British Foreign Secretary Anthony Eden visited Stalin in Moscow in November 1941, the Soviet leader asked him if the Atlantic Charter was intended to stand in the way of the Soviet Union's absorption of these states. Secretary of State Hull had already warned Eden that the United States was opposed to any territorial agreement until the war had been won. Throughout the war the United States refused to acknowledge that the Baltic States had permanently lost their independence; neither did the United States raise the issue. The ensuing struggle pushed the Baltic question into the background, but it remained for a future agenda. Here was a precedent that was to take on new dimensions once the Soviet armies marched into Central Europe.

Admiral William H. Standley, the American ambassador in Moscow, after the Soviet victory in the battle of Stalingrad in February 1943, informed Washington that there was a growing spirit of independence.[8] In midsummer he warned that a movement calling for a second front in western Europe by the British and Americans was in full swing.[9] Standley was not certain of Russian motives, but he acknowledged that the Russians were probably sincere in believing that the second front was delayed for political reasons. The movement, he stated, created in the Russian public an impression that the Americans and the British were guilty of bad faith and that the Soviet Union, standing alone, was winning the war. Standley thought it was possible that the Russian government was preparing the ground for a strong stand in the field of foreign policy. The Russian public would be inclined to assert that they should have the greatest voice in determining the peace.

In the summer of 1943 there was growing speculation about Russian plans. Standley speculated that the USSR might desire a position in Europe or elsewhere that would bring it into conflict with the United States. Distrust was awakened in June when a Free German Committee was created. Standley asked what this might portend. Was the purpose simply to stimulate greater German resistance to Hitler? Was it for home consumption to promote a greater war spirit? The announcement also raised questions in the United States, but Charles E. Bohlen, assistant chief of the Russian section of in the State Department, thought it would be unwise to take any notice of the committee in the absence of any agreement on general policy toward Germany. Bohlen advised: "If and when a three power meeting on the foreign minister level occurs, an opportunity will be presented to endeavor to work on some common understanding in regard to Germany which would permit consideration of the points raised in Admiral Standley's telegram."[10]

The war and the alliance with the Soviets did not dispel the American public's basic distrust of the Soviet

Union. In the Department of State, Loy Henderson, Chip Bohlen, and others thought the Russians were not to be trusted and should be dealt with firmly. Communism continued to be viewed as brutal, inhumane, and untrustworthy. To be sure, there was admiration for the Soviet Union's turning back the German armies. Americans had good reason for wishing the Russians success on the eastern front. But the distrust remained, and the Roosevelt administration feared an outburst of hostility that could disrupt cooperation with the Soviets. Given the military interdependence of the East and West, this was a time to minimize differences. There were Americans who praised the USSR and cleared it of all past guilt. A former ambassador to the Soviet Union, Joseph E. Davies, was the most prominent among those who now had nothing but praise for the Soviets. His book *Mission to Moscow* explained away the purges of the Russian military in 1937, described the Soviets as friendly, and advocated an agreement conforming to Soviet views of the problem of the Baltic States. The movie based on the book went further in portraying the Soviet Union as a fine friend. Others anxious to counteract the traditional distrust made much of the Russian constitution of 1936, maintaining that it had established religious freedom. In 1943 the Soviet government abolished the Cominform, the party apparatus promoting communism overseas. This was heralded by Soviet apologists as evidence of a new Soviet Union, one that indicated a complete turnabout in foreign relations.

The change in American attitude was superficial. The old distrust remained dominant. Elbridge Durbrow in the State Department, discussed the problem with Joseph E. Davies, who hoped that the two countries could reach a basic understanding. Durbrow agreed that this was important both in the immediate future and for the postwar years, but he felt that this was not an easy problem to solve. Durbrow cited the record of the Soviet government. During the past years it had entered the Nazi-Soviet Pact, made war on Finland, taken over the Baltic States, and pursued a bold course in Poland. These tactics were still fresh in the memories of Americans. Joseph E. Davies turned to the question of what mattered now and stated that there was a need for greater realism. He had recently been in England, and what he had learned led him to believe that the British were prepared to concede some territorial changes and would recognize Soviet claims to the Baltic States.

Neither Standley in Moscow nor some segments of the American public delayed in concluding that the creation of the Free German Committee indicated trouble. By July 23, 1943, Standley had decided that the Soviets intended to pursue an independent policy "and at least so far as Eastern and Central Europe is concerned to play a leading role."[11] Together with the Polish question, the Soviet move unleashed a flood of suspicion. Hull was deeply disturbed. He observed that there were at least thirty different boundary questions to be settled in Europe, which must necessarily await the termination of the fighting. Reports of American public opinion were published in Russia and caused public denunciation of the United States.

In that same summer of 1943, Italy surrendered. The Soviets were not consulted about the terms and were only informed of them well after the event. When an American correspondent, Henry Cassidy, protested to Ilya Ehrenburg, a prominent Soviet literary figure, that the Americans and the British had not been consulted about the establishment of the Free German Committee, he replied that the Soviet Union had been wholly bypassed in the making of arrangements with Badoglio, who had taken the place of Mussolini; and he warned that Italy's future was a question of importance. Two could play the game, he said, and the Free German Committee was an answer in advance to any plan that the Americans and British might have for going ahead in Europe without consulting the Soviets.[12] The failure to fully inform the Soviet government on the decision in Italy and to include it in deliberations had widened the rift. Stalin, in a message to Roosevelt, declared: "The United

States and Great Britain made agreements but the Soviet Union received information about the results of the agreements between the two countries just as a passive third observer. I have to tell you that it is impossible to tolerate such a situation any longer."[13] Soviet spokesmen asserted that they too had been fighting Italians on their front and that by engaging German forces on a large scale they had contributed to the victory in Italy. Ambassador Standley thought that the establishment of the Free Germany Committee without consultation with the British and the Americans on the future of Germany was "probably not unrelated to the independence of British and American policy toward France and Italy."[14]

Allied suspicions gained ground as it became clear that by this time the Soviets were confident of defeating Germany. The Germans were being driven back along the entire eastern front. Standley, still in Moscow, reached no firm conclusions about Soviet aims, but he speculated about them. The announcement of the dissolution of the Communist International did not suggest to American officials in the embassy in Moscow that Russia would necessarily refrain from interference in the internal affairs of other countries. Standley thought that the Soviet Union stood to gain from disassociating itself from the Cominform activities. During the upheavals that would naturally take place, Communist parties would be in a stronger position if they were free of the stigma of Soviet control.[15]

In answer to an inquiry by a British correspondent, Stalin answered that abolition of the Cominform would free the Soviet Union of false allegations that it was actively interfering in the internal affairs of other countries, and it would facilitate "the work of patriots in freedom loving countries for uniting the progressive forces . . . , regardless of party or religious faith, into a single group of national liberation."[16] This frank statement suggested future difficulties in countries that were liberated of the German forces.

The Conference of Foreign Ministers in Moscow in Oc-

tober 1943 marked the beginning of the wartime confer-
ences. No agreements had been reached on coordinating
military campaigns or on the postwar questions that
were now beginning to develop as Russian armies were
advancing toward eastern and central Europe. The Soviet
Union and Czechoslovakia were negotiating a treaty that
would bring the Czechs into the Soviet camp. Beneš,
president of the Czechoslovak government in exile, had
initiated negotiations after he concluded that his country
could not rely on the western democracies for protection.
Anthony Eden, British foreign secretary, opposed the negotiating of a separate treaty that would set a dangerous
precedent whereby the Soviet Union would tie up the
postwar world as it took possession of each country in
eastern Europe.

Vital questions affecting the future arose when Italy
surrendered to British and American forces in the summer of 1943. Surrender terms were set by the British and
Americans, and the Soviet government was belatedly informed of the terms. Stalin finally gave his approval, but
insisted that Italy should be under the control of an advisory committee composed of representatives of the
three powers. Churchill at once advised the United States
that giving Stalin the power of veto was impossible.[17]
When the Moscow Conference met in October 1943, the
Soviet Union still did not have a single representative in
Italy.

In that summer of 1943 the future of Poland hung in
the balance as Soviet armies approached. Relations between Poland and the Soviet Union were at their nadir. In
April ten thousand bodies of Polish officers were discovered at Katyn, killed by the retreating Russians. It was
also estimated that the Soviets had carried off more than
1 million Polish soldiers and sent them to Siberia. The
Soviets were convinced that the Poles were ready to stab
them in the back, a conviction that had a long history
and was recently strengthened by the violent opposition
of the Poles after the Nazi-Soviet division of Poland. When
the Poles called for an investigation of the Katyn mas-

sacre by the International Red Cross, the Soviet Government broke off relations with the Polish government in exile in London.

Before the Moscow Conference in October, the Polish ambassador in Washington made a dramatic plea to Secretary of State Cordell Hull, calling for joint military operations by the western allies and the Soviets when the time came for an invasion of Poland. Only if western forces were present was there any hope of establishing Polish independence. The memorandum of the ambassador warned that the Soviet demand to appropriate half of Poland's territory (actually, the Soviets demanded only territory up to the Curzon Line that the Poles had taken over after the war in 1921) "can be interpreted as an intention on the part of the Soviet Government to subordinate the whole of Poland and use it as a spring board for subjugation of Central Europe and Germany."[18] Poland, the ambassador warned, faced dire tragedy unless some understanding was reached before Soviet troops arrived. The president and Hull had heard the plea made in eloquent terms before, and they were too realistic to have any hope of changing the course of events. Hull listened and wrote in his notes that he had "exhibited suitable interest," and he dismissed the plea as "offering nothing new in the attitude of this Government."[19] Neither Roosevelt nor Hull were prepared to be a party to the extinction of Poland, but they were not about to wreck the alliance with the Soviet Union by a futile exercise that would destroy hopes of defeating Hitler. As Hull put it, he was not about to open the Pandora's box of European boundary questions.

In a memorandum to Roosevelt before the Moscow Conference, Hull explained the approach he would take: "It seems to me that it would be well not to be too detailed in suggesting items for discussion but try to keep the exchange of views on the broad basis of general world security, within which framework, if the Soviet Government is willing to cooperate, many of the detailed questions would be more easily solved."[20] Hull did not go to

Moscow to resolve the troublesome questions that were immediately pending. His stand on Poland was much the same as on other issues. This was due to reluctance on the part of the Roosevelt administration to get bogged down in Europe after the war. The approach was also rooted in the importance of military considerations, the necessity of promoting cooperation between the Soviet government and the western allies, if the war was to be won.

At the conclusion of the discussion of the Polish question at the conference Hull sat quietly by, content to say no more than that he considered it more a British problem in view of their treaty agreements with Poland.[21] Again, when the Soviet-Czech treaty was discussed, he took a similar stance, although that was an issue of major importance. Eden had already opposed the treaty on the ground that if the Soviets were to act alone in negotiating treaties with the occupied countries, then the final result would be a Soviet sphere of influence. Hull quietly observed at the close of the discussion that the treaty question was a matter for the British and the Soviets to resolve.[22] He preferred to discuss high principles that he believed would lay the basis for settlement by diplomacy, and his proposed world international agency would provide peaceful settlements.

Hull's principles were stated in the agenda the United States proposed before the conference. Questions such as the future of Germany, joint responsibility for liberated areas, reparations, and Iran should be discussed. The British suggested only minor changes. The Soviets likewise approved, but insisted that the most important item must be the opening of a second front.[23] Once the conference met, it became clear that the United States had two major goals. The first was an understanding about the second front that would assure cooperation on the military front. The second goal of major importance was gaining Soviet approval of the international organization. It was believed that public American support for the proposed United Nations was more likely to be achieved while the war was in progress and before the various minorities, tied to their European homeland, succeeded in stirring up opposition to cooperation with the Soviet Union.

These two limited aims were achieved. At the opening of the conference British and American military representatives laid out before the Soviets in detail the plans and preparations underway for the invasion of western Europe. These included impressing the Soviets with the various types of aircraft and landing craft that would be used: 2,000 fighter planes and 1,900 bombers. The openness of the presentation and the magnificent scale of the operations appeared to assure success, but Lieutenant General Hastings Ismay of England added that the operation was dependent on certain other conditions prevailing. Asked by the Soviet representatives what these conditions were, Ismay and General John R. Deane, head of United States Military Missions in Moscow, explained:

> First, there must be substantial reduction in the strength of the German fighter force in North West Europe between now and the date of the assault. It is expected that the ever increasing Anglo-American bomber offensive will produce this result. The second condition is that the German reserves in France and the Low Countries as a whole must not be more on the day of the assault than about 12 full strength, first quality, mobile divisions. This is, of course, exclusive of coastal training and German Air Force divisions. Furthermore, it must not be possible for the Germans to transfer from other fronts more than 15 first quality divisions during the first two months of the operation.[24]

These final conditions spelled out by General Ismay, explaining that the assault could not take place unless the Soviets cooperated by continuing their aggressive campaigns on the eastern front, testifies to the military interdependence of the allies.

The delay in establishing the second front was not due to Allied trickery calculated to postpone the invasion and leave the Russians to make the sacrifices. The undertaking was a most hazardous one, given the time that the

Germans had to establish strong fortifications on the Atlantic, the strength of their forces, and the superiority that they enjoyed in the air during the first three years of the war. The disastrous British invasion of Dieppe in 1942 testified to the dangers of a cross-channel invasion. General Ismay's testimony at the Moscow Conference clearly spelled out that a premature invasion would probably result in a disaster.

The establishment of firm military cooperation constituted a major achievement. It contributed to the atmosphere of congeniality that dominated the Moscow Conference. The other major ingredient in the cooperative spirit that prevailed came on October 26, when Molotov stated that it was clear that all agreed that the Declaration of the Four Powers must include the creation of what was soon to become known as the United Nations. Molotov asked no questions and proposed that a committee of the powers jointly work out the preliminary questions.[25] This was to be hailed in the United States as a promise that the Soviet Union and Allied democracies could work together.

The congeniality was in part facade. Fear prevailed that the success of the Soviet armies would lead to the establishment of Russian spheres of influence in eastern and central Europe. The draft declaration that Eden submitted to the conference expressed this fear in points 1 and 4. Point 1 read, "That they affirm the people, that each people is free, to choose for itself the form of government and way of life, provided that it respects equally the rights of other people." Point 4 called on the three powers that they "not seek to create any separate areas of responsibility in Europe and will not recognize such for others, but rather affirm their common interest in the well-being as a whole."[26] Eden met such strong opposition that he decided it was necessary to withdraw the proposal to facilitate the work of the conference. When he brought it up a second time, Soviet diplomat Litvinov dismissed it as unnecessary. The Soviet Union, declared Molotov, had no reason to be interested in separate zones or spheres of influence. Eden then stated that he saw no reason to press the point.[27] Molotov's statement stood in direct contradiction to that he had made to the German ambassador in November 1940. The Soviet Union clearly had an interest in establishing spheres of influence.

No clear understanding was reached about the future of liberated countries. It was agreed that during the military operations in any country the power doing the fighting should be in control, but surrender terms should be agreed upon by consultation. There was discussion of a proposal that the three powers "will act together in all matters relating to surrender and disarmament of that other state held by that enemy."[28] This was dropped after Molotov protested that it could be understood as providing for joint occupation. He readily agreed to consultation, a word that was not precise in its meaning that would still allow the Soviets a free hand. Here was a matter of crucial importance.

Eden's efforts to prevent a separate treaty between the Soviet Union and Czechoslovakia also came to naught. He withdrew his proposal after Molotov consented to providing for consultation but objected to giving any power a veto over the decisions of the occupying power.[29]

Months had passed since the surrender of Italy, and yet no Soviet representative was there. When the Soviets had sought a voice in the control of Italy, Churchill had advised the United States, "We cannot be put in the position where our two armies are doing all the fighting but Russians have a veto and must be consulted on any minor variation of the armistice terms which Eisenhower considers militarily essential."[30] That decision was to hold in Italy after the fighting had stopped. Acting Secretary of State Edward R. Stettinius agreed with Churchill.

The three powers likewise failed to come to an agreement that was clear cut and not subject to more than one interpretation on the future determination of frontiers or changes in national boundaries. Hull was satisfied that expansion at the expense of neighboring states and achieved by military means was contrary to the principles of the Four Power Declaration, but he failed to get down to basics. Moreover, his silence at the time these issues were raised appeared as acquiescence to Stalin and Molotov. Harriman, who was present and who discussed the problem with Molotov and Stalin, did not question their sincerity in believing that Hull agreed with them.[31]

The Moscow Conference also failed to come to an agreement on Iran. The western allies favored cooperation on improving conditions in Iran and strengthening its position. Molotov pushed aside the concerns expressed about Iran's weakness. He clearly had no interest in contributing to building up Iran and making it the ward of the three powers.

No one of the three western powers was ready to decide on the future of Germany. The United States presented a skeleton proposal, acknowledged as incomplete, for dividing the country into three parts. Eden supported this and added that Germany should be disarmed. Molotov added in a jocular vein that he would be satisfied with any settlement that left Germany helpless. It was then decided to submit the question to the newly established European Advisory Committee scheduled to meet in London.

Congeniality had prevailed. No one was more impressed with this than Cordell Hull, who placed his faith in the establishment of the world congress. He had somehow convinced himself that there would be no spheres of influence and that questions could be settled by negotiation. It appeared to Hull that there had been an agreement on principles. A younger man, Chip Bohlen, who had spent years in the American embassy in Moscow, firmly believed that Communistic ideology was a governing factor and that Hull's high principles were utterly strange to men who ranked power as the decisive determinant in international relations. The conference, it appeared to Bohlen, had been a success in part because the Russian armies had advanced and in part because the really thorny questions had been avoided.[32] Bohlen perceived what Hull failed to see, that there had been no agreement on the basic question:

The proposals that had been set aside by Molotov at the conference, had they passed, would have limited the free exercise of Soviet power. With their recent successes and bright hopes of victory, the Russians did not want their future actions circumscribed, and in the absence of firm agreements, future settlements would be determined by military successes. In view of the advances of the Russian armies, it was already clear that Russia would dominate eastern Europe.

The Polish exile government immediately attacked the Declaration of the Four Powers. The administration of the occupied territory would be under the control of the Soviet Union. The principles of the Atlantic Charter would be suspended until after the termination of military occupation. The Polish ambassador, Jay Ciechanowski, in Washington, protested that a plebescite after Soviet occupation would remain an empty wish, and with deep emotion he warned, "One cannot hold a plebescite on a cemetery and undoubtedly by that time Poland would have virtually become a cemetery."[33]

Averell Harriman, the new American ambassador to the Soviet Union, in his first dispatch of November 5, 1943, shortly after the Moscow Conference, outlined in detail three major determinants as concerns in future cooperative relations. Harriman warned that it was impossible to overemphasize the importance of a second front in the spring of 1944. Secondly, there was the Polish question, which, he said, was "even tougher than we believed." The Soviets regarded the Polish exile government in London as hostile and they would insist on a "whole hearted friendly neighbor." "They are determined," he asserted, "to have no semblance of the old 'cordon sanitaire' concept in Eastern Europe. Molotov told me that the relations they expect to establish with the border countries did not preclude equally friendly relationships with the British and ourselves. In the Conference, however, it was indicated that although they would keep us informed they would take unilateral action in respect to these countries in the establishment of relations satisfactory to themselves."[34]

The Conference at Teheran began on November 30, 1943. For the first time Roosevelt and Stalin met. The agenda was nonexistent, so that the three leaders felt no restraints as they wandered back and forth over the world's future landscape. One bright light sufficed to push back the shadows that lurked over the future. Agreement was promptly reached on the invasion of western Europe only six months hence. The future was uncertain, but victory was not. It was dependent upon close cooperation between the American and British forces in the west and the vast Soviet armies in the east, and that was agreed to promptly.

Stalin's armies were already well advanced toward east and central Europe. The American forces and the British had yet to cross the Channel. The two democracies also had to acknowledge that the war in Europe was yet to be won, that the military estimated that the war in East Asia would probably last another two years, and that the prospective invasion of Japan would take a half million to a million lives.

None of the three leaders permitted congeniality to obscure the national interests that they represented. Europe was central in their thoughts. Western Europe was a major concern in the minds of the British and the Americans—a Europe like the Europe of the past, where no nation enjoyed hegemony and where the British and the Americans had sustained their economies and the economies of western Europe, and where they were now for a second time putting down the threat of German domination on the continent. Above all they cherished a world of law and order where power rested on financial strength and the influence that went with ability to extend credit, goods, and markets.

Stalin had other thoughts inherited through the history of an isolated and backward Russia, and an ideology that dismissed the fondest ideals and rhetoric of the West as mere camouflage for self-interest. To Stalin, Soviet security and well-being depended on power, and power meant the ability to control and to influence not by economic strength, but by loosening the grasp of western capitalist states over neighboring territories. The Soviet Union was also concerned about its neighbors on the East. The USSR was an Asiatic power sharing a five-thousand-mile border with China. Japan had long been a powerful rival in Manchuria, and the two nations had fought a war in 1905 over who was to dominate. During the turbulent years of the Bolshevik revolution, Japan extended her control over Manchuria and for a time threatened to seize partial hold of Siberia. The two nations engaged in military skirmishes again in the 1930's. Peace between them reigned during the war in Europe thanks to a nonaggression pact signed in April 1941. During the Moscow Conference, Stalin confided to Hull that the USSR would be prepared to enter the war against Japan, once Germany had been defeated.

The British were concerned over their empire in Southeast Asia and hoped to regain control of their former colonies when the war was over. They were equally, if not more, interested in the Mediterranean. Their more immediate objective was victory in Europe. Then, a western Europe that was open to them could shield them from the danger of cross-channel attacks. Their proximity to the continent and their long experience in the international arena made them more willing to strike a compromise including possibly yielding to the Soviet Union on the Baltic States. Their treaties with Poland, and the fact that their loyalty to the Poles was an occasion for declaring war in 1939, added up to an interest in seeking the mildest terms possible for the Poles, but never with any thought of going to war to counter the Soviets.

The United States adhered to the principles of the Atlantic Charter and the creation of a world free of spheres of interest. It supported the settlement of disputes by negotiation, and the freedom of trade. In that world the

United States would hold the upper hand. No possible rival, more particularly the Soviet Union, could compete with American technology, financial strength, and its strong industrial machine. The world of the past met American interests in both security and in the economic sphere.

At Teheran these aspirations were circumscribed by the limits of power. Immediate requirements took precedence over the Wilsonian ideals that were equated with justice, the rights of small nations, and the rule of law. Defeating Germany and Japan remained to be achieved. The western nations confronted their Soviet ally that, in its borderlands, could not be challenged. It was not Roosevelt's policy that was weak; it was his bargaining power. The Soviet Union had lost 20 million citizens, and the country suffered tremendous destruction. It would need assistance after the war, and the United States was the only nation that could offer help. Here was a card for bargaining. Ambassador Averell Harriman was already engaged in lengthy discussions over economic assistance. Harriman placed his faith in the development of cooperation because of the leverage these discussions could give the United States. However, he could not assure the Soviets that assistance on acceptable terms would be available at the close of hostilities. Not once at the Teheran Conference did an offer of economic assistance come into play. Given Soviet distrust, it was most unlikely that it would have been effective. Roosevelt lacked the authority to commit himself to a program With this configuration of power, and the existing difficulties at hand, Roosevelt and Churchill could only appeal to principles, play on the hopes for a peaceful world after the war, and plead for an understanding that would replace western distrust of the Communists with reason and some degree of understanding. The weakness of the United States and Britain was apparent, and Stalin had good reason to believe that they would not challenge him with force.

The settlements reached at Teheran confirmed the agreements already foreshadowed at the Moscow Conference. Once the military agreement was reached on the invasion of western Europe and the British and American support of a strong offensive in the East by Stalin's forces, discussion shifted quickly to postwar questions. The Far East engaged the leaders first. Roosevelt came with the urgent recommendations of the Chiefs of Staff that the Soviet Union could hasten and reduce the cost of the war in East Asia. Stalin was only too ready to accommodate them once Germany had been defeated. Before the war was won in the spring of 1945, General George Marshall regretted the Soviet tentative agreement to enter the war against Japan, but concluded that the Russians would have entered the war in the East anyway.

China, a power vacuum, was a standing invitation to foreign intrusion and exploitation, and had not actively fought a war. Instead, it had focused on the challenge from the Communists. The Japanese intrusion had already been dismissed by Chiang Kai-shek as a disease of the skin, while the Communists endangered the very heart of China. Chiang was content to let the Americans take care of Japan. He exacted a price in loans, one after the other, the latest one for $1 billion after the Teheran Conference. Roosevelt, with his sharp eye for the foibles of the American public, understood that any apparent backsliding in support of China would damage public support of the war. There was the China of corruption and devastating internal divisions, hanging back in the face of the enemy, but Americans were wooed by the myth of a friendly China seeking its way to modernization and looking to the United States for support.

Myths are blessed with the strength to defy facts, and along with the China myth there was the myth of the brave new world that would come after victory. Hull had spread the good news after his return from the Moscow Conference. The approach of victory assured Americans once again that there was no problem they could not solve. American history was a success story that left a deep imprint. Victories at sea and on the battlefield further inflated national self-confidence. President Roosevelt shared these ideals, but within limits.

As at the Moscow Conference, American aims were limited at Teheran. Eastern and central Europe were far away, and there was a striking absence of determination to become involved in that area. Western Europe was another matter, and Stalin made no bids for power there. Consequently, the questions facing the leaders at the Teheran Conference did not involve the whole globe. For all the American talk about a world free of spheres of influence and the right of all peoples to determine their own form of government, Roosevelt did not press for the freedom of the peoples of eastern and central Europe to have the right of self-government free from foreign domination.

It was at a luncheon meeting that the three leaders first discussed the Far Eastern question. Churchill sought to discover Stalin's opinions concerning the recent decisions made at Cairo, where Roosevelt and Chiang had agreed that Formosa should be returned to China and that Korea should be independent. Stalin approved, but added that China should muster her energies and fight harder. After a brief discussion of warm-water ports and the Dardanelles, the president asked Stalin, "What could be done for Russia in the Far East?" Stalin then, in a disarming manner, expressed the view that Russia should have a warm-water port on the Pacific. He pointed out that Vladivostok was only ice-free part of the year. Roosevelt then suggested that creation of a free port farther south would meet the need, and suggested Dairen. Stalin thought there would be objections from China, but Roosevelt saw a way around this by making Dairen a free port under international guarantee.[35]

Unfortunately, the remainder of the discussion was not written into any records that are now available, but Roosevelt later summarized what had been said in a session before the Pacific War Council. What was needed to meet Russian needs seemed innocent enough if one was not familiar with the historical facts. The points raised had been the focus of international rivalries in that part

of the world. Roosevelt reported the plan to which he
thought he had been ready to consent:

> We recounted that (1) Russia having no ice-free port in the
> Far-East, wanted one; and that Stalin looked with favor on
> making Dairen a free port for all the world, with the idea
> that Russian trade could move over the Manchurian railways
> and through this port in bond. (2) Stalin had agreed that the
> Manchurian railways should become the property of the
> Chinese government. (3) Stalin wanted all the other half of
> the Island of Sakhalin and all the Kurile islands for Russia.[36]

This concession was paired with Stalin's statement that
he would enter the war against Japan after the defeat of
Germany. A deal was in the making, but not until the
conference at Yalta was it completed, and then it was
stated in terms that, as Chip Bohlen notes, brought cha-
grin to the president. Talk was not cheap in this instance.

Of all the questions discussed at Teheran none evoked
as strong feelings as the future of Poland. Churchill and
Roosevelt knew only too well of Stalin's utter hatred for
the exile Polish government that had recently ordered the
Polish underground to fight when the Russian armies arrived. They knew too that the Poles had been treated bru-
tally in the interval between the Nazi-Soviet Pact and
Hitler's invasion of the Soviet Union. A century and a
half of denial of the Poles' right to exist as a nation had
nourished Polish nationalism, but now once again it appeared that the Poles' heroic qualities had won them enemies instead of respect. The Poles themselves were not
free of blame since the close of World War I. They had
overreached themselves in fighting with the Russians in
1921 and had incorporated territory beyond the Curzon
Line, territory where Poles were not in a majority. At the
time of Munich they had seized territory that belonged to
Czechoslovakia. But these adventures did not account for
the Polish tragedy. Their fate was sealed by their location
between two powerful neighbors. None of this mattered
to Stalin, who saw Poland as the corridor through which

Russia had been thrice invaded. And now this beleaguered people, ever distrustful of Russia, ruled out revisions of its borders. Nothing the Poles could have offered in the way of a settlement, it appears, would have met Soviet demands.

Neither Churchill nor Roosevelt could assume the role of Don Quixote and spend their precious resources in a lost cause. At Teheran, Herbert Feis notes, Churchill "seems to have appealed to, rather than to have argued with Stalin. He proposed that Stalin resume diplomatic relations with the Polish exile government."[37] Roosevelt thought of the several million Polish-American voters at home and the next election, and excused himself from joining in the discussion, an explanation he made privately to Stalin. It would have been better left unsaid, because in all probability it was understood by Stalin as acquiescence, but the day was to come when he did speak. At Teheran the question was left to Churchill and to Stalin, and nothing could change the aims of Stalin. No decision on Poland was reached.[38]

The real results were not to be recorded in the treaty files, but the discussions produced tentative binding agreements that would be put into written form at Yalta. After the last bomb had been dropped and the Axis powers had surrendered, those decisions were to be labeled as mistakes, but neither Churchill nor Roosevelt chose to see the Teheran Conference as a failure at the time. "Overlord," the military invasion across the channel, was their major consideration. Statesmen have a deep sense of responsibility for interests of their nation and that often calls for unpleasant decisions. But there were also ill forebodings. Chip Bohlen, who was there, wrote a memorandum to Averell Harriman giving his view of the net result.

> Germany is to be broken up. The states of eastern, south-eastern and central Europe will not be permitted to group themselves into federations or association. France is to be stripped of her colonies and strategic bases beyond her bor-

ders and will not be permitted to maintain any appreciable military establishment. Poland and Italy will remain approximately their present territorial size, but it is doubtful if either will be permitted to maintain any appreciable armed force, the result would be that the Soviet Union would be the only important military force on the continent of Europe. The rest of Europe would be reduced to military and political impotence.[39]

Harriman, who was also at Teheran, was not pessimistic. He retained hope that the Allies could achieve a policy of cooperation.

Moscow was in the driver's seat because she had borne the brunt of the fighting. Neither Roosevelt nor Churchill could defy the strength of her military position in eastern Europe without bringing an end to the alliance that was now almost certain to bring about victory.

In October 1944, Churchill visited Moscow and engaged in deliberations in the hope of arriving at agreements that would clear the way for postwar cooperation. He sought answers to such questions as whether Stalin's aims were unlimited, or limited at a given time but likely to expand if new opportunities opened? These questions were left unanswered, and the discussions in Moscow dealt only with the immediate situation.

Reports from Moscow spoke of the exceedingly cordial atmosphere. Stalin appeared to be particularly pleased with Churchill's visit. He was conciliatory toward both Great Britain and the United States. The deputy director of the Office of European Affairs in Washington, H. Freeman Matthews, explained that Stalin's new frankness and friendliness reflected his recognition of the changed situation in the war after the Anglo-American invasion of Europe.[40]

Congeniality could not open the way for a settlement of the Polish question. The two Polish groups hated each other: the Polish government in exile and the Lublin Committee that had been established in Moscow and was now ready to take over in Poland. Efforts were to be made to get them together, and if that failed, then Stalin and Churchill would decide Poland's future. Thus there was no progress on the nature of the future Polish government. Here was the most troublesome question in U.S.-Soviet relations.[41]

During Churchill's visit to Moscow in October 1944, an exceedingly important agreement was worked out in relations to the Balkans, which established separate Soviet and British spheres of influence for the remainder of the war. The division agreed upon accorded with the existing military situation and the interests of the British and the Soviets. In Romania, the Soviet Union was to have 90 percent of control; in Greece, Great Britain was to have 90 percent and Russia 10 percent. Influence in Yugoslavia was to be 50 percent for each, and the same applied to Hungary; and in Bulgaria, Russia was to have 75 percent and the others 25 percent. Harriman, on instructions from Roosevelt sat in on all the discussions. The phrase "spheres of influence" had been used at first, but had been omitted later upon the suggestion of Stalin. Harriman immediately proposed that the larger postwar settlement should be decided by Stalin, Churchill, and Roosevelt after the war. On receiving information of the agreement, Roosevelt did not disapprove and expressed the opinion that it was necessary to make arrangements that would prevent future wars.

The United States chose not to approve or disapprove. The only interest of the United States, according to a memorandum drawn up by Edward H. Stettinius, the under secretary of state, was adherence in any settlement to the principles of the right of people to choose and maintain "for themselves without outside interference the type of political, social, and economic systems they desire"; equality of opportunity as against "the setting up of a policy of exclusion, in commerce, transit and trade; and freedom to negotiate, either through government agencies or private enterprise, irrespective of the type of economic system in operation."[42] Territorial settlements should be left until the end of the war.

Before the Moscow conference ever took place, Roosevelt's special assistant, Harry Hopkins, and Charles Bohlen were alarmed because it appeared that Roosevelt was ready to wash his hands of eastern Europe and had no objections to the creation of spheres of interest. Harriman learned of the projected spheres during the course of the Churchill-Stalin conversations and immediately cabled Roosevelt. When Bohlen learned of the agreement, he was infuriated.[43] Harriman, too, was strongly opposed, as he saw the Russians intent on setting up puppet governments in eastern Europe.[44]

Since there was by now great concern for the future of eastern and central Europe, this United States response was tantamount, in the eyes of the Soviets, to acquiescence, because the agreement would make it inevitable that the power with the most authority would have the upper hand whenever a final settlement was reached. Roosevelt, who was of the view that American troops would not be in Europe for more than two years after the close of the war, appears not to have been overly concerned. Harriman had already expressed concern over failure to take a clear-cut position. In a long cable to the secretary of state on September 20, 1944, the ambassador responded to an inquiry whether the Soviet government had reversed its position and was no longer ready to be cooperative. "I do not believe," Harriman stated, "that Stalin and the Kremlin have determined to reverse their policy of cooperation decided upon by them at Moscow and Teheran."[45] Harriman said that it was difficult for the United States to understand precisely their concept of the agreement that had been reached in Moscow and Teheran. Molotov had stated several times that he considered "that after they had put us on notice of a Soviet policy or plan and we did not at the same time object, we had acquiesced in and accepted the Soviet position."[46] Harriman thought that the Soviets believed that the United States representatives had accepted their plan for the future. They would keep the Allies informed, but they also reserved the right to settle their problems with their western neighbors unilaterally. Difficulty also arose over the meaning of such a term as "friendly governments."[47] In Poland they were insisting on a hand-picked government. In Czechoslovakia, where conditions were more stable, they were satisfied to give assurance that they would not interfere in internal affairs, but, in fact, limited that independence.

As Harriman saw it, the Allies, in effect, had agreed to give Russia a free hand. In his cable, Harriman did not suggest that the Soviets were distorting agreements reached, and we may assume that Harriman believed that Molotov believed that the Americans and British had agreed to giving the Soviet government freedom to decide the future of eastern and central Europe.

Having so stated, Harriman came to the central question: the possible dangers in giving at least tacit approval to the Soviet policy. He acknowledged that American interests need not be concerned over the affairs in this area, but he feared that "when a country begins to extend its influence by strong arm methods beyond its borders under the guise of security, it is difficult to see how a line can be drawn." There was likewise, Harriman thought, the basic issue of what constituted a "friendly government."[48]

Recent experience led the ambassador to ask how the United States could best counter Soviet interference in the internal affairs of another country. "If we give them a free hand with any one country," he thought, "then a precedent would be established." It appeared wiser to pursue a policy of concern. It might be possible "to temper Soviet domination in each situation and I believe we have a chance to lead them to a behavior in international affairs that is compatible with our own concepts." He concluded, "Whenever we find that Soviet behavior offends our standards we should call it forcibly to the attention of the Soviet government." He observed, "I recognize that this will lead to unpleasant situations but for reasons I will explain later I am satisfied that the Soviets will accede at last to a reasonable degree to our insistent demands."[49] He was prepared to counter what he expected to be unilateral Soviet actions in Romania and Bulgaria.

Why then did Harriman believe this proposed policy would be successful? At the close of the same cable he gave his answer. It was his conviction "that Stalin and his principal advisers placed the greatest importance and reliance on the newly won relationship with the British and ourselves and desire above all else to take a leading role in international affairs." The Soviets, he thought, were fearful of the antagonism of the world against them. They were conscious that they were a backward country, but they now took great pride in the strength of the Red Army. Harriman thought they were realists and knew what they wanted. "I believe the time has come," he wrote, "to develop a more positive policy toward them than has been possible up to now." We should be firm, but we should also be sensitive, "meet them much more than half way, encourage and support them wherever we can, and yet oppose them promptly with the greatest of firmness where we see them going wrong."[50] After a residence of ten months in Moscow and close dealings with Stalin and Molotov, Harriman held the view that the overwhelming number of the Russian people and the principal men in government were friendly. He was prepared to institute his new policy.

Harriman's turnabout marks the beginning of what was to evolve into the cold-war policy. It was drafted not long before the Yalta Conference met in February 1945. The conference opened with a discussion of military matters. The Americans and the British had already reached agreement on strategy in preliminary meetings in Malta. At Yalta there was complete agreement among the three leaders about the need for a synchronized final attack on Germany. The Germans had been driven back, but they continued to put up fierce resistance. There was no dissension about the future military operations in Europe.

The second major task was to work out a strategy for defeating the Japanese. All three parties expected the Japanese to put up a tough fight. The American military leaders envisioned that probably half a million lives would be lost in the projected invasion of Japan. The Joint Chiefs of Staff were anxious for the Russians to enter the war and to engage the large Japanese armies in Manchuria. The Soviets set a price on their cooperation, and that included the return of Sakhalin to Russia, the transfer of the Kurile Islands, and "preeminent" rights to the seaport of Dairen, and control of the South Manchurian Railway. According to Bohlen, Roosevelt's expression became somber on hearing the Russian demands.[51] All this was to be done without informing the Chinese, because they could not be trusted to keep a secret, and the Soviet leaders were anxious that Japan not learn of the plan. Again, the agreement contained words that had no clear definition. The word "paramount" was to give the Soviets a basis for claiming that it had been agreed that they were to be in control of Dairen and the railway. There had been another slip. The Americans present were not well versed in the provisions of the Treaty of Portsmouth and therefore accepted as a fact that the Kurile Islands had belonged to Russia before 1905, which they had not. To seek Soviet entry into the war was legitimate. The American generals present had been told that an atomic bomb would be ready by August, but there was no certainty at the time about the planned trial at Los Alamos. The secrecy at the expense of China was to mark the entire Yalta series of agreements with a stain of dishonor.

Poland remained a divisive issue at Yalta. No agreement had been reached on the boundary question or the makeup of the Warsaw government, and the future boundaries received first attention. Churchill had already agreed to the Curzon Line. Roosevelt sought to leave Poland an oil region just east of the line, but he gave way in the face of Churchill and Stalin. The western boundary offered a more difficult question. Stalin proposed that the boundary be set at the more westerly of the two Neisse rivers. Churchill pointed out that setting it even as far west as the Oder would require that some 6 million Germans evacuate lands that they had occupied for centuries. He was not opposed to compensating Poland for the loss of territory in the east, but this extension raised not only a moral question but also the point that there was no need to stuff the Polish "goose so full of German food that it got indigestion."

Roosevelt disliked extending the Polish boundary beyond the Oder and was wary of any settlement. He proposed that the communiqúe state no more than that drawing the eastern boundary at the Curzon Line was acceptable. There appeared to be little justification for setting the western boundary beyond the Oder. Roosevelt for a time proposed that nothing be said about boundaries in the communiqúe. What was on the president's mind is uncertain, but he did say that he had no authority to settle the issue. The Soviets did not have their way.[52] The final agreement stated no more than that the western boundary should be decided at the peace conference, but Charles Bohlen, who was present, states that Churchill and Stalin had virtually agreed on the Oder-Neisse line.[53]

Reaching an agreement on the nature of the future Polish government was infinitely more difficult. The existing government in Warsaw was an extension of the Lublin Committee, which had been set up by the Soviets and was composed of Communists. The Polish exile government was obsessed with utter distrust of Russia, and with good reason. Between them was a raging sea of acrimony. The Soviets knew only too well that the Polish government in London represented a people who had suffered the most extreme terrorism. The assassination of ten thousand Polish officers at Katyn by the Russians and the exportation of a million or more Polish soldiers to Siberia were established facts. On the other hand, the Soviets remembered how the Poles had taken territory east of the Curzon Line by force in 1921 and had incorporated into Poland an area inhabited by as large or even larger numbers of Russians. The Polish underground had fought ferociously against the Soviet takeover after the

Nazi-Soviet Pact. When the Russian armies once again marched into Poland in 1944, the Poles fought fiercely against them.

What the Soviet leaders wanted and what Churchill and Roosevelt aimed at establishing could never be reconciled. The two western statesmen called for the establishment of a government representative of all parties and early elections. The result was an ambiguous agreement that the Lublin government should be reorganized on a broader democratic basis. Given the occupation of Poland by the Soviet armies and the indefinite language of the agreement, it was tantamount to acquiescence in granting the existing Communist Lublin government a free hand. As Churchill was to say at the close of the conference, "This was the best I could get." Roosevelt made a separate appeal to Stalin in which he deplored the effect that a failure to reach an agreement might have on American public opinion.[54] Bohlen saw in the agreement reached on Poland "the shabbiest sort of equivocation."[55]

The final agreement reached at Yalta applied to Germany. The division of Germany into zones of occupation drafted by the European Advisory Committee was approved. The western Allies gained Soviet acceptance of a zone for France and a full place for France on the Allied Control Council that was to administer the zones along lines that were agreed upon. The inclusion of France and the granting to her a voice in the control of Germany was an important gain. Stalin had raised objections, but finally agreed. To some observers the imminent danger of a final defeat on the Polish question was counterbalanced by the alignment of France on the side of the democracies.

The decision at Yalta directly reflected the configuration of existing military power. The vast Soviet armies that far outnumbered the armies of the western Allies and were already in possession of eastern and central Europe were the final determinants. On his way home, Admiral William Leahy observed to the president that the Russians could stretch the agreements and establish complete Soviet hegemony in Europe. Roosevelt did not question this evaluation and could only observe that it was the best he could do.

Prior to the conference, the Department of State had drafted the Declaration on Liberated Europe providing for consultation among the three major powers regarding the developments in the liberated countries and the establishment of broadly democratic governments. Stalin had no objections, but he sought to amend the Declaration to provide support to the people in those countries who had taken the lead in opposing the Nazis, and these were predominantly Communists. When Churchill and Roosevelt opposed this, Stalin withdrew his proposal. Faced with the fact that in the years ahead the Soviet authorities would exercise complete control, the Americans fell back on the Declaration on Liberated Europe. This approach to the problems that arose was futile, but they had no option other than accepting an inevitable Russian sphere of influence.

The Polish question is not one to be dismissed with a simple narrative of events. It has become a major issue for revisionist historians. Gabriel and Joyce Kolko, in their study *The Politics of War* offer a provocative interpretation. The Polish government in London had dreams of becoming a great power, and it was inflexible in its demands, believing that the United States would sooner or later redeem it. The Kolkos suggest that the positions taken by the United States strengthened the Poles' hopes and their inflexibility. Insistence that there should be no territorial settlements until peace had been restored contributed to this. Both Hull and the president were at times impatient with the Poles, but they failed to exert their power to bring about a reasonable settlement, not because of admiration of the leaders in the Polish government in London, but, according to the Kolkos, because they saw Poland as the centerpiece in the broader program of preventing Soviet expansion in eastern and central Europe.[56]

The United States's opposition to Soviet controls in eastern Europe, the Kolkos state, was basically rooted in its economic interests in trade and investment. The reparations question also entered in, because though investments in that part of the world were small, freedom to trade was a matter of principle. The restoration of international trade after the war was always on the mind of Cordell Hull, who had long been the champion of the Open Door policy. As the Kolkos see it, American policy narrows down to the promotion of American economic interests.[57] Would that the problem were so simple.

Foreign policy inevitably includes economic considerations, but these did not have a monopoly during World War II. Furthermore, the Polish question was in several ways a question by itself, and it involved much more than economic interests. It did become the focus of public attention, and the Polish embassy in Washington and Polish spokesmen in the United States promoted it to the headlines and later helped make it a most important part in the postwar criticism of the Soviet Union. In 1943 and 1944, Roosevelt and Hull looked on this development in domestic politics with great alarm.

No final decision on Germany was reached at Yalta other than the decision to implement the recommendations of the European Advisory Committee that had been meeting in London. The British seized the initiative on the zones to be occupied by the three victorious powers. Thanks to Roosevelt's argument with the British over whether the northwest zone should be British or American and his failure to give the American ambassador, John Gilbert Winant, a member of the European Advisory Committee, directions, for which Winant had pleaded, Winant had no influence. The Soviets, having been awarded a very large part for occupation, went along. The committee drafted plans for the Allied Control Council to adjudicate all matters that were national rather than local, but these plans eventually would fail due to the French insistence that Germany must be kept weak.

In the years ahead the Yalta Conference was to be denounced as a bundle of tragic errors revolving around failure to protect British and American interests. Much of this criticism constitutes oversimplification and fails to acknowledge that wartime military strategy resulted in the Soviet Union having the upper hand. There was no practical strategy that could have prevented Russian dominance in East and Central Europe.[58] A respected historian has pointed out that Stalin too could have said, as did Churchill, that the outcome "was the best I could get." He had failed to achieve his primary goals concerning Germany and the reparations settlement he so desperately wanted. Vojtech Mastny, the historian, writes:

> Measured by achievements, Yalta was, despite its later notoriety, the least important of the Allied chiefs' wartime gatherings. No "partition of the world" (as the title of a popular book would have it) was decided there. In all probability "the map of Europe would look very much the same if there had never been the Yalta conference at all." Yalta was certainly not a glorious occasion for Western statesmanship, but neither was it in any tangible way "Stalin's greatest victory." If it stands out as a landmark, this is because of the precipitous breakdown that soon followed, a shock to all its participants.[59]

Adam B. Ulam has placed the Yalta Conference in proper historical perspective. "The essential fact about the Yalta conference," he has written, "is that with victory by now certain and foreseeable in the very near future insofar as Germany was concerned, it represented a perfectly natural process of bargaining among three great allies as to their influence in shaping the postwar world."[60] Each had its strength and weaknesses. Each of the participants sought a settlement that would avoid war for a long time to come. The United States placed its hopes on the founding of the United Nations. Germany's future was not decided. That was to become the major issue in the postwar world.

8

Emergence of the Cold War
1945–1947

THERE is no one broad generalization that explains its coming, but placed in historical perspective, the cold war was not a surprise. The divisions came to the fore over spheres of influence. No balance-of-power order was in place to moderate the fears and the rivalries that were present. On opposite sides of the barriers were two radically different societies, one democratic, operating under a free enterprise system, and the other a society dominated both politically and economically by a highly centralized state. Both were relatively recent in the system of international relations that had been dominated by the nations of western Europe. The United States had isolated itself from the struggles in Europe except in the years 1914 to 1919. It had become an economic giant, the banker of the world, with a closely guarded sphere of interest in the Caribbean and Central America. The Soviet Union, long a backward nation, had become a major industrial power in the 1940's, surpassing Germany in its production by 1943. Ideology and experience had inculcated a deep distrust of capitalist society. Intervention during the Communist Revolution and the refusal of the western powers to accept Russia as a partner during Hitler's rise to power, the Spanish Civil War, and the Munich crisis of 1938, promoted the distrust so that the Soviet nation was viewed as an outcast. Only the highly successful diplomacy of the United States had managed to unite the forces of these two giant colossi and bring about the defeat of Germany. Victory in the war, however, removed the linchpin that tied them together. In the future, with the coming of the nuclear age, there was no prospect of friendship and each had to learn that only if they could live together could human society survive.

A major change took place in Washington after the death of Roosevelt. Whereas the wartime president preferred to play down the conflict between American and Soviet aims and found ways to permit the Soviets to save face publicly, Harry Truman was blunt and did not seek to minimize possible confrontations. We cannot know whether Roosevelt too might have been more direct than he had been during the war. In private conversations he had used strong language during the last few days of his life, indicating that it was hard to do business with the Russians.

While Truman was blunt, he had no intention of giving up Roosevelt's policy of seeking conciliation. The end of the fighting left the new administration facing a welter of problems. The war with Japan had yet to be won, Communists were on the way to power in China and there was the possibility of a civil war in that country. There was debate over the approach to be taken in the forthcoming Potsdam Conference. Whether there existed a possibility of establishing cooperative relations with the Soviet Union, now that the war was over, remained an open question. There were those like James C. Dunn, chairman of the State-War-Navy Coordinating Committee, who, after a discussion of possible Russian objectives, advised: "Furthermore in estimating Russian intentions, we should give full weight to the fact that she is war-weary, over-extended by her great efforts and in the need of years to reestablish her economy, consolidate her gains and recoup her losses, a process in which she requires the substantial support and assistance of the United States."[1] There were others, like Joseph Grew and Loy Henderson of the Near Eastern Division of the Department of State, who were convinced that the time had come for firmness. No one was more convinced of this need than Averill Harriman, the ambassador to the Soviet Union. He rushed home on learning of Roosevelt's death and sounded a note of alarm in the president's office to cabinet members and to the press. Harriman continued to believe that meeting the Soviets with firmness would bring them around to a cooperative attitude. President Truman readily agreed, but he was not ready to abandon Roosevelt's efforts to resolve the issues to be faced. The former senator and leading figure in the Roosevelt administration, Secretary of State James Byrnes, had faith in the art of compromise that distinguished American political life and he was ready to pursue the same course with the Russians.

The immediate question facing these leaders was the Soviet takeover of eastern and central Europe during the course of the war. There was little expectation that the Russians could be induced to relax their monopoly of authority over the Allied Control Councils in Poland, Hungary, Bulgaria, and Romania, but the United States was still not ready to accept a sphere of Soviet influence. Ambassador Harriman concluded that there was little hope of dislodging the Soviets. In Moscow, George Kennan, chargé in the embassy and career diplomat, had confided to his former colleague in the embassy, Charles Bohlen, now a representative of the State Department in the White House, that the Soviet sphere of influence was a fact and that, since it could not be changed, it appeared to be the wiser course to accept it. Walter Lippmann, a well-known columnist and author, deplored making an issue of the Soviet spheres in eastern Europe. Lippman's basic maxim in the making of foreign policy was never to extend your responsibilities beyond the power you had to carry out those responsibilities. He feared that challenging the Soviet Union within its now-established sphere would lead to a war that the United States could not win.

Truman and Byrnes accepted that the United States could not dislodge the Russians, but at the Potsdam Conference in July 1945, and again at the London Foreign Ministers Conference in September 1945, they claimed that the agreements that had been reached provided that the United States should have a role in establishing new regimes in both Poland and Romania. In both instances they were met by firm denials. The rebuffs at the London conference signalled that negotiations offered no hope of the Russians granting any significant concessions.

Why did the United States pursue the fight against the Russian sphere of influence in eastern Europe? As Harriman had stated in 1943, a nation of great power embarked on a course of expansionism must be met with resolve because there was great danger that the nation would expand further where it had no legitimate security reasons for taking over. This was the fear that dominated Truman's associates in the field of foreign affairs. There was also a political consideration, one that Charles Bohlen made explicit in his reply when Kennan had asked, Why not accept the fact of Russian control? Bohlen disagreed. He stated: "To me the acceptance of a Soviet sphere, instead of relieving us of responsibility, would compound the felony. Any formal, or even an informal, attempt to give the Soviet Union a sphere of influence in Eastern Europe would, as soon as the agreement became known, have brought a loud and effective outcry from our Poles and Czechs."[2] Here was a matter that the politicians who sought election could not afford to ignore. It had been a concern to President Roosevelt, the master of American politics, and after the Russians marched westward in 1943, he was rightfully worried that immigrants in America would protest so vigorously that they would endanger any alliance with the Soviet Union.

Equally important, Soviet actions ran counter to the American commitment to the people's right to govern themselves, a precept which had its roots in the political principles of the founding fathers and in the long-standing anticolonialism of the United States. Annexation of the Philippines obviously contradicted this principle, but the American government had already promised them their independence. The principle had most recently occupied a prominent place in the thinking of Franklin Roosevelt, who favored independence for India and French Indo-China.

Western Europe ranked first in the thinking of the foreign-policy establishment in Washington. Society at home and throughout western Europe was the product of three hundred years of common history. Political principles, the role of religion, and the reverence for law were part of a common heritage.

Stalin had not at any time during the war given any indication that his ambitions extended to western Europe with the single exception of Germany, and as Charles Bohlen observed, it appeared that the Soviet Union had no set plan about what should be done there, aside from destroying Germany's capacity to make war once again. Nevertheless, the fate of western Europe remained to be decided.

In 1945 there was a scene of economic catastrophe and political uncertainty in every section of Europe. The United States had gone to war twice to prevent Germany hegemony, because a balance of power in that part of the world was seen as a vital interest. Now western Europe was wholly unable to defend itself should there be a threat. With Europe's potential industrial power, her strategic location, and the traditional ties to the United States, there was fear that both Communist ideology and power considerations could result in a Soviet effort to win control. Economic ties were of major importance to the United States and went hand in hand with the other considerations that gave western Europe the highest priority in American foreign policy. Should Soviet hegemony in the East be confronted with a defenseless, economically bankrupt western Europe, there might well be danger of Soviet intrigue.

No American government could be a party to the establishment of Soviet control in eastern and central Europe, but it was also accepted that the United States could not change what had taken place there. The United States would protest, now that the war was over, if for no other reason than domestic politics, but the central issue in 1945 and 1946 was not the Russian sphere of influence in eastern Europe. The issue was the prevention of further

Soviet expansion. In light of the aggressiveness of the Soviet government in both Poland and Romania and its success in that part of the world, it appeared unlikely that Russia would not move into other areas if opportunities presented themselves, where a virtual power vacuum lay open for exploitation.

The word "containment" had not yet come into everyday use, but it was exactly what was in the minds of associates such as Dean Acheson, assistant secretary of state in 1945, Harriman, and Kennan. It was an elusive word, one that could be stretched like a rubber band to meet the requirements of the speaker. In the American view, holding back the Russians was a defensive measure. In the eyes of the Russians it meant imperialist encirclement, a fear nourished by their experience since 1917, and further by the Soviet political ideology.

Nations, like individuals, are influenced by feelings of pride, fear, suspicion, and trust. In this case the wartime alliance had brought victory but had failed to produce mutual trust. Its absence stemmed from the first days of peace. From the American point of view, neither at Yalta nor at Potsdam was there any evidence of a spirit of give and take. The situation in Poland aroused the strongest feelings. Churchill and Roosevelt agreed to the Curzon Line as Poland's eastern border, but decisions over the western border and the nature of government to be established in Poland caused such sharp differences that communications quickly broke down. At Yalta, Churchill and Roosevelt held firmly to the view that Poland was entitled to a multiparty government, but Stalin was uncompromising on making the all-Communist Lublin committee the controlling force. He agreed to broadening the government by including representatives of other parties, but insisted that real power must rest with the Soviet-sponsored Lublin group. Churchill and Roosevelt insisted that the USSR agree to free elections. After lengthy discussion of the makeup of the government that would immediately take control, with no prospect of agreement, Roosevelt asked how long this government was to be in power before holding elections. Stalin thought elections could take place within a month. If this was so, then the temporary arrangement was less important, and Roosevelt yielded without securing a firm commitment about representation of all parties in the temporary Polish administration. In the approaching election the Polish people supposedly would be free to choose their own representatives. The Soviet Union did make a commitment to holding a free election, but no election ever took place. Neither the Russian nor the Polish Communists were about to hold an election they were certain to lose.

The Potsdam Conference in July 1945 listed an agenda that not only was long but included matters of great complexity. Agreements were reached that were the product of reluctant cooperation and a desire not to break up the conference because that would lead to a dangerous and futile confrontation. Stalin went along with Truman's proposal that the peace treaties be drawn by the Council of Foreign Ministers. The major point at issue, however, was the complete dominance of the Allied Control Councils in Romania and Bulgaria by the Soviets. Allied protests brought no change. The Soviet Union and the acting government had already entered into a treaty about Poland. Disagreement concerning the western boundary of Poland offered a demonstration of how little role reason would play compared to power. Stalin insisted on compensating Poland by extending her boundaries deep into East Prussia, where he would find the most fertile lands and the area of greatest agricultural productivity. Six million Germans had once lived in the area; two million remained, though most had fled to the West. Uprooting this immense population was not only cruel, but also assured that the food production of their area would now go eastward instead of to the American and British zones of occupation. The American and British zones would be flooded with refugees from the East and be a burden to the Americans and the British who would have to feed them. Stalin saw no need to be concerned about the Germans who had acted ruthlessly and engulfed the world in war, and he held one trump card. It was arranged to have representatives of the Polish government come to Potsdam and testify. Among them was Mikolajczyk, former head of the Polish exile government in London and now a member of the new Polish cabinet. He readily cooperated with Stalin and Molotov and argued that a larger Poland and a weaker Germany would contribute to peace. Both Truman and Churchill were bitter, but powerless to rescue the Poles.

Despite lengthy arguments concerning reparations, on this issue an agreement was reached. Truman and Churchill were on firmer ground, for their troops occupied a large part of Germany. They had no success on loosening the Russian hold over Bulgaria and Romania, where their representatives were reduced to spectators as those new governments were firmly subordinated to the Soviet Union. Amidst the rejoicing over the end of hostilities, the scene at Potsdam was not only bleak, but demonstrated that it is sometimes more difficult for the victors to arrange a peace among themselves than it is to make peace with the defeated.

Nothing in the welter of changes and conflicts facing the world at the close of World War II approached in significance the presence of the atomic bomb. This development not only changed methods of diplomacy but ushered in the nuclear age, in which human beings had to live with the chilling knowledge that an entire people could be destroyed in a few seconds. Never in human history had our future appeared so uncertain. A weapon had come into being that changed the nature of warfare.

Those few in the decision-making process in Washington were fully aware not only of the destruction that could be wrought but also that the presence of the bomb would radically alter international relations. They believed that, depending on how and where the bomb was dropped, it would carry its own message to the enemy and to the world. The Target Committee, assigned responsibility for deciding where it should be dropped, agreed that, to have its full effect, it must be dropped in a place where there was less danger of the weapon being lost and that the area should also be large and densely populated. Thus the Japanese would be shocked so that they would make peace, and the entire world would grasp the bomb's importance.[3]

The war spirit, so callous of human life, nourished by almost four years of gruesome destruction, had hardened decision makers. The Pacific War was yet to be won, and after much heart searching, it had been decided that an invasion of Japan would be necessary. Estimates of American casualties ranged from a half million to a million men. There were in Japan those who had long favored peace, but there was also the more-powerful military, who insisted on continuing the war. This faction held that an American invasion offered the opportunity to defeat the Americans.

On August 5, 1945, the bomb was dropped on Hiroshima, destroying the city and killing over one hundred thousand. Thousands of others were maimed for life. The devastation enabled the advocates of peace in Japan to make the first moves to arrange a peace. On the same day that the bomb was dropped, the Soviet invasion of Manchuria strengthened their resolve. Two weeks later a second bomb was dropped on Nagasaki with equally devastating destruction.

It has been suggested that the atom bombs were used to impress the Russians. This is not correct, but after the Potsdam Conference in early July, the American delegates lost hope of a friendly settlement with the Soviet Union,[4] and Secretary of War Stimson reversed his stand on international control of atomic energy.[5] The Soviet Union, he concluded, was a police state and therefore could not be trusted.

President Truman and Secretary of State Byrnes were well aware that the United States could not dislodge the Russians from eastern Europe by force. The Soviet Union's aggressiveness was supported by a superiority in armed forces in that part of the world. The first success of the bomb in the test explosion at Los Alamos appeared to strengthen the diplomatic position of the United States, and the president exhibited a new sense of confidence. That the bomb could be used as a diplomatic weapon against the Soviet Union was an idea that was promptly dismissed. When Byrnes met Molotov in London in September 1945, it became clear that possession of the bomb had not given the United States the upper hand.

The major figure in the formulation of foreign policy after the end of the war was Dean Acheson, whose mind functioned like an efficient computer; and his ability and readiness to counter those who stood in his way sufficed to intimidate those who disagreed. Here was a brilliant man with power.

When in November 1939, Acheson addressed an audience at Yale on foreign policy, he offered an explanation about the forces that had brought the world to the situation it was now in, suggesting that economic changes had brought severe depression and desperate people sought to remedy their difficulties by establishing totalitarian governments and war. The world was on the edge of a complete breakdown of all order. How then could this course of deterioration be reversed? The United States, the most powerful of nations, must do everything within its power to strengthen those weak nations that now faced disaster. Markets for their goods must be opened to them in the United States. The weight of loans due since World War I must be removed so as to encourage the economies of Great Britain and France. The United States must offer at once a program of preparedness. The democracies in western Europe must be provided with all possible help in the way of armaments so that a sense of security could be restored and defeatism replaced with confidence. It was western Europe that was at the heart of Acheson's thinking.[6]

Six years later, the same line of thought determined Acheson's response to the postwar scene. Only if western Europe recovered from the horrible conditions it faced—

food shortages, unemployment, and general economic collapse—could some degree of order and stability be restored to the world. Otherwise, the dismal and desperate conditions in Europe would continue and would inevitably lead to a reaching out for radical solutions. The United States alone could restore a private-enterprise economy and self-government in western Europe.

In his letters and conversations during the course of 1945, Acheson never raised a fear that the Soviet Union would launch a war. In private conversations in 1953, as Acheson was looking back on his years as secretary of state, he said to friends that neither side wanted a general war. He went even further and stated that both sides faced the same problem. Each sought to defend its interests, each sought not to lose face by backing down, and each wondered how to resolve that most important of all questions for both the western Allies and the Soviet Union, the German problem.[7]

Acheson had no sympathy with extremists at home who, in the grip of emotion, substituted denunciation of a moderate course for cold analysis of the problem. He was convinced that nothing was to be gained by dwelling on difficulties in a cynical manner nor by an idealism that was based on dreams at the cost of facts. There had developed antithetical attitudes that were divisive. Acheson wrote: "One is the hard-boiled or cynical attitude. Its advocates, it has been said, are desperately absorbed in the attempt to keep out of the last war. Opposed to this is the Pilgrims Progress attitude in which some nation, often our own, is cast as a valiant struggling with a myriad national embodiments of original sin."[8]

Acheson liked to quote a man he greatly admired, Justice Oliver Wendell Holmes, Jr., who had said:

> I confess that altruistic and cynically selfish talk seems to me about equally unreal. With all humility, I think "whatsoever thy hand findeth to do, do it with thy might" infinitely more important than the vain attempt to love thy neighbor as thyself. If you want to hit a bird on the wing, you must have all your will in focus, you must not be thinking

about yourself, and, equally, you must not be thinking about your neighbor: you must be living in your eye on that bird.[9]

Acheson had to keep his eye on more than one bird: his associates, Harriman, James Vincent Forrestal, Truman; and Congress. His position called for infinite patience with men less disciplined than himself. The American scene was as important in shaping policy as the European scene.

Abba Eban, the Israeli prime minister, a man with many of Acheson's attributes of self-discipline, tells of his first meeting with the statesman:

> He was a complex and subtle figure. His outer elegance, a little too careful and refined, was the reflection of a precise intellect rather than a dandified pose. He was intolerant of excess in rhetoric or emotion. He liked everything to be in balance and the lowest audible key. Perhaps he attached excessive weight to reason as a determining factor in the life of mankind. He sought shelter from the gusts of sentiment, passion and prejudices by pretending that they were not blowing at all, or alternatively, that they would soon subside.[10]

There were other aspects of Acheson's character that played a part in his response to the disarray in the world order. He despised weakness in the face of danger. He accepted that the course he chose might bring unforeseen dangers, developments that would come as a surprise. No one was more aware of fortuitous happenings and the vicissitudes of chance that upset the best-laid plans. In a speech in 1948, Acheson warned that "There is no formula which will remove the difficulties which confront us. Dangers and crises are with us not because the right policy or the right action eludes us, but from the very nature of the situation we face." Much would depend on the course pursued by the Soviet Union. There were dangers ahead, and one of those dangers was war. To this he added the significant warning: "No one can say that the danger of war is precluded, since the decision is not in our hands. But this danger must not make us flinch or waiver in dealing with the problem, whatever it may be, in a careful but forthright and determined way. To say, as some appear to do, that no course is possible unless it precludes the possibility of war is to assure war and invite disaster."[11]

Historians are left with no more than circumstantial evidence about Stalin's plans at the close of the Second World War; however, it appears that we can assert that nothing less than control of the border states was his goal. He had demonstrated that he was firmly committed to this course in 1939 and 1940 during the Nazi-Soviet Pact, and he had adhered to that goal all during the war. Only in Hungary did he permit the establishment of a freely elected government, and even there the established government was at the mercy of a small minority of Communists who had the support of Russian military authorities who were present.

In the 1930's Stalin, anticipating war and the hardships it would bring that could lead to the breakdown of his rule, carried out purge trials and massive assassinations, eliminating generals and lower-rank officers who might exploit military setbacks to overthrow his regime. At the same time he promoted the building of an industrial empire. At the close of the war, faced with a ruined economy and difficulties that would demand ever-greater stringency, which could lead to new challenges to his government, he feared internal revolts. Faced with this threat, he carried out a ruthless suppression of dissent and of all traces of sympathy with western ideals.

Stalin remembered all too well how the disruptions accompanying the disasters of the First World War had enabled a small minority to bring about the overthrow of the old order. The conditions he now faced portended the same danger. The fertile and productive lands where vast armies had fought were now wasteland. Farm laborers had been drafted into the armed forces, and many had no wish to return. Both machinery and fertilizer were in short supply. The production of wheat declined 25 percent after 1940. Peasants, having faced starvation during the war as their produce was transported to the armies, were not ready to face a continuation of austerity after the war.[12]

The new ranks of military heroes could, Stalin feared, become leaders of opposition to his rigid rule. Stalin's solution was to demote them and send them to remote stations in the provinces. The most famous of these was Marshal Zhukov, who had commanded the forces in the Berlin sector. Zhukov was transferred to a distant provincial command.[13]

Confronting possible challenges to his regime, Stalin aroused fears that Russia was surrounded by the treacherous enemies in the West and promoted panicky fears that the greedy capitalist imperialists were aiming to encircle the country. Given such a danger, internal unity was essential and further sacrifices were necessary. The greater the dangers of the capitalist enemies, the greater the justification for stringency at home.

The internal situation accounts, in part, for the shift in Soviet foreign policy in 1945. The demands of Molotov at the London Conference of Foreign Ministers marked the change. He demanded a Soviet trusteeship over Tripolitania, the Italian colony in Africa; equal participation with the United States in the occupation of Japan; and bases in the Mediterranean. The same spirit of boldness was exhibited in Romania and Bulgaria. A belligerent speech by Stalin the following February widened the breach between East and West.

Shifting public attention from internal difficulties at home to dangers abroad is an ancient strategy. Also important in promoting the shift in foreign policy was the way the Soviets viewed what was taking place in the West. Their understanding was colored by the long-term distrust of capitalist states fostered by communist ideology and by experience. To the Soviets, American support for the United Nations appeared unrealistic. No international organization would be strong enough to hold in check a drive by powerful states, and could not possibly assure Russia of security. The American insistence that France and China have a voice in decision making was seen by the Soviets as nothing more than the United States' lining up votes against the Soviet Union. What right had these two nations, both weak and defeated, to participate with the Big Three in decision making? Likewise, the American effort to defend the rights of small states impressed the Soviets as an effort to consolidate the West and encircle the Soviet Union.[14]

Stalin did not have a master plan for world conquest. Time and again during the last days of the war, Averill Harriman had testified that Stalin and Molotov wished for peace and hoped to establish a degree of cooperation with the Allies. Firmness, Harriman thought, would alter the Soviet course. There were other reasons to question the dark forebodings. At the close of hostilities Stalin had yet to indicate that he had plans to intervene in western Europe. He ordered various national Communist parties not to foment revolutions. Palmiro Togliatti, leader of the Italian Communists, was instructed to work for a coalition government, which he did. Stalin pursued the same course in France. He did not stipulate that the major offices be given to Communists. He acted cautiously in Austria, and he permitted a free election in Hungary. In Poland, Romania, and Bulgaria he went to the other extreme.

Among those responsible for American policy there arose a dangerous illusion of omnipotence because the Soviet Union faced devastation and the United States was the only nation in a position to be of aid. However, there was likewise over-anxiety that gave rise to discussions of preventive war. Party warfare took on new life at the close of the war, and any concessions to the Communists aroused alarm. There had long been questions about the future course of the Soviet Union, and these continued. Excessive rhetoric took the place of sober thinking. No agreement emerged immediately after the war about the policy that should be pursued.

Developments in Austria in 1945 contrasted sharply with the quick takeovers in Poland and Romania. What took place was foreshadowed at the Moscow Conference in October 1943. In a puzzling turn of events it was agreed that Austria should not be treated as an enemy, but as a state that had been liberated, subject only to the provision that it should pay reparations. In the meantime, the European Advisory Committee in London set up the divisions of Austria and Vienna into three zones of occupation in each area.

In April 1945 the Russian army marched into the town of Gloggnitz, where the last president of the democratic parliament, Karl Renner, resided. Renner called on the Russian colonel to urge that he restrain the troops from looting and committing rape. In subsequent meetings it was agreed that Renner should draw up a series of proclamations to announce the convening of surviving members of the last parliament. Renner, on his arrival in Vienna, found that there were already three parties that were well organized, and so he negotiated with the leaders. A Russian officer was present but did not intervene. A temporary government was established that included four Socialists, four members of the People's Party, three Communists, and two specialists without party affiliation. From the beginning, Renner aimed at giving the ruling group a broader base. He was successful, and a coalition government came into being.

What the coalition achieved in the succeeding months was truly remarkable, considering the extreme dislocation in the country, the breakdown of the economy, the complicated procedures for rooting out the Nazis, and the measures necessary to restore the economy. A major hurdle was the restoration of order. Russian soldiers committed thievery and rape of the most brutal kind, but a police force, made up in large part of Communists, gradually restored order. The secret of Austrian success was the determination to cooperate, despite several shades of political opinion. Conditions in Austria were grim. Recovery was slowed further by the divisions of the country into three sectors and the tardiness of the United States in granting it recognition. This made it difficult to plan for the future and to negotiate trade treaties with neighboring powers so that exports could be increased. The large-scale Soviet seizures of machinery and other goods in the name of reparations increased the difficulties, while at the same time creating a flood of complaints to the American representatives.

A weakness of the American policy in Austria lay in the decision not to recognize any Austrian political group and to ban meetings of a political nature. This stood in the way of cooperating with democratic leaders, some of whom had fought in the resistance movement in Austria during the war, and others who were determined to drive out the Nazis, whose measures of repression were barbaric. A second difficulty arose in implementing the policy of denazification. The American military government, fearful that innocent people might fall victim to the highly emotional drive to rid the country of Nazis, insisted that denazification was to be carried out by occupation authorities. It soon became clear that the Austrians themselves, since they had lived in association with the Nazis, were the better judges.

The aim of the occupation authorities was to restore Austria politically and economically to a self-governing and independent nation. In the early months the focus of concern was not on the Communist question. The Communist party was weak, and the population at large looked to the West rather than to the East. At times the highly respected representatives of the Office of Strategic Services were dismayed by the policies of the military authorities, who were inflexible in carrying out orders that added up to treating Austria as an enemy nation the same as Germany and thereby impeded recovery.

So rapid was the progress that two able representatives of the Office of Strategic Services who had scouted the country from province to province and engaged in long interviews with leaders of all three parties arrived at the conclusion that the Austrians could best govern themselves and that the wisest move in terms of Austrian interests would be a removal of the occupying authorities.

An American representative, a man of broad experience and monumental common sense, summed up his feelings in a letter to his wife:

> Every day I become more confirmed in my opinion that we should get out of this country as soon as possible and that an end should be put to the absurd situation now prevailing. The red-tape involved in policy making is such that if the Powers decided tomorrow to get out, I suppose they would negotiate a year or so about the method of withdrawal, who should get out when, etc.[15]

Not until some months had passed did the Communist question arise. Before the occupation there was uneasiness on both sides about future relations, but this attitude was shortly replaced by a feeling that the Russians were desirous of cooperation. A report from an American representative read:

> The personal relationships between the members of the Mission and their Soviet hosts, initially correct but slightly aloof, developed during the ten day visit into strong mutual admiration and friendship. In the cordial atmosphere produced by daily professional associations and frequent social gatherings not only the officers but also the enlisted men found the Russians only too anxious to demonstrate the warmth of their feelings for their Allies.[16]

There was a word of caution: "Unless and until such relationships are permitted to develop with the full knowledge and approbation of Moscow, it would be a mistake to exaggerate their significance as indications of a friendlier Russian attitude or even an improved understanding of doing business."[17]

Questions arose in September 1945 about long-range Soviet intentions, thanks to Soviet efforts to negotiate with the Austrian government in Vienna to hand over to them the Zistersdorf oil wells. The Allied Control Council refused to give its approval. The Russian move was not dictated by a need for oil. Experts estimated that Russia would shortly be able to export large amounts of oil.

In November 1945, Lieutenant Leonard Hankin of the

Office of Strategic Services submitted a lengthy report on Soviet policy in Austria. He concluded:

> A review of the foreign policy of the USSR indicates that Russia regards Austria as one of those countries in which she seeks to have an influence at least equal to that of any other power. It appears that Russia's desire is to bring Austria as close as possible to her own political and economic orbit in the Balkans and at the same time to prevent the country from being used as the jumping-off point for any Western anti-Soviet alliance.
>
> . . . Her stake in Austria is not so great, however, that she will so antagonize the Western powers in Austria to endanger further the achievement of those broader aims which are necessary to establish Russia as a world power.[18]

In Austria friendly relations existed between the Renner government and the Soviet mission, and to a great degree this was also true between the western missions and the Soviets. For instance, in the fall of 1945 there was unanimous agreement that Austria should go ahead and establish an Austrian government. Each recognized that the cumbersome occupational machinery stood in the way of economic reconstruction. Renner called a conference of representatives of the several provinces, which opened in Vienna on September 24. In a communication to the Joint Chiefs of Staff, General Mark Clark, head of the American mission, warmly endorsed the Renner government as the sponsor of the conference.[19] The government had been established by the Soviets, but it had done a remarkable job. He explained that one of the advantages of the step being taken by the Renner government was its friendly relations with the Soviets. Above all, it enjoyed great popular support. Shortly after the conference met, the Soviets said they were prepared to recognize the provisional government and that they favored free elections. In the election held on November 25, the People's Party received 49.84 percent of the vote, the Socialists 44.54 percent, and the Communists 5.44 percent. The new provisional government was granted recognition by each of the four occupying powers. The Allied Control Council, however, remained the supreme authority.[20]

The new leader of the provisional government, Leopold Figl, met with General Clark, who assured him of support but also warned that he feared that there might be some change in Soviet policy. This caused him to say to Figl that if at times he appeared to be critical of the Soviets, "it was only because he was trying to be helpful and that to get anywhere he had to employ different strategies on different occasions."[21] Because he had talked very frankly with Marshall Koniev, the Soviet representative, he had developed the best of relations with him, and he would do the same with Figl.

The promising beginnings in the reconstruction of Austria came to a halt in 1947. The foremost issue concerned Soviet claims to reparations. The Russians based these claims on the Potsdam agreement. The western powers argued that Soviet demands would leave Austria impoverished and her independence endangered. Austria expressed a willingness to pay a high price to be free of the thousands of occupation troops. The United States and her Allies stood firm on any settlement that could be seen as a surrender to the Soviet Union. The cold war now embraced Austria's future.

Soviet concerns about developments in the border states mounted as the local regimes demonstrated strong nationalistic trends. The most glaring example of tension was Hungary. In a free election in 1945 the Smallholders party, a liberal group, gained a majority and was in control of the parliament. Side by side with this development, the Soviets were in a position to support the small Communist party, thanks to the presence of Soviet troops. Moreover, the minister of the interior was a Communist and controlled the police. To the Hungarians it appeared that the real political power resided with the Communist minority. Late in 1946 a small number of the ruling Smallholders party were charged with a conspiracy to overthrow the existing government. A series of arrests of members of parliament followed. These actions were seen by Prime Minister Ferenc Nagy as aimed at a Communist takeover. The conspiracy was a fact, and Ambassador Bedell Smith in Moscow declared that the evidence clearly indicated that this was so.[22]

The United States sought to bolster the hopes of the Hungarian public and to strengthen the Smallholders' will to resist by increases in various forms of economic support. An appeal was also made to the chairman of the Allied Control Council for an investigation of the current situation by a committee of representatives of the three powers. This action inspired a quick response that the Soviet Union could not agree to intervention by the United States in the internal affairs of Hungary.

Increasing pressure from the Soviet Union on the government in Hungary originated in part from concern over Hungary's commercial relations with the United States. The Soviet Union was determined to reverse this trend and to strengthen economic ties between the two countries. Prior to leaving for Switzerland, Prime Minister Nagy had a long conference with H. F. Arthur Schoenfeld, the United States representative in Hungary. Schoenfeld inquired whether Nagy shared the view that the strain in Hungarian-Soviet relations was caused in part by efforts of the Hungarian government to maintain economic ties with the United States. Nagy agreed "that this was unquestionably so" and added that "it would be unrealistic for Hungary to sever economic ties with the United States."[23] That this was a central issue is further affirmed in a memorandum handed to the secretary of state by the Hungarian minister in Washington. Imports from the Soviet Union were costly, and the costs of reparations were deemed unjust. In June the Soviet Union was pressing Hungary to enter a new trade agreement.[24] The great financial strength of the United States, and conjecture about how that strength could be used to establish ties among the countries on Russia's borders, caused alarm in Moscow.

The alleged conspiracy to overthrow the government was a Communist action to remove Nagy and his associates of the Smallholders party. In the spring and summer of 1947, after the signing of a peace treaty stipulating that Hungary was to be free and independent, the small Communist party, which had polled only 15 percent of the votes in the first election, continually intervened. In preparation for an election to be held in August, the Communist police stipulated who could serve as candidates of each of the parties and disfranchised some 20 percent of the voters. Investigation found that some of the charges were grotesque. The United States representative of the Allied Control Council charged interference in the domestic affairs of Hungary and repeated aggressive attempts at coercion.

The countries stretching from Iran to Turkey and Greece posed even greater dangers of confrontation. Here both sides had vital interests at stake. Free and unlimited access to the Mediterranean through the Dardanelles had been a major goal sought by Russia all during the nineteenth century. Control of the Mediterranean was no less important to the British, who had long opposed Russian efforts. Persia (Iran) had also been the scene of rivalry between the two countries. Iran lay at the head of the Persian Gulf, and its strategic location had been magnified a hundred times by the need for oil. During World War II, Iran had been the gateway through which western supplies reached Russia. It had also become a major source of oil for the British and, to a lesser extent, the United States.

In World War II the three major powers were present in Iran, and the country was unable to defend its own interests amidst their rivalry. Along the Iranian northern border the Soviet Union conscripted primitive native transportation and siphoned off the wheat grown in the northern province of Azerbaijan. The Anglo-Persian Oil Company, partially owned by the British government, was a state within a state. The United States first became involved because of Lend-Lease shipments, but it had a major interest in the oil of the neighboring state of Saudi Arabia.

Until World War II the United States took no interest in Iran, but this changed as the country became one of the major passageways for sending military aid to the Soviet Union. The three outside powers benefited while Iran suffered. The American minister in Iran was deeply concerned about the abuse of the natives and the shady dealings in Lend-Lease materials. The Soviet Union and the British were intent on preserving their privileged positions after the war. Concerned over the troubled scene, the Near East Division in the U.S. State Department set to work on a plan to improve conditions. A memorandum was drafted by John Jernegan, who served in the American mission in Iran, that proposed strengthening Iran so that it would be able to stand as an independent nation at the close of the war. Self-denying pledges were to be sought from the British and the Soviets. To enable Iran to achieve strength, the United States should provide assistance. Secretary of State Hull gave his approval before forwarding the memorandum to the president. John Jernegan explained his motives some weeks after his note had been submitted. He stated that the United States had a vital interest in future oil development and an immediate concern in upholding the principles of the Atlantic Charter. Should Iran fall victim to outside pressures, it would greatly weaken the chances of carrying forward plans for a new world order. At that time the United States controlled 42 percent of the proved oil reserves of the Middle East.[25]

At the Teheran Conference President Roosevelt had asked Patrick Hurley, secretary of war under Hoover, to draft a declaration that could be set before the Soviets and the British with some hope of adoption. Hurley's statement called on all three powers in Iran, England, the Soviet Union, and the United States, to help that nation economically and support its integrity and independence during and after the war. This was no more than an abbreviated version of the policy that had been set forth in the Jernegan memo. Approval of the declaration started Hurley on the development of a broader program calling for the United States to furnish advisers who were to help modernize and strengthen Iran. These advisers, who were to be paid by Iran, were to work in cooperation with the State Department. The draft also called for the United States to take charge of all Lend-Lease supplies so that the alleged shady dealings of the Soviets and the British could be stopped.[26] The Near East Division, acutely aware of the complexity of the situation, and also well informed about the many weaknesses of Iran and the internal forces that would oppose modernization, took a critical view of the Hurley proposal. Eugene Rostow called it "hysterical messianic globaloney." Dean Acheson likewise opposed it as impractical.[27] Their concern was with the immediate problem of winning the war and not with rescuing a country enmeshed in internal disputes and subject to the powerful influence of the Moslem clergy. Members of the State Department read Hurley's program and were amused by such terms as "modern nation," "free enterprise," and "self-government," all of which were irrelevant to the tangled situation in Iran.

Due to his close connections with the oil industry, Hurley was well informed, and his biographer suggests that his concern may have had less to do with reform in Iran than with his close ties to Harry Sinclair, the Tulsa oil magnate.[28] The new interest in Iran was clearly related to the recent awareness of the shortage of oil. Iran's rich oil resources, and its location at the head of the Persian gulf and next door to Saudi Arabia, could scarcely be overlooked.

Relations with the British in Iran were far from friendly and were constantly marked by bickering among the representatives of the two countries. This harmful rivalry led to Stettinius's mission to London in April 1944, where discussions led to a recognition that the two countries had a community of interest. It was agreed that they should cooperate, and both British and American agents in Iran were ordered to cease their complaints about each other.[29]

The increased activity of the Russians and their new intrusions had brought about that change. Azerbaijan, the province northwest of Teheran, became the headquarters of the new Tudeh party, which concentrated its program on the grievances of the population. This was the province that had the closest trade ties with the Soviet Union, and these ties opened the door to Soviet political activities. The division of the population among several minority groups likewise offered the opportunity to exploit local feelings.

In the fall of 1944, after the Moscow Conference, the Soviets supported the policies of the Tudeh party in a major campaign against Iran's national government, which had its seat in Teheran. This, in turn, alarmed some of the American friends of Iran, who saw in the Soviet intrusions challenges to the principles set forth in the Atlantic Charter, and the result was a program calling for the three major powers to commit themselves to the enunciated principles, including equality of commercial opportunity. Iran promptly became another major point of conflict between the East and the West. As Bruce Kuniholm, an authority on the Near East, observes: "Unquestionably, the application of the Charter's principles to Iran threatened to discriminate against Russia's interests. Her less-developed and less-sophisticated oil technology, for example, could not compete with that of the United States."[30] Because of the danger of a confrontation, the three powers now turned to finding some more realistic formula that would secure the interests of all three powers. Efforts were made to work out a solution both in the Teheran Conference and at Yalta, but met with firm opposition from Molotov, who had no intention of getting the destiny of its important neighbor wrapped up in an agreement that would give the United States and the United Kingdom future leverage.

It was against this background that events moved toward a crisis after World War II. The government in Teheran, so long weakened by the presence of powerful intruders, sought the withdrawal of all foreign forces in accordance with the treaty of 1943, which provided that each of the three powers present should withdraw all troops no later than six months after the war. At the Potsdam Conference the British, the Americans, and the Soviets reaffirmed that accord, but postponed any coming to terms with the long-range problems. In the meantime the Soviets increased their activities, and the Tudeh party, which was dependent on Soviet support, carried on a vigorous campaign against the government in Teheran, warning that if national troops came into Azerbaijan there would be a civil war. In August 1945 the Soviets organized a new party in Azerbaijan that was fully committed to Communism and then attacked the Tudeh party. The new Democratic party promptly opened a campaign against the government. By November the Democratic party, with the armed support of the Soviet Union, had established a new government in Azerbaijan.[31]

The creation of an independent government in Azerbaijan and the Soviet warnings to the government in Teheran challenged the United States. Was it willing to confront the Soviet Union? It soon made it clear that Teheran could count on American support in the United Nations. The Soviets now backed down, and when Teheran moved into Azerbaijan, that government collapsed and the Soviet Union took no further action. This did not bring an end to American concern. It was assumed that the Soviet Union would attempt coercion again at some more propitious time.[32]

Before leaving for Moscow in December 1945, Secretary of State Byrnes received instructions to insist that Soviet troops be removed, but instead of doing so, he reached an agreement with Molotov removing Iran from the agenda of the meetings. However, a telegram from Assistant Secretary of State Acheson reported the urgency felt in Washington. When Byrnes approached Stalin on the question, Stalin replied that the Soviet Union enjoyed the right to station troops in northern Iran under an older treaty, that the oil fields in Baku were in danger, and denied that the Russians planned to take over in Iran. James Byrnes pressed Molotov further at the next session only to be put off because of the earlier agreement that Iran was not on the agenda.

The impact of these events in Washington was decisive. To members of the Near Eastern Division of the Department of State led by Loy Henderson, it appeared that the Soviet Union was embarked on the course it had followed in Poland and in Romania. These feelings were confirmed by a discovery in captured German documents that a major issue in prewar German negotiations with the Soviets had been the establishment of Soviet bases in the Dardanelles and of military garrisons in specified Turkish districts. James Byrnes' failure at the Moscow Conference and the actions of the Soviet Union now led the president to demand that the Russians be faced with boldness.

The momentum of the controversy over Iran inevitably carried forward long-held convictions on both sides. On February 9, 1946, Stalin delivered his speech charging that the Soviet Union faced encirclement by imperialist powers on all sides. He warned that the Soviet Union must rearm to be ready for the war that the capitalist world was moving towards. The speech led Justice William Douglas of the Supreme Court to confide to Secretary of the Navy James Forrestal that it was "the Declaration of World War III."

At the close of February, George Kennan sent his famous "Long Telegram." What Kennan stated he had said many times before, without ever getting a hearing as far as he knew, but this telegram catapulted him into prominence. Kennan had long taken a pessimistic view of working with the Soviet government. Shortly after the Nazi attack on the Soviet Union and Churchill's extension of aid, Kennan wrote to Loy Henderson in the Near Eastern Division warning of danger.[33] He did not oppose aid for the Soviet Union, but thought it dangerous to welcome the Russians as an associate in the defense of democracy. Should we do so, Kennan said, we would identify ourselves "with the Russian destruction of the Baltic States, with the attack against Finnish independence, with the partitioning of Poland and Romania, with the crushing of religion throughout eastern Europe, and with the domestic policy of a regime which is widely feared and detested throughout this part of the world and the methods of which are far from democratic."[34] Aid should be extended only after realistic consideration of our own interests. Throughout the war Kennan continued to depict the Soviets in the darkest of terms. Because America depended on cooperation with the Soviet Union if Germany was to be defeated, Kennan's messages necessarily could only be set aside as not being helpful in solving the immediate and overwhelming problem of defeating Germany.

By early 1946 the situation had changed, and the immediate problem was no longer winning the war but winning the peace. Kennan had not been alone in his distrust of the Soviets. In the final months of war and immediately after, Harriman had cautioned the Department of State and President Truman that firmness was required.

Kennan's mastery of prose and the care he gave to drawing upon Russian history and analyzing Communist ideology—together with his perception that nationalism now overshadowed ideology in the minds of the leaders of the highly centralized Soviet State—arrived at a time when Americans faced perplexity, confusion, and divisiveness. The long telegram of eight thousand words gave to those already advocating firmness, and those still suffering the pangs of uncertainty, a resolution of their difficulties. Kennan did not advocate war; he expressed faith in the possibility that a restrained and not-unfriendly policy based on realism would eventually result in relations of a cooperative nature. Once it reached Washington, the telegram was duplicated hundreds of times and passed around among the many people concerned.

Because the telegram was not specific about the course

to be followed and because of its forceful language, it left room for different interpretations, some of which did not fit into Kennan's thinking. To bolder spirits such as James Forrestal, who was already panicky over the Soviet Union, it was a call to arms.

Rhetoric soon again added to the crystallization of opinion. On March 6, 1946, in Fulton, Missouri, Winston Churchill coined the ringing phrase "the Iron Curtain" to describe how the Soviet Union had separated eastern and western Europe all the way from Warsaw to Sofia. Churchill's speech had been read by Truman before it was delivered, and the president's presence on the platform suggested that he endorsed it. There was criticism of Churchill, but it has appeared to John Gaddis, the highly regarded historian of the cold war, that the British stateman's views were shared by the majority of the American public and by the inner circle of the Truman administration.

As the rhetoric mounted, the Iran question reached a climax with both the British and the Americans urging that all major powers remove their troops by March 2 in accordance with the treaty of 1943. The Soviets explained that they did not have plans to take over Iran, that the Iranians and their government were hostile, and that the Russian troops were there to keep the peace. Teheran appealed to the United States for help and then decided to put the controversy before the United Nations Security Council. American and British troops withdrew, but Soviet troops remained after the deadline. The Security Council met on March 25. On that day the Soviet newspaper *Tass* announced that all troops would be withdrawn within five to six weeks, unless unforeseen developments intervened.

The final days in February and the first weeks of March were momentous ones. Foreign affairs, particularly the conflict over the withdrawal of troops from Iran, made newspaper headlines. A feeling prevailed that America was at a crossroads. On the final day of February, Byrnes spoke before the Overseas Club at the Waldorf Astoria in

New York. He declared that the United States would back the United Nations with force, called for strengthening the military, and advocated military conscription. The following day, Senator Arthur H. Vandenburg of Michigan, a prominent Republican, spoke before the Senate and asked what the Russians were up to. President Truman and the cabinet had met earlier to discuss a change in foreign policy. All except Henry Wallace, former vice president and now secretary of commerce, opposed what had by now been labeled the appeasement policy. Two members, if we may believe a report, pointed to the "rising tide of indignation throughout the Nation as the result of the continued retreat by the State Department before Soviet demands."

Withdrawal of Soviet troops did not occur. The Soviets pressured the government of Teheran, repeatedly seeking to place in control leaders friendly to the Soviets. At the same time the Soviet ambassador warned that there would be war if Teheran sent its troops into Azerbaijan, where a separate government had been established. These Soviet declarations and their demands on Turkey during the fall of 1946 brought a change in American foreign policy. Instead of appealing to the Security Council, the government assumed a readiness to use force if the United Nations could not bring a halt to Soviet intrusions in Iran.[35]

The change in policy was one of great significance. The United States had concluded to make developments in Iran a test case for Soviet intentions. Charles Bohlen had protested that the United States was not a signatory to the treaty of 1922 on which the question of the Soviet position in Iran hinged and therefore the United States lacked legal grounds for taking such a position. More important, Bohlen said, the United States was truly unable to confront the Soviet Union in Iran. The American army was weak due to demobilization. If force was to be used, the United States would be in a stronger position in western Europe. Action by the United States, said Bohlen, was likely to be considered as a bluff by the Soviet Union. It might call the bluff, and then the United States would be left fighting a war where it would be at a disadvantage. This was not the point of view taken by Loy Henderson in the Near Eastern Division of the State Department. His turned out to be the decisive vote. Yet a critic might honestly ask whether or not the United States was not unwisely carrying a chip on its shoulder.[36]

The Soviet Union had warning of this change from Ambassador Bedell Smith, and also in the economic aid that was being extended to the three nations that were in trouble. In turn the government in Teheran moved its troops into Azerbaijan. The rebel government there collapsed immediately. When the Russians did not intervene, it became the opinion in Washington that the Soviet Union only backed down because the United States was ready to use force.

Because Iran has a long common border with the Soviet Union, the conflict of the two very different societies and the mutual distrust turned the country into the arena where the use of force became a distinct possibility. There was no one public response to the events. The *San Francisco Examiner*, a newspaper that gloried in scandal and conspiratorial charges, hailed James Byrnes' speech as a departure from appeasement, but commented that Senator Vandenburg was wrong in stating that we should be as realistic as the Russians. We could not act like the Soviets "for we do not have the despotic purposes of Russia, or its perverted ideals, or its bad morals."[37] One of the leading and most respected newspapers, the *Atlanta Constitution*, responded to Byrnes' speech because "in a time when hysterical and irresponsible radio commentators and news columnists are speaking of a third world war— merely for the effect on readers and listener interest," and "at a time when special interests are insisting that war with Russia is inevitable," Byrnes was calm and reasonable.[38]

There were clear-cut reservations about the change in policy and the furor that had caused the Russians to withdraw their troops. As early as 1943, Walter Lippmann had urged that the United States accept that the Soviet Union would never again tolerate anti-Russian regimes on the Soviet border. Lippmann accepted spheres of interest as inevitable, but he too favored a firm policy. Churchill's Iron Curtain speech aroused Walter Lippmann's wrath. That evening Walter and Mrs. Lippmann were dinner guests of Dean Acheson. The speech, said Lippmann, would enlarge Soviet fears of encirclement, stimulate an arms race, and lead to war.[39] At a later dinner party, Lippmann and Bohlen exchanged views on the Iran question. Lippmann charged that such a belligerent policy would destroy the effectiveness of the United Nations and could eventually lead to war. Bohlen obviously felt compelled to defend the steps that had been taken. Mrs. Lippmann, who had served as a nurse during the First World War and as director of the nursing program in World War II, turned to Bohlen and said, "Well, Chip, all I can say is that in your war I won't be a nurse's aide!"[40] Lippmann was no less critical of the Soviet Union than George Kennan or Dean Acheson, but believed that firmness was giving way to belligerence.

The Russians sought to avoid dramatizing the Iran question. Submitting it to the Security Council meant that the Soviets were denied face saving. Byrnes' action at this point was a reaction to the critics who were charging that he was appeasing the Soviets. He acknowledged that he had been subjected to criticism for yielding too much. The very perceptive and disciplined historian John Lewis Gaddis states that Byrnes action "stemmed chiefly from domestic considerations."[41] As so many times in our history, party politics and public pressures exerted an undue influence.

The Iran question was only one of several topics relating to the Soviet Union that made headlines late in the fall of 1945 and during the winter of 1946. In March 1946 the newspapers featured Russian looting in Manchuria. James Byrnes protested to the Soviet Union and assured the public that there was nothing in the secret agreements that condoned looting. Also swirling through the news reports of the day were the heated debates over

Truman's proposal to extend foreign loans. Rumors of a billion-dollar loan to the Soviets opened the way for further denunciation of the administration. The question of the atomic bomb was also on the front pages. Secretary of State Stimson pleaded for the sharing of information. He contended that it was inevitable that scientists elsewhere would soon master the secret, and failure to bring this new and frightening technology under international control, while there was still time, could lead to war. The public mind was not yet set in an inflexible mold on future relations with the Soviet Union, but it was on a course that led in that direction. Dean Acheson held out for an agreement on atomic energy, but had been overruled by the president.

Also in the fall and winter of 1945–46, the Coordinating Committee of the secretary of state, the secretary of the army, and the secretary of the navy were chiefly concerned about the "civil war" in Greece and the assistance that the revolt was receiving from forces inside Yugoslovia and Bulgaria. Soviet demands on Turkey called for a grant of territory and the establishment of two military posts on the Dardanelles. Vital Soviet concerns about the Dardanelles, through which German ships had been free to pass during the war, were recognized in that it was accepted that the Russians must have free access to the Aegean Sea, but at the same time it was agreed that they must not be allowed to infringe on Turkey's independence.

The take-off point in American thinking was that the Soviets might repeat what they had done in Poland and in Romania. Iran was an intimate part of this syndrome in the eyes of the Near Eastern Division and the secretaries of the Army and Navy. Acheson shared these views. The Russians had only moved where their armed forces were in a position to act quickly. Iran, Turkey, and Greece were readily open to being taken by the Soviet armed forces.

The most important question remained unsettled. Germany was of major importance to both the Soviet Union and the western democracies. The plan of occupation devised by the European Advisory Committee divided Germany into three spheres. At Yalta it was agreed that France should also have a sphere, a decision advocated by the United States. Local affairs were to be under the control of the power to whom the zone was granted, while all questions that were broader in scope and essentially national were to be subject to the Allied Control Commission. This plan of organization had inherent weaknesses. The zones tended to become more and more completely separate divisions that stood in the way of trade, so that the needs of one zone could not readily be met by making available the superfluities in another. The decision to make reparations a zonal matter further complicated the restoration of the economy so that it could meet even minimum German needs. Another difficulty stemmed from the requirement that actions by the Allied Control Council were subject to a unanimous vote by the four powers. Given the differences in national interests, rivalry would have a higher priority than subordination of these interests to a common goal.

Contrary to studies that appeared immediately after the war, it was France that caused the major breakdown. Weakened by the war and internal divisions, France was determined to prevent the rise of a strong German state. It set forth claims that were as great as those that France had set forth at the Versailles Peace Conference. Having suffered through two wars, France was intent on security, and this called for the annexation of the Saar, the Rhineland, and the Ruhr. The Department of State in Washington had decided before the end of the war that the United States had a vital interest in strengthening France so that she would not fall prey to Communism, and could be counted on to check Soviet advances. The opposition of France to all measures that signalled Germany's future power created tensions, but the United States, thanks to the Department of State, did not challenge them. France, in turn, refused to yield unless its demands were met. In addition to arguing its case on the ground of security from Germany, France also voiced its opposition on the ground that a centralized occupation authority in Germany would bring the Soviets as neighbors.

The intransigence of the French contributed to desperate conditions in Germany. In the absence of food shipments from the Soviet zone, and because of the removal from Germany of large quantities of machinery, plus the complete uncertainty about Germany's future, the American and British zones became dependent on support from the United States. General Lucius Clay protested repeatedly that the occupation was crippled and that measures must be taken toward centralization if the situation was to be improved. In this he had the support of the United States Army because it was being held responsible for the failure of the occupation.

From the first days of the occupation it was the position of the United States that it would not make the mistake it had made after World War I and finance German recovery. The recovery must be achieved by enabling Germany to pay for imports by a renewal of the Germans' ability to export. Clay's efforts went for naught in his attempts to remedy this situation. At the same time he gradually concluded that reparations must cease until the economy recovered.

In his scholarly study, John Gimbel has concluded that it was the actions of the French that forced Clay to act.[42] On May 3, 1946, Clay announced a suspension of reparation payments from the American zone. At the time, Clay explained that the French opposition to centralization measures made his decision necessary. The Russians favored centralization and had been cooperative. Gimbel's evidence for his conclusions is weighty and has not yet been contradicted.

Clay's announcement had far-reaching effects. It was followed by the combination of the British and American zones and energetic efforts to revive the German economy. This promptly caused the establishment of a separate currency for the combined zones and, subsequently, the Berlin blockade. Once the payment of reparations was suspended, it became commonplace for the Department of State to blame the Russians. Gimbel states that this was not because of an intellectual conception or a rational plan. He sees it as a result of long-term experience with the Russians and a slow and gradually acquired habit of thought and orientation that influenced the judgment of ongoing developments.[43]

Viewed in broader terms, the failure of the occupation was not the fault of any one power. All were to blame for the tragic economic situation in Germany during 1946 and 1947.[44] It became apparent that without recovery there, there could be no recovery in Europe at large.

Developments throughout 1946 convinced Acheson and Loy Henderson that the Soviet Union was intent on pursuing a course that would reduce Iran, Turkey, and Greece into client states. The Soviets had retreated in Iran early in the year, rather than invite a confrontation, but its maneuvers in Iran left doubts about its ultimate aims. The United States was fully informed of these actions. Turkey, in desperate economic straits, was also weak militarily. She would not be able to resist Soviet demands. Greece was in the midst of chaos, thanks to a corrupt government and a Communist movement supported by Yugoslavia.[45]

This area had long been a sphere of influence of the British, who had wanted control of the eastern Mediterranean to secure the passageway to India. Thanks to developments during the war, the United States had gradually come to view this part of the world as a vital interest. The decline of Great Britain and the desperate economic situation it faced were well known in Washington, and there were clear indications that Britain would not long be able to play its traditional role.

Soviet action further promoted examination of what course the United States should pursue. The discussions involved the Department of State, the Pentagon, and the

Treasury. Acheson and Loy Henderson of the Near Eastern Division prepared the way for a change in the course of the United States. In these discussions there was no exhibition of excessive rhetoric.

The final major decision came about when Truman received an aide-mémoire from the British on February 21, 1947, stating that they could no longer carry the costs of maintaining troops in Greece. Acheson at once ordered his staff to prepare position papers calling for aid to both Greece and Turkey. The assistant secretary of state was well aware that he was now inviting a momentous decision. At a meeting between Secretary of State George Marshall, Patterson, Acheson, and Chief of Staff of the Army, General Dwight D. Eisenhower, "Ike" whispered to Acheson, asking whether he thought the president fully understood all possible consequences. Acheson asked the president, who took out a set of the maps of the area and then gave his unqualified assent. He won the assent also of Secretary of State George Marshall. It was the final wording of the message to be delivered by the president that stirred doubts among a few. Was the president's message to Congress to be low-key? Was it to be no more than a call for aid to stricken Greece? Aid had been rendered to several war-torn countries. Or was it to be a ringing declaration in broad terms that added up to a bold confrontation, one that would summon the public to support a broad new and unprecedented policy? And would the proposed measures suffice to restrain Soviet expansion?

Kennan protested that it was a mistake to lay down a policy stating that the United States would resist Soviet advances anywhere in the world. He felt that it would be wiser to take into account the many considerations that would be relevant in each situation as they arose. He likewise saw in the first drafts the danger of raising the conflict into a military confrontation.[46] Kennan was overruled.

The message to Congress was a product of emotion as well as ripened convictions that the Soviet Union was bent on unlimited expansion. In their book *The Wise*

Men, Walter Isaacson and Evan Thomas describe Acheson's state of mind as he met with members of the Congress.

> The situation, he declared to the doubting congressmen, was unparalleled since ancient history. Not since Athens and Sparta, not since Rome and Carthage, had the world been so polarized by two great powers. The U.S. and the U.S.S.R. were divided by "an unbridgeable ideological chasm." The choice was between "democracy and individual liberty" and "dictatorship and absolute conformity."[47]

To these emotional appeals he added a metaphor. "If Greece fell, 'like apples in a barrel infected by a rotten one,' Asia Minor, Egypt, then even Italy and France would fall prey. Before long, two-thirds of the world's population and three-quarters of its surface would be red."[48] In its final form Truman's statement announced that, "It is the policy of the United States to give support to free peoples who are attempting to resist subjugation from armed minorities or from outside forces."

It has been said with good reason that only by embedding the appeal for aid to Greece and Turkey in the context of a global setting could the administration obtain the support of Congress, which had recently denied two requests for aid. Certainly, it was a bold step to describe the move in broad global terms. The result could be that this very-general policy takes the place of careful examination of each situation as it arose. In the ensuing years the United States was seized with an apocalyptic vision born of the combination of ideology and dangerous rivalry. That outcome was the product of other forces than the Truman Doctrine, but Acheson's appeal to political considerations was more than shrewd politics. His own convictions told him that there was no alternative.

Placed in a historical perspective, the cold war was not a surprise. The breakdown of long-established governments in Europe, the weakness of Great Britain, and the collapse of France and Italy had left a power vacuum. The future of Europe was a question of vital interest to the Americans, who also believed that they were on the defensive. Continuation of the desperate European economic conditions would probably lead to revolution and open the way to Soviet hegemony. That was the fear.

Neither Truman, Acheson, Kennan, nor Bohlen expected the Soviets to go to war, and war in the future was unlikely if it was made clear to the Soviets that on certain crucial and strategic points they would meet with resistance. Most American leaders were cautious and avoided tactics that would force the Soviets to react. At the same time they hoped that the Soviets would not challenge them at points where they would be forced to act.

This delicate imbalance, in which there was much room for miscalculation by both sides, became even more hazardous because of the ideological, political, and social differences between the two societies. Opinions differ as to the role of ideology, but it was in the ideological realm that the East and the West found justification for their postures. This made compromise difficult. Capitalism connoted the evil of exploitation by the ruling class, in the thinking of Communist ideologues. Communism was then interpreted by the West as synonymous with brutal repression and the denial of humanistic values. These rigidly held opinions, in a world already living at the edge of nuclear disaster, acquired ever-greater strength.

Epilogue

THE sixth of the major transitions analyzed in the fore-
going pages has come to a close. The twenty years following the pronouncement of the Truman Doctrine in March
1947 were marked by a painful search for the twin goals
of security and peace. Never before had the nation faced
such an upheaval in relations with the outside world.
Given the goals, the period was marked by success. Western Europe was restored and a balance of powers was
achieved. But the world now lived amid the terror of
hydrogen bombs, guided missiles, adolescent exaggera-
tion, and legitimate fears. The Korean War and the Vietnam war, both costly in human life, generated disillusion. Never was the search for a world order of stability
more difficult to achieve. The time is arriving when historians will have gained a historical perspective of this
latest transition.

An understanding of what has taken place requires that
the public recognize that this can be achieved only by
taking into account the nation's previous two hundred
years of experience in foreign relations. It is necessary to
begin far earlier than 1914 or 1945. The diplomacy of a
state is molded by its heritage and perception of its past,
and its conception of the world. The American experience extends over six major transitions. No one was isolated from its predecessor. All were a part of an on-going
process. Party warfare, spicy language, exaggerated pho-
bias, and pride entered in from the earliest days just as
they have in the recent past. Moderation and realism
have marched hand in hand with occasional adventurism,

an absence of limited aims clearly defined, and a dangerous tendency to reduce issues to moral dimensions. Time
and again, it has been mistakenly assumed that human
rights were exportable. Rights, as Edmund Burke told us,
are slowly learned and not achieved by drawing a new
blue print. The rights of a free society cannot be exported.

There are many indications that the cold war is at
an end and society is about to make another transition.
States will continue to seek their physical survival, preservation of their institutions, and prosperity. It will be
necessary to limit ambitions and to advance understanding rather than ascribe satanic characteristics to rival
states. The close-knit world of today no longer permits
hasty judgements. Presidents, thanks to the increasing
importance of foreign relations, are likely to achieve more
power. They, as former senator William Fulbright warns
us, must be men of stature and should be chosen by improved procedures.

Notes

1. Foreign Policy Rooted in Society, 1763–1783

1. Max Savelle, *The Origins of American Diplomacy: The International History of Angloamerica* (New York: Macmillan Co., 1967), p. 547.

2. Ibid., pp. 540–41.

3. Ibid., p. 542.

4. Thomas Hutchinson, *History of Massachusetts Bay*, vol. 2, ed. Lawrence Shaw Mayo (Cambridge, Mass.: 1936), quoted by Savelle, op. cit., page 543.

5. Savelle, *Origins of American Diplomacy*, pp. 544–45.

6. *The Life of Benjamin Franklin Written by Himself*, ed. John Bigelow, vol. 2 (Philadelphia: J. B. Lippincott, 1874), p. 285.

7. Ibid., pp. 314–15.

8. Lawrence Henry Gipson, *The British Empire before the American Revolution, Zones of International Friction: The Great Lakes Frontier, Canada, the West Indies, India, 1748–1754*, vol. 5 (New York: Alfred A. Knopf, 1942), pp. 125–32.

9. Gary Nash provides a detailed analysis of the social changes in the leading cities in the years immediately following the Seven Years War. He writes: "Although no social revolution occurred in America in the 1770's, the American Revolution could not have unfurled when or in the manner it did without the self-conscious action of the urban laboring people—both those at the bottom and those in the middle—who became convinced that they must create power where none had existed before or else watch their position deteriorate, both in absolute terms and relative to that of others. Thus, the history of the Revolution is in part the history of popular collective action and the puncturing of the gentry's claim that their role was legitimized by custom, law, and divine will." Gary B. Nash, *The Urban Crucible: Social Change, Political Consciousness, and the Origins of the American Revolution* (Cambridge: Harvard University Press, 1979), pp. 383–84.

10. John Rutledge to John Jay, June 29, 1776, *Letters of Members of the Continental Congress*, ed. Edmund C. Burnett (Washington, D.C.: Carnegie Institution, 1923), 1:375–77.

11. Committee of Secret Correspondence to Silas Deane, March 3, 1776, Burnett, *Letters* 1:375–77.

12. Richard Henry Lee to Landon Carter, June 2, 1776, Burnett, *Letters* 1:469.

13. *Journals of the Continental Congress, 1774–1789*, ed. W. C. Ford (Washington, D.C.: Government Printing Office, 1906), 5:128.

14. *Diary and Autobiography of John Adams*, ed. L. H. Butterfield (Cambridge: Harvard University Press, 1961), 2:338.

15. *Journals of the Continental Congress, 1774–1789* 5:128.

16. Jonathan R. Dull, *A Diplomatic History of the American Revolution* (New Haven: Yale University Press, 1985), p. 124.

17. *Journals to the Continental Congress* 5:770.

18. Edward S. Corwin, *French Policy and the American Alliance* (Princeton: Princeton University Press, 1916), p. 109.

19. *The Correspondence and Public Papers of John Jay* 1:249–50.

20. Ibid., 1:266–67.

21. Ibid., 1:322–23.

22. Ibid., 1:329.

23. *The Revolutionary Diplomatic Correspondence of the United States*, ed. Francis Wharton (Washington, D.C.: Government Printing Office, 1889), 4:135.

24. Corwin, *French Policy*, pp. 197–98 and pp. 267–68. See also Wharton, *Revolutionary Diplomatic Correspondence* 3:488–90 for letter of Luzerne to Congress, February 2, 1780.

25. John Jay to Count de Vergennes, September 22, 1780, Wharton, *Revolutionary Diplomatic Correspondence* 4:140.

26. Wharton, *Revolutionary Diplomatic Correspondence* 4:64.

27. *The Correspondence and Public Papers of John Jay* 1:433.

28. Wharton, *Revolutionary Diplomatic Correspondence* 4:743.

29. Ibid.

30. Jay reported: "The Count admitted this, and made several observations to show the importance of this object to Spain and its determination to adhere to it, saying with some degree of warmth that unless Spain could exclude all nations from the Gulf of Mexico, they might as well admit all; that the king would never relinquish it; that the minister regarded it as the principal object to be obtained by the war, and *that obtained*, he should be perfectly easy whether or not Spain procured any other cession; that he considered it far more important that Gibraltar." Wharton, op. cit., 4:146.

Americans to this day have been slow to recognize Spain's contributions to American victory. Jonathan Dull corrects this error. He holds that "it is almost inconceivable that France and the United States could have defeated Britain without Spanish help." See Dull, *Diplomatic History of the American Revolution*, pp. 109–11.

31. Ibid., 5 : 649.

32. Richard Morris, *The Peacemakers: The Great Powers and American Independence* (New York: Harper and Row, 1965), p. 248.

33. Gerald Stourzh, *Benjamin Franklin and American Foreign Policy* (Chicago: University of Chicago Press, 1954), pp. 47–48, 99.

34. Morris, *Peacemakers*, p. 308.

35. Ibid., pp. 360.

36. Ibid., pp. 305–306.

37. Ibid., p. 307.

38. Ibid., pp. 308–10.

39. Ibid., p. 330.

40. Ibid., p. 345.

41. Ibid., p. 459.

2. The First Transition: The Difficulties of a Client State, 1789–1815

1. Lance Banning, *The Jefferson Persuasion: Evolution of a Party Ideology* (Ithaca: Cornell University Press, 1978), pp. 57, 77, and 128.

2. Lance Banning, "The Hamiltonian Madison: A Reconsideration," *Virginia Magazine of History and Biography*, January 1984. Reading this article in its entirety is most necessary and delightful. See pages 20–23 in particular.

3. The most outspoken defender of Hamilton and critic of Jefferson is probably Forrest McDonald. He charges both Jefferson and Madison with being inept and demagogic. Forrest McDonald, *Alexander Hamilton: A Biography* (New York: W. W. Norton Co., 1979), p. 192.

4. Henry Adams, *The Life of Albert Gallatin* (reprint, New York: Peter Smith, 1943), p. 159.

5. "An Account of the Receipts and Expenditures of the United States for the Year 1792," "Abstract of the Net Amount of Duties on Imports and Tonnage Which Have Accrued in the United States during the First and Second Quarters of the Year 1793," *The Papers of Alexander Hamilton*, ed. Harold G. Syrett, vol. 15 (New York: Columbia University Press, 1909), pp. 475–545, 575.

6. E. A. J. Johnson, "Federalism, Pluralism, and Public Policy," *Journal of Economic History*, December, 1962, pp. 427–444.

7. Dumas Malone, *Jefferson and His Time*, vol. 2, *Jefferson and the Rights of Man*, (Boston: Little, Brown and Co., 1951), p. 35.

8. *Hamilton Papers*, "An American," no. 1, 12:157–64; "Catullus," no. 3, 12:498–506.

9. In the first of his attacks on Jefferson, Hamilton said that, if the people recognized the importance of credit and "if they are willing, that the powers granted to it should be exercised with sufficient latitude to the ends they had in view in granting them and to do the essential business of the Nation," they could not side with the opposition." Catullus, no. 3, *Hamilton Papers*, 12:498–506.

10. *Annals of Congress*, 1st Cong., 1st sess., p. 182.

11. Ibid., pp. 201–202.

12. Ibid., 3d Cong., 1st sess., p.329.

13. Dumas Malone states that Jefferson, as secretary of state, was careful to adhere to established diplomatic practice and he did not permit his pro-French feelings to influence his actions. Privately he gave vent to fervent opinions, but as a public man he imposed "extraordinary restraint on himself." Dumas Malone, *Jefferson and Time*, vol. 3, *Jefferson and the Ordeal of Liberty*, p. 46.

14. Alexander Hamilton to John Jay, April 8, 1793, *Hamilton Papers*, 14:297–98.

15. Rufus King to Alexander Hamilton, April 24, 1793, and Edward Carrington to Alexander Hamilton, April 26, 1793. *Hamilton Papers*, 14:335–36, 346–52.

16. Ibid., p. 375.

17. Ibid.

18. Ibid., "Pacificus," no. 4, July 10, 1793, 15:85.

19. Thomas Jefferson to James Madison, June 2, 1793, James Madison Papers, Library of Congress.

20. *Hamilton Papers* 15:72–73.

21. *The Writings of Thomas Jefferson*, ed. Paul Leicester Ford, vol. 1 (New York: G. P. Putmam's Sons, 1895), pp. 253–254.

22. Cabinet Meeting, Opinion on the Fitting out of Privateers in the Ports of the United States, August 3, 1793, *Hamilton Papers*, vol. 15.

23. Dumas Malone, *Jefferson and His Time*, vol. 3, *Jefferson and the Ordeal of Liberty*, p. 135.

24. Ibid.

25. Ibid.

26. "No Jacobin," no. 8, August 28, 1793, *Hamilton Papers* 15.

27. Stephen Higginson to Alexander Hamilton, August 24, 1793, *Hamilton Papers* 15:273–76.

28. David Ross to Alexander Hamilton, August 30, 1793, ibid., pp. 309–10.

29. *Annals of Congress,* 3d Cong., 1st sess., pp. 213–15.

30. James Madison to Thomas Jefferson, March 14, 1794, James Madison Papers, Library of Congress.

31. *Annals of Congress,* 3d Cong., 1st sess., p. 290.

32. *American State Papers: Foreign Affairs* 1:472–74.

33. *Annals of Congress,* 4th Cong., 1st sess., pp. 977–87.

34. Jerald A. Combs, *The Jay Treaty: Political Background of the Founding Fathers* (Berkeley: University of California Press, 1970), p. 158.

35. Ibid., p. 183.

36. Gallatin from his first days in Congress confronted questions dispassionately and rarely indulged in personalities. In the Gallatin papers we find evidence of these traits in a note he wrote giving his judgment of his congressional colleagues. He praises men on both sides of the aisles. He states that two were superior, Fisher Ames and John Marshall. Fisher Ames' speech in support of the treaty impressed Gallatin as "the most brilliant and eloquent" of the many speeches. Ames' speech created such a deep impression that the House was hushed and men wept.

Henry Adams wrote of Gallatin: "His temper was under almost perfect control. His power lay in courage, honesty of purpose, and thoroughness of study. Undoubtedly his mind was one of rare power, perhaps for this special purpose the most apt that America has ever seen; a mind for which no principle was too broad and no detail too delicate; but it was a scientific and not a political mind." Henry Adams, *Life of Albert Gallatin,* pp. 154–55.

37. The best account of the relations between the United States and England in the ten years after the Jay Treaty is Bradford Perkins, *The First Rapprochement: England and the United States* (Berkeley: University of California Press, 1962).

3. Manifest Destiny and Crisis in the Midnineteenth Century, 1820–1850

1. Albert Gallatin, "Letters on the Oregon Question," no. 3, Gallatin Papers, New York Historical Society.

2. William Binkley, *The Texas Revolution* (Baton Rouge: Louisiana State University Press, 1952), p. 14.

3. David Weber has enriched our understanding of the decay along the entire frontier from California to Texas. His is the only study of what was taking place in the border areas and adds a new dimension to earlier writings: David J. Weber, *The Mexican Fron-*

tier, 1821–1846: The American Southwest Under Mexico (Albuquerque: University of New Mexico Press, 1982).

4. William Binkley, *The Texas Revolution*, pp. 3, 27–28.

5. Ray Allen Billington and Martin Ridge, *Westward Expansion: A History of the American Frontier* (New York: Macmillan, 1960), p. 408.

6. David Weber, *The Mexican Frontier*, p. 252.

7. Marquis James, *The Raven: A Biography of Sam Houston* (Indianapolis: Bobbs-Merrill, 1929), p. 217.

8. Ray Allen Billington, *The Westward Movement*, pp. 516–20.

9. Ibid., p. 524.

10. Paul A. Varg, *New England and Foreign Relations, 1879–1950* (Hanover, N.H.: University Press of New England, 1983), p. 154.

11. Ibid., p. 155.

12. Caleb Cushing of Massachusetts was a prominent leader in pushing for a settlement of the Oregon question. Cushing held that the United States had exclusive rights to not only the Columbia River valley but also all of the territory up to 54°40′. Cushing spoke of the Hudson's Bay Company, which exercised sovereignty in Oregon. While professing admiration for the British, he contended: "On us they must not encroach. Whilst our territorial expansion is restricted to this continent, hers must be excluded from it." Cushing reported a bill providing for the protection of the citizens of the United States in the territory of Oregon. A report prepared by Cushing accompanied the bill, of which 10,000 copies were ordered to be printed. Papers of Caleb Cushing, Library of Congress.

13. Daniel Webster to Edward Everett, January 27, 1843, Papers of Edward Everett, Massachusetts Historical Society, Boston.

14. William Ellery Channing, *The Works of William E. Channing* (Boston: American Unitarian Association, 1889), pp. 752–79.

15. Secretary of State Abel Upshur to Edward Everett, minister of the United States to Great Britain, October 16, 1843, Instructions of the Secretary of State to the United States Minister in London, National Archives.

16. Daniel Webster to Edward Everett, November 30, 1843, *The Papers of Daniel Webster* 5:322.

17. Daniel Webster to Robert C. Winthrop, April 28, 1844. *The Papers of Daniel Webster* 6:46.

18. Charles Sellers, *James K. Polk, Continentalist, 1843–1846* (Princeton, N.J.: Princeton University Press, 1966), pp. 48–49.

19. Daniel Webster to Abijah Bigelow, January 23, 1844, *The Papers of Daniel Webster, Correspondence,* 6:12–20.

20. E. D. Adams, *British Interests and Activities in Texas, 1838–1846* (Baltimore: Johns Hopkins University Press, 1910), p. 162.

21. Ibid., pp. 167–70.

22. Ibid.

23. Ibid.

24. Ibid., p. 172.

25. David Pletcher, *The Diplomacy of Annexation: Texas, Oregon, and the Mexican War* (Columbia, Mo.: University of Missouri Press, 1973), p. 160.

26. Sellers, *James K. Polk, Continentalist*, pp. 83–88.

27. Ibid., p. 72.

28. Moses Norris, *Congressional Globe*, 28th Cong., Special Session, Appendix, p. 184.

29. Ibid.

30. A. P. Stone, ibid., p. 224.

31. Levi Woodbury, ibid., p. 297.

32. Andrew J. Donelson, American chargé d'affaires in Texas, to Secretary of State Buchanan, William B. Manning, *Diplomatic Correspondence of the United States* (Washington, D.C.: Carnegie Endowment for International Peace, 1939), 13:448–52.

33. Richard S. Coxe to Secretary of State James Buchanan, August 4, 1845, papers of James Buchanan, Pennsylvania Historical Society, Philadelphia.

34. William Parrott to Secretary of State James Buchanan, July 26, 1845, Manning, *Diplomatic Correspondence* 8:472.

35. Sellers, *James K. Polk, Continentalist*, p. 332.

36. Wilbur Devereux Jones, *Lord Aberdeen and the Americas* (Athens, Ga.: University of Georgia Press, 1958), p. 69.

37. Ibid., p. 73.

38. Ibid., p. 71.

39. Sellers, *James J. Polk, Continentalist*, p. 333.

40. *Diary of James Knox Polk*, March 28, 29, 30, and April 3, 1846, Papers of James K. Polk, Library of Congress.

41. *Congressional Globe*, 29th Cong., 1st sess., p. 786.

42. Ibid.

43. *Papers of Daniel Webster: Diplomatic Papers*, ed. Kenneth Shewmaker (Cambridge, Mass.: Harvard University Press, 1967), p. 29.

44. Edward Everett to Daniel Webster, October 17, 1842, Papers of Edward Everett, Massachusetts Historical Society.

45. Daniel Webster to Edward Everett, January 9, 1843, Despatches to the United States Minister in London, National Archives.

46. Edward Everett to Secretary of State Abel Upshur, August 17, 1843, Despatches from the United States Minister to Great Britain, National Archives.

47. Ibid., November 14, 1843.

48. Diary of Edward Everett, March 29 to April 18, 1845, Everett Papers, Massachusetts Historical Society, Boston.

49. Edward Everett to Secretary of State Buchanan, April 16, 1845, Everett Papers, Massachusetts Historical Society.

50. Pletcher, *The Diplomacy of Annexation*, pp. 247–48.

51. Aberdeen to Pakenham, April 18, 1845, Aberdeen Papers, BM, AM, vol. 43123, files 249–50, quoted in Pletcher, *Diplomacy of Annexation*, p. 243.

52. Pletcher, *Diplomacy of Annexation*, pp. 244–45.

53. On September 30, McLane interviewed Aberdeen on Pakenham's blunt rejection of Polk's offer to settle for the forty-ninth parallel. Aberdeen stated "that if Mr. Pakenham had communicated the American proposition to the government here, as [he] was instructed to have done, he, Lord Aberdeen, would have taken it up as the basis of his action, and entertained little doubt that he would have been able to propose modifications which might ultimately have resulted in an adjustment mutually satisfactory to both Governments; and he observed that if it had not been withdrawn, after Mr. Pakenham's note, he would have disavowed his rejection, and proceeded to treat it as an open proposition." Louis McLane to Secretary of State Buchanan, October 3, 1845, Despatches from United States Minister, National Archives.

54. Diary of James K. Polk, August 30, 1845, Papers of James K. Polk, Library of Congress.

55. Ibid.

56. Ibid., October 21, 1845.

57. Ibid.

58. Ibid., November 29, 1845.

59. *Congressional Globe*, 29th Cong., 1st sess., February 26, 1846, p. 432.

60. Ibid., March 16, 1846.

61. Edward Everett to Lord Aberdeen, November 14, 1845, Everett Papers, Massachusetts Historical Society.

62. Edward Everett to Lord Jeffrey, December 15, 1845, Everett Papers.

63. Edward Everett to Lord John Russell, December 28, 1845, Everett Papers.

64. Pletcher, *Diplomacy of Annexation*, pp. 244–46.

65. Albert Gallatin, Letters on the Oregon Question, Papers of Albert Gallatin, New York Historical Society.

66. Albert Gallatin to Gales and Seaton, February 27, 1846, Papers of Albert Gallatin, New York Historical Society.

67. Polk, Diary, January 4, 1846, James K. Polk Papers, Library of Congress.

68. Ibid., March 7, 1846.

69. *Congressional Globe,* 29th Cong., 1st sess., March 5, 1846, p. 460.

70. Pletcher, *Diplomacy of Annexation,* pp. 406–407.

71. Edward Everett to Robert Winthrop, February? 1848, Everett Papers, Folger 271, Massachusetts Historical Society.

72. "What Impression We Make Abroad," *Putnam's Monthly Magazine,* October, 1853.

4. Rethinking Foreign Policy: A New Ideology, 1890–1917

1. Charles S. Campbell, *The Transformation of American Foreign Relations, 1865–1900* (New York: Harper & Row, Publishers, 1976), p. 337.

2. Ibid., p. 255.

3. David F. Trask, *The War and Spain in 1898* (New York: Macmillan Publishing Company, 1891), pp. 373–74.

4. Ibid., p. 353.

5. *Congressional Record,* 55th Cong., 3d sess., p. 1431.

6. Ibid., pp. 959–60.

7. *The Papers of Woodrow Wilson,* ed. Arthur Link (Princeton: Princeton University Press, 1971), 11:93.

8. Ibid., p. 66.

9. Paul Kennedy, *The Rise and Fall of the Great Powers: Economic Change and Military Conflict from 1500 to 2000* (New York: Random House, 1987), pp. 200, 244.

10. Ibid., p. 244.

11. Ibid.

12. Ibid., p. 245.

13. Ibid., p. 210.

14. Salvador Madariaga, literary figure and diplomat, was a prolific writer whose articles were widely published in the United States in the late 1920's and early 1930's. He was highly amusing in his satirical pieces. See his series of six articles in the *Forum* from January to July 1928 entitled "our Muddling World."

15. Thomas Jefferson to James Madison, January 30, 1787, *The Papers of Thomas Jefferson,* ed. Julian Boyd (Princeton: Princeton University Press, 1955), 11:92–97.

16. Edward Everett, "Phi Beta Kappa Address," Everett Papers, Massachusetts Historical Society.

17. "Address by Secretary of State Elihu Root Before the Trans-

Missouri Commercial Congress," November 20, 1906, *United States Foreign Relations, 1906* (Washington, D.C.: Department of State, 1906), pp. 1457–1469.

18. For a full discussion of the difficulties in developing the China market, see Paul A. Varg, *The Making of a Myth: The United States and China, 1897–1912* (East Lansing: Michigan State University, 1968), chap. 3, "The Myth of the China Market."

19. Dana G. Munro, *Intervention and Dollar Diplomacy in the Caribbean, 1900–1921* (Princeton, N.J.: Princeton University Press, 1964), pp. 535, 536.

20. Richard Challener, *Admirals, Generals, and American Foreign Policy* (Princeton, N.J.: Princeton University Press, 1973), p. 418.

21. Paul A. Varg, *Missionaries, Chinese, and Diplomats* (Princeton, N.J.: Princeton University Press, 1958), p. 3.

22. Ibid., p. 68.

23. *Interdenominational Conference of Foreign Missionary Boards and Societies in the United States and Canada* (New York: E. G. Jenkins Son's Printing House, 1893), p. 3.

24. Varg, *Missionaries, Chinese, and Diplomats*, p. 64.

25. Ibid., p. 79.

26. Mahan to Newton W. Rowell, July 9, 1913, *Mahan Papers* 3:501–503.

27. Charles Henry Fowler, *Missionary Addresses* (Cincinnati: Jennings and Graham, 1906), pp. 44–45.

28. Howard K. Beale, *Theodore Roosevelt and the Rise of America to World Power* (Baltimore: Johns Hopkins University Press, 1956), p. 174.

29. David Trask suggests that there was no plot on the part of Roosevelt and Lodge to annex the Philippines. In ordering Dewey to attack the Spanish fleet in Manila, Roosevelt was acting in accordance with naval planning. The purpose was to ensure that the Spanish squadron could not be used elsewhere. Roosevelt did not originate the order; he simply decided the time for its transmission. David Trask, *The War with Spain* (New York: Macmillan Publishing Company, 1981), p. 81.

At the close of 1898, Alfred Thayer Mahan wrote stating that he had envisioned a free Cuba "but I confess the Philippines, with all they mean, had not risen above my mental horizon. As you know, I am one of those who looked with anxious speculation toward the Chinese hive; but I never dreamed that in my day I should see the United States planted at the doors of China, advancing her outposts and pledging her future, virtually to meeting the East more than half way." Mahan to J. B. Sterling, December 23, 1898, *Letters and Papers of Alfred Thayer Mahan,* ed. Robert Seager (Annapolis, Md.: Naval Institute Press, 1975), 3:619. See also Robert Seager, *Alfred Thayer Mahan: The Man and His Letters* (Naval Institute Press, 1977), pp. 392–93.

30. William E. Livezey, *Mahan on Sea Power,* rev. ed. (Norman: University of Oklahoma Press, 1980), p. 84.

31. Alfred Thayer Mahan, "Motives to Imperial Federation," *National Review,* May, 1902, quoted in Livezay, *Mahan and Sea Power,* p. 288.

32. Alfred Thayer Mahan, *The Problem of Asia* (Boston: Little, Brown, and Company, 1900), p. 168.

33. Ibid.

34. "When a nation finds thrust upon it a number of communities, for the moment politically helpless, there is a presumption—though by no means a certainty—that God means it to do something for them. I do not for a moment claim that my view of what is required is hereby demonstrated; but I feel reasonably sure that the true course is to be found by a devout recognition of the divine hand in all this and a prayerful effort to see what is right to do in the light of actual conditions; not in the light of stock phrases, applicable to conditions at different times and to communities of different character." Mahan to the editor of *The Churchman,* September (?), 1899, *Letters and Papers of Alfred Thayer Mahan, 1847–1889 2:663.* ed. Robert Seager (Annapolis, Naval Institute Press, 1975), p. 663.

35. Livezey, *Mahan on Sea Power,* pp. 212–13.

36. As early as 1897, Mahan expressed fear of Germany and of the probability that she would challenge the Monroe Doctrine. "There is nothing, I believe, for which our people would be more ready to fight at a moments notice than any actual attempt at a European expansion here. . . . If our people get roused as to Germany, it would naturally draw their attention not only *from* the traditional jealousy of Great Britain, unhappily not yet at an end, but *towards* better appreciation of your truly great work in India and Egypt and the fact that on this side and in the Pacific we are natural allies." Mahan to James R. Thurfield, December 1, 1897, *Mahan Papers* 2:529.

Again, at the time of discussions of arbitration treaties he sounded the alarm. This time he warned that if Germany was successful in changing international law so that Great Britain would not be free to exercise control of the seas in wartime, Germany would have the way to victory. Mahan to Theodore Roosevelt, July 12, 1906, *Mahan Papers* 2:165.

37. Mahan to Roosevelt, July 12, 1906, *Mahan Papers* 3:165.

38. Ibid.

39. Mahan to James Ford Rhodes, April 16, 1897, *Mahan Papers* 2:503.

40. Ibid.

41. Brooks Adams' writing acquired a new interest in the early years of the cold war, and the book was reprinted. In the preface Marquis Childs wrote that the book could have been written in 1946, that Adams would have had to alter scarcely anything to relate it to that time. Brooks Adams, *America's Economic Supremacy* (New York: Harper and Brothers Publishers, 1947).

42. The author is indebted to Howard H. Beale for his perceptive interpretation of Theodore Roosevelt, as readers will readily recognize. For Roosevelt's basic postulates, see Howard H. Beale, *Theodore Roosevelt and the Rise of America to World Power* (Baltimore: Johns Hopkins University Press, 1956), pp. 23–28.

43. Ibid., pp. 38–39.

44. Ibid., p. 56.

45. Ibid., pp. 32, 70, 160–62.

46. Ibid., p. 161.

47. Ibid., p. 162.

48. Ibid., pp. 161–62.

49. William Langer, *The Diplomacy of Imperialism, 1890–1902* (New York: Alfred A. Knopf, 1965), p. 385.

50. Ibid., p. 488.

51. Ibid., p. 507.

5. Implementation of the New Ideology, 1898–1917

1. Walter Wellman, "Shall the Monroe Doctrine Be Modified?" *North American Review,* December, 1901, pp. 837–44.

2. Captain R. P. Hobson, USN, *North American Review,* October, 1903, pp. 548–54.

3. Paul A. Varg, *United States Foreign Relations, 1820–1860* (East Lansing, Mich.. Michigan State University Press, 1979), pp. 222–28.

4. A. E. Campbell, *Great Britain and the United States, 1895–1903* (London: Longmans, Green and Co., 1960), p. 50.

5. Bradford Perkins, *The Great Rapproachment: England and the United States, 1895–1914* (New York: Atheneum, 1968); Campbell, *Great Britain,* p. 55.

6. Beale, *Theodore Roosevelt and the Rise of America to World Power,* pp. 107–109.

7. J. G. S. Grenville presents a particularly useful explanation of questions that disturbed the British cabinet in *Lord Salisbury and*

Foreign Policy: The Close of the Nineteenth Century (London: Ashlane Press, 1964) chap. 16.

8. John Bartlet Brebner, *North Atlantic Triangle: The Interplay of Canada, The United States, and Great Britain* (New Haven: Yale University Press, 1945), p. 260.

9. Beale, *Roosevelt and America's Rise*, p. 127.

10. Beale provides a detailed account of Roosevelt's maneuvering, Lodge's pushing, and Hay's embarrassment and reluctance, pp. 115–29.

11. Beale, in part, justifies Roosevelt, who did not insist on a settlement. He would have been content to live with a modus vivendi that gave the Canadians temporary use of the land at the head of the Lynn Canal. It was the Canadians who pushed for a showdown.

Roosevelt's nomination of three men who were not impartial jurists as called for by the treaty came only after two members of the Supreme Court declined to serve. Beale also observes that the strategy employed was not wholly Roosevelt's. It had been agreed upon after a long discussion at a conference with Ambassador Choate, Secretary of State John Hay, and Secretary of War Elihu Root. Beale, *Roosevelt and America's Rise*, p. 130.

12. Warren Kneer, *Great Britain and the Caribbean, 1901–1913: A Study in Anglo-American Relations* (East Lansing, Mich.: Michigan State University Press, 1975), pp. 68–75.

13. Richard D. Challener, *Admirals, Generals, and American Foreign Policy, 1898–1914* (Princeton: Princeton University Press, 1973), pp. 62–64.

14. Ibid., p. 111.

15. Kneer, *Great Britain and the Caribbean*, p. 22.

16. Challener, *Admirals, Generals*, pp. 111–13.

17. Kneer, *Great Britain and the Caribbean*, p. 37.

18. Ibid.

19. Ibid., pp. 39–40.

20. Ibid., pp. 42–43.

21. Ibid., p. 44.

22. Dana Munro defended Roosevelt. He concluded that all that he undertook to do was to nominate customs collectors for appointment by the Dominican government. He was strongly opposed to taking over the government and there "is no reason to suppose that he regarded the customs receivership as a first step toward a more complete control." Dana Munro, *Intervention and Dollar Diplomacy in the Caribbean* (Princeton, N.J.: Princeton University Press, 1964), pp. 106–107.

23. Dana Munro, *Intervention and Dollar Diplomacy*, p. 92. The author gladly acknowledges his indebtedness to Dana Munro for his judicious and scholarly treatment of the Santo Domingo question.

24. Akira Iriye, *Across the Pacific: An Inner History of American East Asian Relations* (New York: Harcourt, Brace and World, 1967), p. 80.

25. Paul A. Varg, *The Making of a Myth: The United States and China* (East Lansing, Mich.: Michigan State University Press, 1968), chap. 3, "The Myth of the China Market."

26. Varg, *Open Door Diplomat: The Life of W. W. Rockhill* (Urbana: University of Illinois Press, 1952), pp. 45–48.

27. Beale, *Roosevelt and America's Rise*, p. 307.

28. Varg, *Open Door Diplomat*, pp. 73–74.

29. Beale, *Roosevelt and America's Rise*, p. 312.

30. Varg, *The Making of a Myth*, p. 151.

31. Ibid., p. 155.

32. Ibid., p. 156.

33. W. W. Rockhill to the Secretary of State, August 23, 1905, National Archives.

34. Editor, "The Fakumen Railway," *Far Eastern Review* 6 (November, 1909): 228–29.

35. C. F. Remer, *Foreign Investments in China* (New York: Macmillan Co., 1933), p. 58.

36. Ibid., p. 76.

37. George Bronson Rea, "Railway Loan Agreements and Their Relation to the Open Door: A Plea for Fair Play to China," *Far Eastern Review* 6 (November, 1909): 214–17.

38. J. Newton Nind, "A Study of Trade Conditions in the Orient," *The Far Eastern Review* 6 (July, 1910): 40, 57.

39. "Imperial Railways of North China," *Far Eastern Review*, (November, 1909), p. 234.

40. William C. Redfield, "America's Export Trade," *Far Eastern Review* 8 (March, 1912): 327–29.

41. Varg, *The Making of a Myth*, pp. 101–102.

42. Varg, *Open Door Diplomat*, p. 111.

43. Ibid.

44. Gordon Levin develops this facet of Wilson's thinking at length in *Woodrow Wilson and World Politics: America's Response to War and Revolution* (New York: Oxford University Press, 1968), pp. 13–19.

45. For an exposition on Wilson's views, see Lloyd Gardner, "Woodrow Wilson and the Mexican Revolution," *Woodrow Wilson*

and a Revolutionary World, 1913–1921, ed. Arthur S. Link (Chapel Hill: University Press of North Carolina, 1982), chap. 1.

46. *Papers of Woodrow Wilson*, ed. Arthur S. Link (Princeton, N.J.: Princeton University Press, 1983), 30:472.

47. Ibid., 31:13–14.

48. John W. Coogan, *The End of Neutrality: The United States, Britain, and Maritime Rights, 1899–1915* (Ithaca: Cornell University Press, 1981), pp. 125–47.

49. Ibid., pp. 160–68.

50. Ibid., pp. 174–81.

51. Ibid.

52. Arnold A. Offner, *The Origins of the Second World War: American Foreign Policy and World Politics* (New York: Praeger Publishers, 1975), p. 20.

53. Robert H. Ferrell, "The Price of Isolation: American Diplomacy, 1921–1945," *The Unfinished Century: America Since 1900* (Boston: Little, Brown and Company, 1973), p. 466.

54. The tragedy of Wilson is understandingly presented by Robert Ferrell in his book, *Woodrow Wilson and World War I* (New York: Harper and Row Publishers, 1985).

55. *Papers of Woodrow Wilson* 41:527.

6. The Coming of a Revolution in American Foreign Policy, 1932–1941

1. Arnold A. Offner, *The Origins of the Second World War: American Foreign Policy and World Politics* (New York: Praeger Publishers, 1975), pp. 49–51, 65.

2. The Acting Chairman of the American Delegation to the Disarmament Conference, Hugh Wilson, to the Secretary of State, June 17, 1935, *Foreign Relations of the United States* [hereafter *USFR*] (1935), 1:708–709.

3. Hajo Holborn, *A History of Modern Germany, 1840–1945* (New York: Alfred A. Knopf, 1969), pp. 673–74, 677–80.

4. Akira Iriye, *Across the Pacific: An Inner History of American–East Asian Relations* (New York: Harcourt, Brace and World, 1967), pp. 172–73.

5. *Report of the Commission of Enquiry of the League of Nations, Signed at Peiping, September 4, 1932*, pp. 247–48.

6. Stanley K. Hornbeck, "Brief Statement of the Policy of the United States with Regard to the Far East," Hornbeck Papers, box 20, Hoover Library, Stanford University.

7. For a helpful account of these efforts, see Dorothy Borg, *The*

United States and the Far Eastern Crisis of 1933–1938 (Cambridge, Mass.: Harvard University Press, 1966), p. 247.

8. Ibid., p. 79.

9. Ibid.

10. Ibid., p. 81.

11. Ibid., pp. 92–98.

12. Joseph Grew to the secretary of state, May 14, 1937, *USFR* (1937), 3:96–100.

13. Ibid., March 17, 1937, 3:48–52.

14. Ibid., July 23, 1937, 3:251–53.

15. Ibid., July 14, 1937, pp. 164–66.

16. Ibid., August 27, 1937, pp. 485–88.

17. Secretary of state Cordell Hull to Joseph Grew, September 2, 1937, *USFR* (1937), 3:505–508.

18. Ibid.

19. Paul A. Varg, *Missionaries, Chinese, and Diplomats.* (Princeton, N.J.: Princeton University Press, 1958), and *The Making of a Myth: The United States and China.* (East Lansing, Mich.: Michigan State University Press, 1968).

20. Memorandum by Hugh Wilson, assistant secretary of state, November 16, 1937, *USFR* (1937), 4:194–96.

21. Memorandum of Conversation by Stanley Hornbeck, January 21, 1938, *USFR* (1938), 3:44–47.

22. Memorandum on Possible Peace Terms for Communication to the United States Government, February 14, 1938; "Analysis and Comment by the Department of State," *USFR* (1937), 4:194–96.

23. Ibid.

24. Ibid.

25. *USFR* (1938), 4:48–53.

26. *USFR, Japan* (1931–1941), 1:478.

27. Joseph Grew to the Secretary of State, January 31, 1938, *USFR* (1938), 4:587–90.

28. Joseph Grew to the Secretary of State, February 14, 1938, *USFR* (1938), 4:590.

29. Joseph Grew to the Secretary of State, May 2, 1938, *USFR* (1938), 4:596–600.

30. Ibid., 4:599.

31. Joseph Grew to the Secretary of State, December 1, 1938, *USFR* (1938), 4:401.

32. Ibid.

33. William L. Langer and Everett Gleason, *The Challenge to Isolation, 1937–1940* (New York: Harper and Brothers, 1952), p. 12.

34. German Chargé d'Affaires in the United States to the Ger-

man Foreign Ministry, September 12, 1938, series D, vol. 6, "The Last Months of Peace, March–August 1939," pp. 726–32.

35. Speech by Senator Tom Connally, April 29, 1937, *Congressional Record*, 75th Cong., 1st sess., p. 3946.

36. Raymond Leslie Buell, "The New American Neutrality," *Foreign Policy Reports*, January 15, 1936, pp. 287–88.

37. Robert Dallek, *Franklin Roosevelt and American Foreign Policy, 1932–1945* (New York: Oxford University Press, 1979), p. 127.

38. Ibid., p. 293.

39. Ibid., pp. 300–301.

40. Ibid., pp. 302–303.

41. Two excellent analyses of isolationism and the America First Committee are Selig Adler, *The Isolationist Impulse: Its Twentieth Century Reaction* (New York: Abelard-Schuman, 1956) and Wayne Cole, *America First* (Madison: University of Wisconsin Press, 1953).

42. This aspect began to be emphasized early in 1940. Adolph Berle spoke on the subject before the National Farm Institute early in February. His speech was published in the *Department of State Bulletin*. Henry Grady spoke on the same subject before the New School for Social Research in the same month. Anne O'Hare McCormick of the *New York Times* wrote lengthy and forceful arguments that appeared there in June 1940. Douglas Miller, former commercial attaché in Berlin, had already published his book *You Can't Do Business with Hitler*, and it was a best seller.

The economic argument that Germany's foreign-trade policy meant a closing of the door to the United States occupied a prominent place in the debates on the Lend-Lease Bill. The focus was on Germany rather than Japan, but speakers did portray the danger of the United States facing Japan's New Order in Asia on the one side and a European economy controlled by Hitler on the other side.

43. Douglas Miller, *You Can't Do Business with Hitler* (Boston: Little, Brown & Co., 1939).

44. Offner, *Origins of the Second World War*, p. 193.

45. Microfilm of the Morgenthau Papers, reel 1, Roosevelt Library, Hyde Park, N.Y.

46. Published excerpts from the Morgenthau Papers, containing interoffice memos and printed committee reports, entitled *Morgenthau Diary* (Washington, D.C.: Government Printing Office, 1965), 1:198.

47. My account of the discussions in Washington leading to the embargo is based on Herbert Feis, *The Road to Pearl Harbor: The*

Coming of the War Between the United States and Japan (Princeton, N.J.: Princeton University Press, 1950), pp. 88–94.

48. International Military Tribunal for the Far East, microfilm edition, 30917. The proceedings were edited by R. John Pritchard and Sonia M. Zaide and published as *Tokyo War Crimes Trial* (New York: Garland Publishing, 1981), 22 vols.

49. International Tribunal for the Far East, microfilm edition, 30917, 10241.

50. Ibid., 30917, 10241.

51. Hull to Chargé in France (Mathews) September 2, 1940 *USFR* (1940), 4:104–105; Memorandum of Conversation, by the secretary of state, September 16, 1940, ibid., pp. 120–121.

52. William L. Neuman, *American Encounters Japan: From Perry to MacArthur* (Baltimore: Johns Hopkins University Press, 1963), chap. 12, "The Unwanted War."

53. Cho Yukio, "An Inquiry into the Problem of Importing American Capital into Manchuria: A Note on Japanese-American Relations, 1931–1941," *Pearl Harbor as History, Japanese-American Relations, 1931–1941*, ed. Dorothy Borg and Shumpei Okamoto (New York: Columbia University Press, 1973), pp. 388–91.

7. Origins of the Cold War, 1940–1945

1. David Eisenhower, *Eisenhower At War, 1943–1945* (New York: Random House, 1986), p. xii.

2. Norman Rich, *Hitler's War Aims: Ideology, The Nazi State, and the Course of Expansion* (New York: W. W. Norton, 1973), p. 180.

3. *Documents on German Foreign Policy, 1918–1945* (Washington, D.C.: Government Printing Office, 1960), 11:8–10.

4. Ibid.

5. Ibid.

6. Ibid., pp. 567–68.

7. Ibid., pp. 714–15.

8. Ambassador William M. Standley to the Secretary of State, March 10, 1943, *USFR* (1943), 3:504–505.

9. Standley to the secretary of state, July 3, 1943, *USFR* (1943), 3:553–54, and August 10, 1943, 3:560–63.

10. Ibid., p. 575.

11. Ibid., p. 553.

12. Ibid., p. 555.

13. Ibid., pp. 555–57.

14. *USFR* (1943), 2:553–54.

15. Standley to the secretary of state, May 25, 1943, *USFR* (1943), 2:534–35.

16. Ibid.

17. *USFR* (1943), 1:554.

18. Memorandum by the Polish ambassador to Secretary of State Cordell Hull, October 6, 1943, *USFR* (143), 3:468–71.

19. *USFR* (1943), 3:467–68.

20. *USFR* (1943), 1:521.

21. Ibid., p. 622.

22. Ibid., p. 635.

23. Ibid., pp. 744–48.

24. Ibid., p. 642.

25. Ibid., p. 737.

26. Ibid., pp. 638–39.

27. Ibid.

28. Ibid.

29. Ibid., p. 597.

30. Ibid., p. 554.

31. In a letter to President Roosevelt dated November 5, 1943, Harriman wrote: "Although Soviet territorial questions were never raised at the Conference, it can only be inferred that the Soviet Government expects to stand firmly on the position they have already taken in regard to their 1941 frontiers. I believe they have."

32. Charles E. Bohlen, *Witness to History, 1929–1969* (New York: W. W. Norton & Co., 1971), p. 130.

33. Jay Ciechanowski, Polish ambassador to Dunn, November 17, 1943, copy to the Secretary of State from Polish Ambassador, *USFR* (1943), 3:478–79.

34. Harriman to Roosevelt, November 5, 1943, *USFR* (1943), 3:1012–15.

35. Herbert Feis, *Churchill, Roosevelt, Stalin: The War They Waged and the Peace They Sought* (Princeton, N.J.: Princeton University Press, 1957), p. 255.

36. Ibid.

37. Ibid., p. 284.

38. Bohlen, *Witness to History*, p. 153.

39. Ibid.

40. Freeman Matthews sent a lengthy memorandum summarizing the discussions including the spheres-of-interest arrangement. The Polish question was also discussed by Churchill and Stalin. Churchill supported drawing the boundary at the Curzon Line, but the Poles still held out for the boundary established in 1921. *USFR* (1943), 3:1016–19.

41. In the course of the meetings Eden, Harriman, and Molotov met. Harriman reported to Roosevelt that he had an opportunity "to explain how important it was in our relations with Russia for

the American people to be satisfied that the Russians were being generous to and patient with the Poles in their difficulties and that in the United States the Polish question was looked upon as the first real test of collaboration in dealing with world problems. Eden and I both got the impression that for the first time, Molotov was really interested in understanding the public reaction in England and the United States to the Polish question." This observation was prophetic. The situation in Poland was most prominent during 1945 and created distrust of the Soviet Union. *USFR* (1943), 3:1012–15.

42. Edward R. Stettinius, Secretary of State, to President Roosevelt, November 8, 1944, *USFR* (1944), 4:1025–26.

43. Walter Isaacson and Evan Thomas, *The Wise Men: Six Friends and the World They Made* (New York: Simon & Schuster Inc., 1986), p. 243.

44. Ibid., p. 244.

45. Harriman to the secretary of state, September 30, 1944. *USFR* (1944), 4:992–98.

46. Ibid.

47. Ibid.

48. Ibid.

49. Ibid.

50. Ibid.

51. As Stalin listed his demands, the president said several times that he had not had a chance to discuss these terms with the Chinese. Bohlen later wrote that it was obvious that the president was bothered by what he was doing. Bohlen was of the opinion that the Chinese, if they had been informed, would not have received better terms from the Russians. He added that the principal fault with the agreement was that it turned out to be unnecessary. Bohlen, *Witness to History*, p. 198.

52. Feis, *Churchill, Roosevelt, Stalin*, pp. 522–25.

53. Bohlen, *Witness to History*, p. 187.

54. Roosevelt's letter is published in Bohlen's *Witness to History*, pp. 188–96. In it he stated: "You must believe me when I tell you that our people at home look with a critical eye on what they consider a disagreement between us at this vital stage of the war." Bohlen thought this unwise because Stalin considered references to American public opinion in the same category as nonsense.

55. Isaacson and Thomas, *The Wise Men*, p. 246.

56. Gabriel and Joyce Kolko, *The Politics of War* (London and New York), p. 99.

57. Ibid., pp. 166–67.

58. Vojteck Mastny, *Russia's Road to the Cold War: Diplomacy,*

Warfare, and the Politics of Communism, 1941–1945 (New York: Columbia University Press, 1979).

59. Ibid.

60. Adam B. Ulam, *Expansion and Coexistence The History of Soviet Foreign Policy, 1917–67* (New York: Frederick A. Praeger, Publishers, 1968), pp. 368–69.

8. Emergence of the Cold War, 1945–1947

1. Minutes of State-War-Navy Coordinating Committee, National Archives, reel 2, file 14, of microfilm copy prepared by Scholarly Resources Co.

2. Charles E. Bohlen, *Witness to History*, p. 177.

3. Martin Sherwin, *A World Destroyed: The Atomic Bomb and the Grand Alliance* (New York: Alfred A. Knopf, 1987), p. 229.

4. Ibid., p. 228.

5. Ibid., p. 238.

6. *Princeton Seminar Letters of Dean Acheson*, microfilm copies, reel 1, no. 0000074 Truman Library, Independence, Mo.

7. Ibid., no. 0000305.

8. Ibid., no. 0000146.

9. Ibid.

10. Abba Eban, *An Autobiography* (New York: Random House, 1977), pp. 155–56.

11. *Princeton Seminar Letters of Dean Acheson*, reel 1, no. 0000305.

12. The changes in the Soviet Union and Stalin's retreat from Leninism and adoption of a policy of promoting coalitions in the liberated countries are fully treated by William McCagg, *Stalin Embattled* (Detroit: Wayne University Press, 1978).

13. Hugh Thomas, *Armed Truce: The Beginnings of the Cold War, 1945–1946* (New York: Atheneum, 1987), pp. 77–78, 102–103, 525.

14. Adam B. Ulam, *Expansion and Coexistence History of Soviet Foreign Policy, 1917–1967* (New York: Praeger Publishers, 1968), pp. 400–405.

15. Paul Sweet to his wife, Katherine, June 28, 1945, *Gesellschaft und Politik am Beginn der Zweiten Republik*, ed. Oliver Rathkolb (Vienna: Hermann Bohlaus Nachf., 1985).

16. Charles Thayer, OSS, July 14, 1945, *Gesellschaft und Politik am Beginn der Zweiten Republik*, p. 284.

17. Ibid.

18. Leonard J. Hankin, November 20, 1945, ibid., pp. 330–31.

19. Mark Clark, United States military commissioner to the Joint Chiefs of Staff, September 29, 1945, *USFR* (1945), 3:610–13.

20. The United States political adviser for Austrian affairs (John G. Erhardt) to the secretary of state, November 27, 1945, 4:footnote, p. 665.

21. *USFR* (1945), 4:3.

22. *USFR* (1947), 4:276.

23. Ibid., pp. 297–99.

24. Ibid., p. 304.

25. Bruce Robellet Kuniholm, *The Origins of the Cold War in the Near East: Great Power Conflict and Diplomacy in Iran, Turkey, and Greece* (Princeton, N.J.: Princeton University Press, 1980), pp. 157–59.

26. Russell D. Buhite, *Patrick Hurley and American Foreign Policy* (Ithaca, N.Y.: Cornell University Press, 1973), pp. 125–30.

27. Ibid., pp. 130–31.

28. Ibid., p. 132.

29. Kuniholm, *Origins of the Cold War in the Near East*, p. 186.

30. Ibid., p. 163.

31. Ibid., p. 274.

32. Ibid., pp. 394–96.

33. George Kennan, *Memoirs, 1925–1950* (Boston: Little, Brown and Company, 1967), pp. 133–34.

34. Ibid., p. 132.

35. Kuniholm, *Origins of the Cold War in the Near East*, pp. 394–96.

36. Ibid., p. 322.

37. *San Francisco Examiner*, March 2, 1946.

38. *Atlanta Constitution*, March 3, 1946.

39. Ronald Steel, *Walter Lippmann and the American Century* (Boston: Little, Brown and Company, 1980), p. 439.

40. Ibid., p. 430. Lippmann was a strong supporter of rearmament and of a firm policy. He and Kennan criticized the concentration on Iran and Greece; Lippmann saw the danger as the economic deterioration in western Europe and thought it was a gross error to take on responsibilities throughout the free world. Kennan believed that Turkey would be able to stand her ground against the Soviet Union and did not think that Iran was in danger.

41. John Lewis Gaddis, *The United States and the Origins of the Cold War* (New York: Columbia University Press, 1972), p. 312.

42. John Gimbel, *The Origins of the Marshall Plan* (Stanford: Stanford University Press, 1976), p. 130.

43. Ibid.

44. Alan S. Milward, *The Reconstruction of Western Europe, 1945–51* (London: Methuen and Co., 1984), p. 395.

45. Kuniholm, *Origins of the Cold War in the Near East,* pp. 380–81.

46. George Kennan, *Memoirs, 1925–1950* (Boston: Little, Brown and Co., 1967), pp. 316–321. Kennan explains fully his objections. He thought Turkey, while she would be in a precarious position, would be able to withstand Soviet pressures. As to Iran, he pointed out that the Soviets were not doing well in their efforts and that they would meet stubborn resistance in trying to impose their ideology on Moslems. Kennan firmly believed that the real danger was in western Europe and that was the most important area. It was there that we should put our efforts. He particularly disliked the flamboyant language in the president's message.

47. Walter Isaacson and Evan Thomas, *The Wise Men: Six Friends and the World They Made* (New York: Simon and Schuster, 1987), p. 395.

48. Ibid.

Index